P9-CFW-987

DE GAULLE: IMPLACABLE ALLY

De Gaulle

IMPLACABLE ALLY

⚜

ROY C. MACRIDIS

Professor of Politics
Brandeis University

With a special introduction by
Maurice Duverger, Professor, Institut d'Études
Politiques and Faculté de Droit et des Sciences
Économiques, Université de Paris

Harper & Row • Publishers

New York and London

WITHDRAWN

copy 1

DE GAULLE: IMPLACABLE ALLY   Copyright © 1966
by Roy C. Macridis. Printed in the United States of America. All
rights reserved. No part of this book may be used or reproduced in
any manner whatsoever without written permission except in the case
of brief quotations embodied in critical articles and reviews. For information address Harper & Row, Publishers, Incorporated, 49 East
33rd Street, New York, N.Y. 10016.

Library of Congress Catalog Card Number: 66-12560
C-Q

To Kathleen, Peter,
and Stephen

. . . Therefore, as the organization of anything
cannot be made by many, because the divergence
of their opinions hinders them from agreeing
as to what is best, yet, when once they do
understand it, they will not readily agree to
abandon it.

Machiavelli, The Discourses

DC
373.
G3
A25

CONTENTS

❖

Preface
Special Introduction: A Man of the Nineteenth or the Twenty-
     first Century, *by Maurice Duverger*
General Introduction *1*

PART I THE CONDITIONS OF INDEPENDENCE

1. THE INSTITUTIONS   33

The State and the Political Parties *36*
The Temptation of Dictatorship *39*
The Gaullist Constitutional Charter *41*
The Conditions of a Return to Power *43*
The Constitution of the Fifth Republic *45*
The Powers of the President *48*
Popular Election of the President *51*
Vote for De Gaulle and My Reform! *54*
The New Electoral System *55*
The Elections of November 18, 1962—Vote for De Gaulle and
     My Deputies! *56*
The Constitution Works—De Gaulle's Interpretation *59*

2. THE ECONOMY   64

Economic Renovation and Social Reform *65*
How to Get the Country's Economy Moving *71*
Industrial Greatness *75*

Progress and Its Infantile Diseases *78*
We Are On Our Way *80*

3. THE EMPIRE   84

The Future of the Colonies—the Brazzaville Conference *85*
Community and Independence *87*
The Address at Dakar: You Can Have Your Independence *89*
Decolonization is . . . Inevitable *91*

PART II THE MARGIN OF INDEPENDENCE

4. THE CLAIMS OF FRANCE   97

The First Appeal *98*
The Dark Years: Claims and Anxieties *99*
The Memorandum of September 23, 1958 *103*
The East-West Conflict and Conditions for a Summit Meeting *103*
Reflections on the Failure of the Summit Conference *106*
Assertion of French Leadership *111*
The Burdens of Independence *113*

5. THE GAME OF BALANCE   116

Flirtations with England *116*
The Franco-Soviet Pact: La Belle et Bonne Alliance *119*
The Appeal to the Vatican *121*
The Crime of Crimea . . . *122*
. . . Is Unacceptable *125*
Potsdam: The Destruction of the European Balance *126*

6. THE FRENCH ARMY AND THE NUCLEAR SWORD   128

Reflections on the Weakness of France *130*
The Defense of France Must Be French *132*
The Imperative of Nuclear Force *136*
Yes—We Shall Conduct Our Tests *137*
Why We Are Not Interested in Disarmament *139*

The Test Ban Treaty Does Not Change the Situation   *141*
Alliance and Independence   *142*
Our Independent Nuclear Policy—A Summing Up   *147*

PART III   FRENCH INDEPENDENCE

7. THE EUROPEAN VOCATION   155

The Prospects of Unity   *156*
The Basis of Cooperation   *157*
The Fallacies of Integration   *159*
A European Europe   *163*

8. THE ATLANTIC COMMUNITY   168

The Need for Division of Labor   *170*
Defense: A National Problem   *171*
Changing Conditions and NATO   *173*
The Need to Overhaul   *174*

9. GERMANY—THE PERENNIAL PROBLEM   176

The Defender of the Status Quo Unless . . .   *178*
A Clear Eye and a Firm Heart   *182*
Better Cooperation   *184*
The Treaty   *186*
The German Problem is a European Problem   *191*

10. "NO" TO ENGLAND   196

"No" to England   *198*

11. EUROPE'S DAUGHTER—THE UNITED STATES   203

Elementary Feelings   *205*
Franklin Delano Roosevelt   *206*
The Conversation with Hopkins—Franco-American Relations in
     1944   *210*
Truman Simplifies Everything   *213*

Twenty Years After: France Is Independent *216*

12. THE "SO-CALLED" UNITED NATIONS   223

The Birth of the United Nations *223*
A Scene of Disturbance *225*
The Big Five *227*

13. FRANCE HAS INTERESTS EVERYWHERE   230

The Salute to Mexico *231*
The Concern for Vietnam *232*
China: A Great People *233*
France Must Participate in the Settlement of Southeast Asia *236*
We Have Become Independent *239*

Index *243*

Charles De Gaulle and his policies have long been an annoyance
and an enigma to American leaders and political commentators.
The usual argument is: De Gaulle is a nationalist; he has failed
to act as a "faithful ally"; he has balked at European unity and
has by his acts and gestures weakened NATO. This austere
French officer has never appealed to American political leaders
and proved to be more than an irritant to many of his British
allies during World War II. Churchill found the "Cross of
Lorraine" heavy to bear; Roosevelt dismissed him as a prima
donna. In turn, De Gaulle had only critical remarks to make for
many of the American statesmen he met, seeing behind their
noble expressions and plans an American design to dominate the
world; he was also constantly on guard against what he assumed
to be British designs to seize some of the more desirable parts
of the French Empire. In 1958, at the age of sixty-seven, long
after Roosevelt and Stalin had died and when Churchill and
Truman were well out of the political scene, he became President
of the French Republic, with vast powers to govern and to shape
the defense and foreign policy of France under a constitution
tailor-made for him. His seven-year term in office expired in
December 1965, and he was reelected for a second seven-year
term in the same month, but only after encountering and over-
coming strong opposition, which indicated for the first time a
decline in his popularity. How severe and permanent this is remains to be seen. Whatever the case his reelection gives him the
opportunity to continue his rule and to prepare for his succession.

    This, then, is an appropriate time to present to the American
public some of De Gaulle's most representative pronouncements
on domestic and international questions. Like Churchill, he is a

speaker and writer of considerable eloquence. His *Memoirs,* written in the years of his political retirement (1953-1958), are undoubtedly on the same level of literary excellence and political introspection as Churchill's. His earlier publications, although mostly military and technical, nevertheless show a man with a philosophic depth and a grasp of history that few statesmen command. As President of the Republic he has held twelve carefully prepared press conferences, covering a variety of issues. Herein are displayed a depth and breadth of interest, a remarkable incisiveness, a strong, firm, and even stubborn mind when it comes to charting and pursuing a course of action, and at times even flashes of wit that show him, despite what his critics say, to be a man capable not only of devastating irony but also of humor. But these instances are rare. De Gaulle is a dedicated man—committed to the greatness of France and to the return of his country to the status of a world power. This is not only an act of faith but a political act, based upon what he rightly or wrongly considers to be the essentials of a new balance in the world, a balance that will inevitably replace the American-Soviet duopoly.

The theme of these selections is centered on a subject that best exemplifies De Gaulle's career—that of French independence. I have divided the presentation in three parts. In the first I deal with what I call the *Conditions of Independence.* Throughout the duration of the war De Gaulle was preoccupied with laying down these conditions as carefully as possible; he has done little more than to implement them since he became President. In the second part I deal with the *Margin of Independence*—the why and how of the restoration of a European and world balance and the role of France therein. In the third part—*French Independence* —I deal primarily with De Gaulle's major pronouncements since 1958. A note of confidence can now be discerned in his speeches as he feels that his claims are being heeded and as he sees a more prosperous France, equipped with atomic weapons, ready to play the role of a world power. By the same token, an impatient, even strident tone toward those who seem to interfere with his claims —particularly the United States—can be detected.

I have drawn my selections from De Gaulle's *Memoirs,* and

I wish to acknowledge with thanks the permission granted to me by Simon and Schuster to reproduce passages from their three-volume translation, *The War Memoirs of Charles de Gaulle* (Volume I: *The Call to Honour,* Volume II: *Unity,* and Volume III: *Salvation*). I have drawn extensively from the fine collection of major speeches and press conferences that were compiled by the French Embassy's Press and Information Service. Occasionally, I have used the collection of De Gaulle's major wartime speeches and conferences—*Discours et Messages 1940-46* (Berger-Levrault, Paris, 1946). In presenting the material I decided to use a topical rather than a chronological order, inserting notes and introductions to guide the reader.

In addition to my hope that this volume will bring De Gaulle closer to the American reader, I also think that it will benefit the student of French and international politics. Like Churchill, De Gaulle has had to face stark realities of political action and choice. Like Churchill, he will leave behind him not only an impressive body of accomplishments but also the legacy of a man who has thought earnestly on the political problems of our shrinking world and on the means by which man can shape his political universe.

I wish to take this opportunity to thank some of the people who gave me assistance in this undertaking. Stanley Hoffmann of Harvard University sent me a listing of what he considered to be De Gaulle's most representative pronouncements; Serge Hurtig of the University of Paris read and commented on my general introduction. Rollin Posey of Harper & Row was a constant source of help and suggestions. Miss Mary DiGiacomo aided me with innumerable clerical tasks. But the main burden of editing, collating, and putting the selections into their final shape fell upon Mrs. Margaret Cox, and I am much indebted to her. I am also grateful to the State University of New York at Buffalo and to Brandeis University for the financial and other assistance they gave me to defray various clerical and secretarial expenses. Lastly, I wish to thank my friend and colleague, Maurice Duverger, for the special introduction he prepared at short notice.

Waltham, Massachusetts   ROY C. MACRIDIS

A MAN OF THE NINETEENTH OR THE TWENTY-FIRST CENTURY

⚜

by Maurice Duverger

Most Americans, many Europeans, and a number of French think of General De Gaulle as an old gentleman who belongs to a different age. His appearance, his style, his utterances, his thoughts—even his political actions—appear to be archaic. He replaced the parliamentary regime by a republican monarchy. Some even think that he would like to restore a true monarchy— "a monarchical monarchy" (as he would say!)—but he knows that this is impossible. His diplomacy rests on the principle of nationality, like that of Napoleon III. France seems to be governed by a man of the nineteenth century.

We must not forget, however, that twenty years ago De Gaulle was one of the few military leaders in France, England, or the United States who refused to conceive of the coming war in terms of the principles and tactics of the past and who laid the basis of a new strategy. The fact that the solitary general of 1935 was right when most allied generals were wrong does not necessarily prove that the solitary Chief of State of 1965 is right and the other political leaders are wrong. It simply shows that the theses developed by the author of the *Edge of the Sword* and *The Future Army* have a feeling for the new and a capacity for adaptation coupled with a penchant for the archaic and the old-fashioned. His policies with regard to Algeria, Africa, and the underdeveloped world show that he is able to understand the future and to prepare for it. Perhaps the same is true for some of his views concerning the evolution of Europe. In addition, some of his domestic policies show an innovating spirit. He has accelerated the modernization of the economic, political, and social structures in France. Can it be

then that the Chief of State of 1965, like the young Colonel of
1935, is really a modern spirit concerned with the advent of the
twenty-first century rather than with the restoration of the
nineteenth? It is hard to answer this question by reading De
Gaulle's speeches, partly because he naturally prefers, like Bos-
suet and Chateaubriand, the elevated style, rather than the dry
and succinct formula common to administrative reports. De
Gaulle speaks and writes well—but his language is ancient,
more classic in style than modern. He intentionally uses outdated terms and formulas. Frequently his speeches are intended
to disguise his thoughts rather than to clarify them. He thinks
that the great designs should never be clearly revealed and that
the art of statecraft always requires a certain degree of obscu-
rity. During the war in Algeria, the exigesis of the General's
speeches was just about as subtle as that of the Bible in the
Middle Ages.

We must then judge the General by his acts rather than by
his words, especially since the latter help to camouflage the
former. It is what he does rather than what he says that makes
it possible to answer the question we have raised. But what he
does is not always easier to understand than what he says!
He often does contradictory things, either at the same time or
over a period of years. He believes that a statesman must have
many irons in the fire in order to be able to use one or the other,
depending upon the circumstances. He intentionally practices
what he called in the past *la politique de contreassurance* or *la
diplomatie de revers.* Above all, he adapts to the circumstances
when he cannot do otherwise, and this leads him to revise a policy
when he finds that it cannot succeed. He gave independence to
Algeria and French-speaking Africa between 1960 and 1962, after
having inspired the colonialist doctrine of the Gaullist Party—
the R.P.F.—in the fifties. Today he is trying to disrupt NATO,
after having declared in 1958 his desire to participate in its
direction.

The General's realism has often forced him to do what he did
not wish to do. The contradiction in his policies reflects the
fundamental contradiction between the personality of the man
and the period in which he lives. A soldier, De Gaulle (the *de*

without being a proof of his aristocratic lineage, is nonetheless
so interpreted in France), a son of a professor of a Catholic
school, a practicing Catholic himself, a pupil of the Jesuits, he
combines in his person all the traits of a French conservative. It
is true that the force and the originality of his personality
helped him overcome the attitudes of his class, his caste, his
religion, his profession, and his education. One notes that in
1939 he manifested a certain sympathy for *Le Temps présent*,
a Catholic weekly, which, without being progressive, was opposed to the traditional conservative right. In his tastes and
predilections, his contacts and his behavior, De Gaulle is conservative. He is not at home with the century in which he lives.
He prefers the past (as his great interest in history shows).
But General de Gaulle knows that time is irreversible and that
one cannot turn back the clock. He loves to repeat that "things
are what they are." His personal tastes obscure his insights
only in part. He looks at the world fairly realistically as it is,
at least in its broad contours. He knows that he has to take it
as it is. Not being able to do what he wishes, he does what he
can to bring it close to what he wants. His policies are a mixture of the conservative and the progressive, of the archaic and
the modern. Some think that the portions of mixture are different in domestic and international politics. There are some
who think that the General is a conservative in domestic affairs
and a progressive in international affairs. Others think exactly
the opposite—that he is innovating in domestic affairs by putting
an end to the instability and the impotence of the governments
and that he is a conservative—even a reactionary—in foreign
affairs by using nationalism to destroy European and Atlantic
integration. This shows, incidentally, how differently the character of the Gaullist policy is appreciated and interpreted.

I

In his domestic policies, the General is rather conservative, as
many French think. His goal is to affirm the authority of the
State in order to assure public order and civic obedience. His
temperament also is authoritarian. He has established a pater-
nalistic regime, vastly different from a dictatorship, ·in which

both civil and individual rights are maintained. But the regime is equally different from a democracy because the people have little real say over decisions. The General's ideas on the reform of the State, as he expressed them in the Bayeux speech, and as applied in the constitution of 1958 (prior to the reform of 1962) are ideas and conceptions that the French Right had defended for over a century. They are the ideas of MacMahon in 1876, of Millerand in 1924, of Doumergue in 1934, of Tardieu in 1938: reinforce the powers of the Chief of State independently of direct popular suffrage (since he was to be elected indirectly by the notables who are traditionally conservative), give him the right to veto the decisions of the National Assembly elected directly by the citizens. This corresponds to the old theories formulated by Benjamin Constant one hundred and fifty years ago, and applied in France by Louis XVIII around 1820 and by Louis-Philippe between 1830 and 1848. All the nations of Europe experienced this stage of parliamentary monarchy only to overcome and adopt a parliamentary democracy. In trying to return to it, De Gaulle has shown himself to be a man of the nineteenth century.

We find similar conservative signs in his economic and social policies. He favors private initiative and is opposed to socialist institutions and principles. His two Ministers of Finance thus far—Antoine Pinay and Valery Giscard d'Estaing—are men of the right and anxious to apply orthodox economic principles. The banks and big business have a great influence upon the government. De Gaulle himself is more sensitive to the demands of business men and their associations than to those of the trade unions. His regime favors the business men, the bankers, the speculators, and is relatively insensitive to the claims of the salaried groups and wage-earners, many of whom have a low standard of living, General De Gaulle is closer to Poincaré than to Léon Blum. But, again, this conservative man was between 1944 and 1946 at the head of the most leftist government France had known since 1848, with the exception of the Popular Front. His government, in which the socialists and the communists held many cabinet posts, realized fundamental structural reforms. It nationalized the coal mines, gas and electricity,

four of the larger banks, and the Renault automobile factories. It established a comprehensive system of social security.
It initiated a flexible mechanism for planning, which was copied
by many in Western Europe. Only the Léon Blum government of 1936–1937 and the De Gaulle government of 1944–
1946 realized in the twentieth century such large-scale reforms.
If we add that De Gaulle contributed to the destruction of
the remnants of the dictatorship of Marshal Pétain and to
the reestablishment of the republican institutions and individual liberties—in one word, democracy—we see why we cannot call him a conservative. Since his return to power in
1958, De Gaulle has been following more closely his own personal preferences. He did not question the reforms of 1944–1946
but has left the nationalized industries vegetate while favoring
private firms. Air-France was obliged to relinquish her better
African franchises to a private company. The National Corpora-
tion of Renault is in a weaker position today than Citröen or
Peugeot, both private firms. The planes for the *force de frappe*
are being built by the private company of Dassault and not by
the public firms as provided for by the legislation of 1935.
State control and direction of the private sector of the economy
is less today than it was in the past, something that undermines
state planning. Thus, the creator of the First Economic Plan
has contributed to the weaknesses of the Fifth.

In still a different sphere, General De Gaulle is acting now in
a manner contrary to the way he did twenty years ago. After
the Liberation he abolished the government subsidies to the
private (mostly Catholic) schools. In 1959, subsidies were restored more generously than ever before, and he still continues
to favor the private schools. To be sure, the question of *laïcité*
is no longer the fundamental criterion that separates the Right
from the Left in France; but it remains important. In 1944
De Gaulle was *laïc,* that is to say, he allotted the funds of
the taxpayers to the public schools, which are open to all. Since
1959 De Gaulle has become *clerical,* that is to say, he has
subsidized the Catholic schools with public funds. This is a sign
of a right-wing orientation.

But it remains true that there are progressive elements in

De Gaulle's policies during his "second reign." His fight against the activist military and the right-wing fanatics during the war in Algeria may well have averted a fascist adventure in France. To fight against the O.A.S. *(Organisation de l'Armée Secrète),* De Gaulle relied upon the same majority of 1944–1946, including the trade unions and the Socialist and Communist Parties. Above all, in his constitutional reform of 1962, he replaced the parliamentary monarchy of the nineteenth-century type, which he had incorporated in the Constitution of 1958, with a modern semipresidential system which may well help France in the direction of an efficient democratic system adapted to our times. This regime, contrary to the Gaullist theories and to the Constitution of 1958, had been outlined by some intellectuals of the Left in 1956. It was supported by a number of organizations opposed to De Gaulle, notably the Club Jean Moulin. The fact that the General is able to use and apply the ideas of his adversaries is characteristic of the realism that we mentioned earlier.

Some believe that De Gaulle is surely the expression of comprehensive and profound transformation in France. Until 1939 France remained close to the nineteenth century. The importance of agriculture, the predominance of small and middle-sized firms, protectionism and the lack of a dynamic export policy, a tendency to vegetate and a reluctance to expand were the signs of a rejection of technological progress. In 1945, however, France entered the twentieth century. The reduction of the number of farmers and the transformation of agriculture, the modernization of industry and the growth in size of industrial firms, a dynamism and a will to expand all express the progressive adjustment of an old country to the modern world. This adjustment is not taking place without pain or without opposition. We see, for instance, among the French Right the forces representing both the old and new capitalism. The first were reflected in 1956 in the Poujadist Movement. Today they are expressed through the parties of the traditional Right, notably the Independents of Antoine Pinay. The second is expressed primarily through the "Gaullist" groups.

It may well be that we have oversimplified and that the situation is more complex. But I think my analysis corresponds in general terms to what has been happening. It is remarkable for instance that the electoral strength of Gaullism is greater in the more industrialized, the more developed, and the more modern regions of France, and weaker in the backward rural areas. It is also noteworthy that Gaullism is stronger up to a certain degree (but less clearly so) among the young than among the old.

Thus, De Gaulle is playing in the twentieth century a little bit the same role that Disraeli played in England in the nineteenth. He is adapting the traditional conservative ideas and methods to the new realities of our century. In doing so he is attracting, as Disraeli did, a part of the Left, which is unable to innovate on its own. We must not forget that a good number of socialists and communists vote today for De Gaulle and his supporters. Before 1958 the Communist Party received about 25 percent of the votes; since 1958 it has received less than 20 percent. It has lost about one million votes, of which some have gone to the Gaullists—at least so it seems. But we cannot be sure that De Gaulle's successor will also benefit from a similar transfer of votes. The reforms of Disraeli continued to influence the British Conservative Party—a party that existed before and since his time. Born with De Gaulle, the new Gaullist Party— the U.N.R.—*Union pour la Nouvelle République*—does not have much of a chance of surviving him.

II

De Gaulle's foreign policy is just as complex and ambiguous as his domestic policy. One thing is clear—its guide line is nationalism. France is the only passion of this austere man, the only belief of this skeptic, the only system of this empiricist. Because of this, he is considered abroad as an anachronistic person who acts as a break in the evolution of the world in the direction of broader integrated wholes, such as the European or the Atlantic community. Such a judgment is rather superficial. A lot is being said about the old-fashioned character of nationalism. Certainly in theory the development of communications and the interdependence of peoples make national paro-

chialisms seem absurd. All nations should disappear to be replaced by a worldwide state. But there is not chance for such a
state to emerge. Instead, both in the East and in the West,
something else has been emerging—empires, that is to say,
"superstates" or "supernations." Empires in which the strongest
nation dominates the weaker ones. Moscow attempted to establish its dominion over all communist countries and Washington its "leadership" over the Western world. The two Empires
have attempted to attract in their orbit those who wished to
stay out. As a result, the nationalism of the small- and middle-
sized countries takes the form of a resistance of their peoples
to the domination of the giants that favor the abandonment of
sovereignty, integration, and fusion. But this is in essence a
rationalization for *their* own nationalism, which smaller nationalisms endanger. The superpowers give up nothing and refuse to integrate. Their power is too great to be limited or
qualified by the other members of the "communities" they promote. On the contrary, their decisions, instead of applying only
to their own countries, apply to the whole territory of the "pseu-
do-community." To speak frankly, the USSR has nothing to fear
from the establishment of a European Community of Eastern
Europe, nor the United States in the establishment of an Atlantic community. Moscow and Washington simply enhance
their national power by undermining the smaller nations.

Nationalism has had always two different meanings. For a
weak state it is the expression of freedom against a stronger
one. The right of self-determination, as we used to say, is not
any more old-fashioned than individual liberties. Both express
fundamental and permanent values. Only the nationalism of a
stronger state that attempts to impose its will upon a weaker
one is old-fashioned, as is the case also with a dictatorship and
absolutism that destroys individual rights within a nation-state.

The national independence movements of not only the nineteenth, but also of the twentieth century, correspond to the
first type of nationalism. This is the case with the efforts of
the popular democracies to throw off the Russian yoke and with
the efforts of Latin American countries to assert their autonomy
vis-à-vis their "big brother" in the North. All forms of im-

perialism, colonialism, and expansion, no matter how disguised and how seductive their labels, correspond to the second type of nationalism.

The originality of Gaullist nationalism is that it is axed on both kinds of nationalism and it is sometimes the one and sometimes the other. If the General had the power, it is likely that he would have used nationalism in order to extend the influence of France as Louis XIV and Napoleon did. But confronted with the two giants—the USA and the USSR—he cannot do it. Thus, three courses of action remain open in order to play an important role in the world. Either participate in the Western bloc side by side with the United States—this was the policy of the "directorate of three" suggested in the Memorandum of September 23, 1958; or work for the creation of a Western European bloc independent of the United States in which France would have a dominant position—this was the policy underlying the Franco-German Treaty and the rapprochement with Chancellor Adenauer—or finally help the small nations against the hegemony of the giants by becoming the champion of nationalism: this is the policy he has practiced vis-à-vis the underdeveloped world, extended to Eastern Europe. This is what he would also like to practice in Western Europe.

The first of these three courses of action is unmistakably imperialistic. It gives some freedom to France but only by giving her a part in the domination of other nations. De Gaulle prefers it. He tried to follow it at first and he abandoned it only when he had to. He would, no doubt, return to it if the United States accepted the idea of a "directorate of three." The second is more liberal since its purpose is to free Western Europe from the tutelage of Washington. But it is only in order to replace it in part with a French tutelage. Nor is, finally, the third policy free from imperialist traits. Aid to the former colonies, now independent nations, is full of ambiguity. It can be an instrument for the continuation, under a new form, of the influence of the metropolis. De Gaulle attempted first to arrest the African nationalisms by using force in Algeria and various expedients in French-speaking Africa. He did not become reconciled to the idea of independence until he realized that he had no alternative. But even then, he continued with neocolonialist methods inspired by the American "Big Stick" diplomacy, i.e., the intervention of French parachutists in Gabon in 1964. He has not given it up even while extending aid and support to the various national independence movements in Latin America, Asia, and Eastern Europe.

In foreign policy, as in domestic policy, therefore, we find the same contradiction between De Gaulle's preferences and his acts. This conservative is an innovator despite himself. This man of the right is pushed toward the left by the force of things. The contradiction between the man and his work is more manifest in international than in domestic affairs. It is not true that De Gaulle is doing the policy of the Right in domestic affairs and the policy of the Left in foreign affairs—he simply borrows from both Right and Left. But the conservative traits are greater in domestic affairs and the progressive elements more noticeable in foreign affairs. No other French government for instance, could follow a diplomacy more independent vis-à-vis the United States, more favorable to the national liberation movements, more open toward the East than that of General De Gaulle. This explains the irritation of the Americans and of many Western Europeans. But both should examine calmly two questions: (a) Is it possible for De Gaulle's successor to abandon this nationalist diplomacy and return to a loyalty to the Atlantic world (b) Is the diplomacy of the General really more prejudicial to the interest of the West, or isn't it on the contrary more to its advantage? These questions may shock the reader, but it is impossible to evade them.

III

On both sides of the Atlantic, many think that the nationalist diplomacy of France is due to the personal sentiments of General De Gaulle rather than in accord with the feeling and opinion of Frenchmen. When they are told that the foreign policy of De Gaulle is approved by the majority of the French, as the opinion polls indicate, they then claim that this is the result of a temporary case of "psychological regression." A nation that was the first in the world, that considers itself still superior intellectually, is now reduced by the course of the events to second-rate power. It is not prepared to accept this demotion. But yet it knows it to be inevitable. Rejecting the present status that it detests, it finds refuge in the past. De Gaulle speaks the same language of Jeanne d'Arc, of Louis XIV, of Robespierre, and of Napoleon. He makes the French believe that the days of glory are still here. Yet he cannot blind the French completely. This is clearly shown by the peculiar ambivalence of the French toward De Gaulle; on the one hand they criticize and mock him—on the other they admire him and vote for him. When De Gaulle disappears, this ambivalence will cease and a better perception of reality will prevail.

This thesis assumes that the French nationalism is something special and abnormal in Europe and that it cannot be found elsewhere. But this is not so. Despite all appearances to the contrary, France is not more nationalistic than the United States or Great Britain. Its nationalism is expressed in a different manner because it has to be so expressed—this is all. Let us take the case of the Americans. They are not less nationalistic than the French, simply their country is in a position completely different from that of France. The United States, being by far the strongest nation of the West, can play a leading role in the Atlantic community. Their participation in the community does not limit their power but on the contrary extends it. NATO does not limit the freedom of the President of the United States —in no case can he be forced to submit to the collective will of the other members of the Organization. On the contrary, it is his will that commands them. No considerations of "partnership" can modify the actual relations of forces. The equality among the members of NATO will remain purely abstract because of the overwhelming superiority of the United States vis-à-vis the other allied nations. The notion that a better balance of forces could be established if all the nations of Western Europe united, and that a European community would represent a force about equal to that of the United States is equally illusory. In order for Europe to balance the power of the United States, within NATO, it must become as homogeneous and politically unified as the United States. Such a unity may well

be realized one day—but it is still a long way from now. Neither
our generation nor the next will see this day. As long as the
United States acts with one voice, one government, elected by
one nation, they will be infinitely more powerful than a Europe
speaking with many voices, making decisions through many
governments elected by many nations, even if the European
whole is materially on a level of equality with that of the American whole. For a long time to come, the Atlantic community
will not limit American nationalism—on the contrary, it will
give it a vaster field of action.

There are not any greater differences between the British
and the French nationalisms either. The special ties that unite
England with Washington allow the British to participate up
to a certain point in the leadership of the West. This is simply a
privileged situation that Great Britain enjoys alone among the
allies; it has no real relevance as to the relative distribution of
power. British nationalism appears to be satisfied with this
situation. French nationalism would have also been. Let us not
forget that the first act of the General, after his return to
power, was to ask that France be treated by the United States
in the same manner. The anti-NATO and anti-American diplomacy of the Fifth Republic is nothing but a substitute, developed only after the United States turned down De Gaulle's
Memorandum of September 23, 1958, in which he suggested that
the directorate of two (United States and Great Britain) be replaced by a directorate of three (United States, Great Britain,
and France). If this directorate had been established, the General would have been today one of the staunchest supporters of
the Western Alliance. His nationalist policy turned against
NATO because he was not allowed to act through NATO as
Britain did.

There is also no difference in the intensity of nationalism
between France and the other nations of Western Europe. The
Benelux are too small to develop their own diplomacy. Any comparison that we can make should therefore be limited to the
Federal Republic of Germany and to Italy. Both are, relatively
speaking, new states in comparison to France. The French nation has existed as an independent community for over one

thousand years, while Italy was founded in 1864 and Germany in 1871. Even more, the German Empire and the Weimar Republic were federations. Germany was not really fully unified until the period of 1939–1945. As for Italy, it remains torn between two traditions that correspond to her two periods of greatness—the unitary tradition of the Roman past and the tradition of the independent states of the Middle Ages and the Reformation. To be sure, there is a genuine Italian nationalism, but it is not as old and well rooted as that of France. The German national sentiments are even more fragile. In addition, the present division of Germany and the probability that reunification will not take place in the near future account for the fact that the Federal Republic is not a true nation. It is also true that both Germany and Italy have emerged from dictatorship, a situation that produced a reaction against nationalisms and suggested greater circumspection. In Rome and in Bonn, a leader like De Gaulle would evoke the memories of Hitler and Mussolini rather than those of the resistance! Also, the Germans and the Italians were defeated in 1945 and were reduced almost to complete impotence. Their position in NATO therefore represents for them a great step forward in the direction of national independence when compared to their predicament twenty years ago. France, which was then among the victorious nations and signed the armistice along with Great Britain, the United States, and the Soviet Union, and later joined the Big Four, on the contrary found her position in NATO second to that of the United States and Great Britain and only equal to that of Italy and Germany. For France this amounted to a degradation. Finally, neither Germany nor Italy can effectively have a foreign policy different from that of the United States. Neither one nor the other can say *no* to the United States. Italy does not have the force to do it—economically, politically, or militarily. West Germany has perhaps the power—with a large population and stable political system, greater wealth and industry. But its international status, barring adventures that nobody in Germany wishes to contemplate, places her at the discretion of the United States. The security of West Germany and the status of Berlin depend essentially on the United States. In theory, one may well imagine Bonn playing the game of balance and turning toward the Soviet Union in order to realize its reunification at the price of sovietization. In practice, no political leaders can seriously entertain the thought of becoming a citizen of a communist state. Besides, everything leads us to believe that the Soviet Union in no way wishes a unified Germany—even a communist one.

So it is only France that possesses both adequate power and adequate freedom of maneuver to play the Gaullist game and have an independent policy. If the other European nations do not imitate her, it is more because of lack of power than virtue or prudence. Some say that French freedom of maneuver and power are to a great extent illusory, because they cannot be exercised except under the military protection of the United States. De Gaulle cannot flirt with the East unless he is protected by the American shield. But this does not change the problem at all. If the United States continues to militarily protect France, despite De Gaulle, it is less because they love France than because American security requires that Paris does not fall under the domination of the Soviet Union. A neutral or a "titoist" France would be protected by the American force, just as a France that remains a faithful ally within NATO, simply because a sovietized France would be a terrible threat to the whole of Western Europe. If Western Europe came under the control of Moscow—the future of the United States would be in jeopardy. The absolute imperative for Washington to protect France against a Soviet threat, *of any kind and at any time,* gives freedom to the French government to conduct a relatively independent diplomacy. De Gaulle has understood this better than his predecessors. But he also benefited from a more favorable situation. Indeed, the fact that French nationalism has developed more under the Fifth Republic is due to world developments rather than to the personality of General De Gaulle. Impaled in the war in Indochina and later in Algeria, France did not have freedom to act. The independence of the French diplomacy was asserted after 1962, that is, after the end of the Algerian war and not in 1958, when De Gaulle returned to power. It is interesting to note that during the Fourth Republic there was also a manifestation of diplomatic independence expressed under Mendès-France by the rejection of the European Defense Community. This period coincided with the end of the war in Indochina and the beginning of the Algerian war (July to November, 1954). There is no doubt, however, that the personality of General De Gaulle remains important. He has influenced the natural course of events further and faster than any other political leader could have done. De Gaulle has taught the French—and others—that one can say *no* to Washington without courting disaster. This will not be forgotten. It is impossible to govern after he leaves the political scene as one governed before—with regard to either domestic or foreign policy matters. In the same way in which it is impossible to return to the parliamentary games of the Fourth Republic with cabinet crises every eight months, in the very same way it is impossible to return to the unconditional Atlantic attachment of the fifties.

IV

Because the United States and Great Britain did not give to De Gaulle the place he demanded for France in NATO, and because the policy of a Franco-German condominium in Western Europe failed, De Gaulle has adopted a new and totally different course. He moved closer to the East; he followed a neutralist stance and he launched the idea of a greater Europe "from the Atlantic to the Urals" while at the same time appearing as the champion of the underdeveloped nations in Africa, Asia, and Latin America. For most Americans, and many Europeans, this Gaullist diplomacy is tantamount to treason because it appears to weaken the West vis-à-vis the communist world. This judgment is inspired by a manichean conception of the world divided into two blocs, and is of doubtful validity. In fact it has been rendered obsolete by contemporary developments. De Gaulle's policy, despite its old-fashioned appearances, may in fact be more progressive and modern than the one followed by his critics. In 1965 the situation is vastly different from the one John Foster Dulles confronted in the fifties. The Eastern bloc is in the process of disintegration. China is in open revolt against the Soviet Union. The rivalry of the two communist

powers is beginning to be just as serious as that of the Protest-
ants and the Catholics four centuries ago. The popular democracies in Europe no longer accept the domination of the Soviet
Union and follow separately their own paths toward socialism in
terms of national considerations that are more and more in
evidence. The result has been to weaken Russia. The very fact
that the Soviets are forced to let the Americans bomb a communist nation that has not committed any open act of aggression
(as it was the case with North Korea fifteen years ago) and
that they limit themselves only to verbal protestations, gives a
measure of their weakness. On the contrary, the Western bloc
appears stronger. The time is past when the Prime Minister of
Great Britain, with the moral support of the other countries of
Europe, was able to limit American intervention in Asia. Today,
neither Prime Minister Wilson nor anybody can change the decision of President Johnson. The authority of Washington in the
West is stronger in 1965 than in 1950 (except in Paris). In
addition, the European rearmament and the atomic force of the
United States give to the West a formidable military superiority. The United States, which controls in fact the bulk of the
forces of the West, is in a better position than ever.

The establishment of a third bloc among the nonaligned countries was the dream of the organizers of the Bandung conference and has not materialized. Its potential members are not in
agreement. The different political regimes, national rivalries,
and the conflict between Peking and Moscow have all aggravated
their differences. But even if they could unite, the underdeveloped countries could not compare even remotely in strength
with the Soviet Union and even less with the West. The nonaligned countries are the objects rather than the initiators of
policies; they are pawns rather than actors. But they retain a
considerable importance. Nobody believes any more that the
nations of the West will ever espouse communism in the forsee-
able future or that the nations of the East will return to capitalism. The rivalry between communism and capitalism is taking
place in Africa, Asia, and Latin America—it is only there that
radical changes are likely to occur in the coming decades. But
it is there that the Western bloc, despite its greater political co-

hesion and its greater military and economic strength appears weak when compared with the communist countries. The states of Latin America, Asia, and Africa have no offensive power— they have no freedom to act beyond their frontiers against either the East or the West. But they retain a considerable defensive power, thanks to their revolutionary and guerilla tactics. The resistance of a people cannot easily be broken by foreign armies, no matter how powerful and modern they may be. The war in Vietnam clearly shows this. Victory will belong to those who can convince the uncommitted nations rather than force them. The West is therefore in an unfavorable position. Capitalism is not an answer to the needs of the poor, exploited, and downtrodden peoples. Communism appears to them to be a better answer, a special brand of socialism would suit them even better. But the great majority of Americans and many Europeans do not distinguish between socialism and communism. They oppose socialism as well—thus forcing these nations into a choice between capitalism *or* communism—a choice that is contrary to the interests of the West. Acting with greater circumspection, General De Gaulle serves better the long-range interests of the West. This is clear when we compare Algeria with Cuba. After their respective revolutions, neither the one nor the other was communistic. In both, communists were a well-organized but small minority. Both countries wanted their own socialisms different from the regimes of Moscow and Peking. The material support given to Algeria by France, even if its regime was not particularly approved by the Gaullists, and the establishment of a new kind of agreement for the joint exploitation of oil resources contributed to the weakening of the communist influence in North Africa. The refusal on the other hand by the United States to understand the Cuban expropriations and nationalizations; the suspension of the purchase of sugar, which obliged Castro either to submit to Washington or to seek support elsewhere, on the contrary contributed to the growth of communism in the island. The only problem about the Gaullist policy in the underdeveloped societies is that the material means of France are not adequate. But if the United States adopted the same goals, they would have the means to realize them.

In Europe, the diplomacy of General De Gaulle appears also to be better adapted to the international situation. When the Iron Curtain separated hermetically the East and the West, when the popular democracies were obliged to close their ranks behind Moscow, it was natural to reinforce the ties among the Western European nations in order to better resist the Communist pressure. But things have changed. The Iron Curtain has been slightly parted. The nations of Eastern Europe are manifesting, one after another, a relatively greater independence toward the Soviet Union, which does not have the means to force them to obey. It is naturally to the interest of the West to favor this development. The disappearance of terror, the softening of dictatorships, the liberalization of Communism—these are the real beginnings of the way to democracy. This is the only conceivable form of a roll-back, because a roll-back by force, imagined by some, would result in an atomic war.

The policy of European integration, whose foundations were laid some fifteen years ago, does not take into consideration these recent developments. It forces the countries of Eastern Europe to fall into the arms of Moscow instead of accelerating their march toward independence. It brings the Iron Curtain down again. The efforts of General De Gaulle to develop better ties with the popular democracies, his idea of forming a greater Europe bringing together the countries of the East and West, corresponds better to the situation in 1965 and to the foreseeable trends. Nor does it imply that the integration of Western Europe is to be abandoned. On the contrary, it will be rather pursued as long as it is not an obstacle to the rapprochement with Eastern Europe—that is to say, as long as it is addressed to the economic and technical rather than to the political sphere.

The European diplomacy of the General has another advantage. It permits a frank confrontation of the German problem instead of perpetuating the double talk of the other Western powers. Officially, the United States and its allies demand the German reunification and they support Bonn's demands. In fact, only a few American politicians believe what they proclaim. Neither Great Britain, nor Italy, nor the Benelux countries, nor the Scandinavians, nor the French wish to see the rebirth of a reunified Germany. The participation of the Federal

Republic in the Atlantic Community destroys every possibility
of reunification. The Soviet Union will never accept the formation of a great Germany allied to the West. They will wage war
to prevent it. If the Western powers wanted they might have
been able to make the Federal Republic relinquish all claims
for reunifications some fifteen years ago. It is too late now and
as a result the diplomacy of the United States and of their allies
gets deeper and deeper into a contradiction that is getting more
and more dangerous. It is not wise to support nationalist claims
that affect so deeply a divided and torn country when it is impossible to satisfy them and when in fact there is no intention
to bring them about. There is risk of provoking the most dangerous situations. General De Gaulle has defined better the conditions of a possible reunification. By showing that it presupposes the acquiescence of Eastern Europe and the Soviet Union
and that the rapprochement of the two Germanies presupposes
also the rapprochement of the two Europes, he has dispelled the
lies and the illusions that prevent the citizens of the Federal
Republic from facing reality.

V

In ideal terms, the Gaullist diplomacy is superior to the official diplomacy of the West. As a policy, however, that can be
effectively pursued by France, it is too vulnerable, because
France has no adequate means to implement it. But even this
should not be exaggerated. It is a mistake to think that the
General's policy is completely unrealistic and that it does not
have a direct impact upon events. One may distinguish three
spheres of action. The first is Africa. There De Gaulle has the
means, both material and psychological, to realize his aims. The
financial aid France is giving to the former colonies does not
exceed her means. The popularity of De Gaulle is great, among
both the governments and the peoples who appreciate his independent stance vis-à-vis Washington. By becoming the champion
of French nationalism, he also becomes in their eyes the
champion of all nationalisms and particularly theirs. The second
sphere is that of the other underdeveloped countries in Asia
and Latin America. Here the goals of French foreign policy

have only psychological appeal. For the Latin Americans as for the Asians, De Gaulle incarnates the resistance against the hegemony of the United States and is the champion of self-determination. But De Gaulle does not have the adequate material means to extend his influence. He asks for neutralization in Viet Nam but he cannot support it especially against the double pressures from Peking and Washington. He proposes the Liberation of the Latin Americans from the economic tutelage of the "gringos," but he cannot provide a financial aid that can replace that of the United States. His diplomacy can succeed only in part. The same is true, generally speaking, for Eastern Europe. The popular democracies derive moral support from the nationalism of General De Gaulle and his anti-Americanism so that they can continue the struggle for independence they have been waging ever since 1956 against the Soviet Union. Everything that weakens the rigidity of the two blocs and attenuates the conflict between East and West favors also the political liberalization of their regimes. The rapprochement between Moscow and Paris gives them a green light to move ahead with their own rapprochement with the West. But France has little economic and political strength beyond the moral support that Gaullism provides.

Western Europe constitutes the third sphere of diplomatic action. Here Gaullism can provide neither material nor moral support. The French atom bomb cannot replace the American nuclear shield. French capital cannot replace the American private investments. This may not perhaps be critical since in the last analysis Western Europe must be defended by the United States—even if it abandoned NATO. As for the private American investments, they could be controlled if the Europeans so decided. What is important is that De Gaulle has failed in his policies in Western Europe because he has been unable to convince the European nations of the necessity of becoming independent of the United States. This is due to the predicament of some, for instance Germany, but also to the defeatist attitude of their citizens. The attitude of many Europeans toward the United States is reminiscent of the attitude of the Greeks toward Rome. Tacitus used to say that "they wallowed in their servitude." Another cause for the Gaullist failure lies also in the inability of General De Gaulle to choose between a European nationalism and a French nationalism. One cannot ask the Europeans to abandon American protection in order to accept French protection. They naturally prefer the domination of a strong power rather than that of an equal, of a wealthy country rather than that of one that is not that prosperous, of a distant country rather than of a neighbor. Because they believed that De Gaulle wished to dominate Europe, the Germans, the Italians, the Dutch, and, to a lesser degree, the Belgians reinforced their ties with the United States. Thus their dependence grew despite De Gaulle's efforts to promote independence.

Failure in Western Europe may well account for the collapse of the Gaullist diplomacy. To put an end to the American hegemony in Europe, to support the underdeveloped world, to liberate itself politically, and to develop economically, to favor the liberalization of the popular democracies and their integration in a larger Europe—this immense task is beyond the means of France. But it could be undertaken by the group of nations that lie between England and the Danube, that constitute together the third greatest industrial concentration in the world, with technical and intellectual resources, provided they could unite. The tragedy of Europe in 1965 is that nobody is trying to lead her in this direction. De Gaulle wishes Europe to be independent but refuses to help unite it. The other heads of states favor European unity but are unwilling to work for independence. The first wishes a return to a "concert of Europe"; the second favor a status that provides only a little more independence than say that of the Philippines. The General cannot even hope to make France's position similar to the one Yugoslavia enjoys vis-à-vis the Soviet Union. He is too much involved in the Common Market and benefits from it so much that he may be unable to withdraw. And if the "five" continue to say "yes" to the United States, the solitary "no" of France will inevitably be drowned.

De Gaulle's passion dominates his realism exactly where the two come into conflict. In Africa, in Latin America, in Asia, and in Eastern Europe French nationalism corresponds to the fundamental goals of Gaullist policy, because it is also in accord with the local nationalisms through which resistance to the domination of Moscow and Washington is expressed. Here the man of the nineteenth century is in tune with the needs of the twentieth. In Western Europe, on the contrary, French nationalism is an obstacle to the development of a European nationalism, which alone would provide the tools for the resistance of the Old World against the domination of the New. The General knows it and speaks sometimes of a "European Europe." But he has not abandoned his attachment to France, his "certain idea of France" as he put it in his *Memoirs* which has guided all his life, in favor of a "certain idea" of Europe, which alone would be in accord with his diplomacy. In order to prepare for the twenty-first century, De Gaulle should abandon the nineteenth. It is unlikely that he will. Yet it would be an error to assume that he is the only one who refuses this drastic shift in favor of a European nationalism and that the other Heads of State are more progressive. The present-day use of Big Stick diplomacy, like the nationalism of De Gaulle, has roots in the nineteenth century, and even earlier.

DE GAULLE: IMPLACABLE ALLY

GENERAL
INTRODUCTION

❖

When Charles De Gaulle was thrust upon the world scene he was almost totally unknown, except among French and, ironically enough, some German military circles. His first two books, *La Discorde chez l'ennemi* and *Le Fil de l'epée*,[1] attracted little attention, but his *Vers l'Armée de métier*,[2] which was published in 1934 and in which he advocated the creation of a highly specialized and mechanized army relying upon mobility, quickly became the subject of controversy in France; it was later destined to become the source of his own vindication. He became Under-Secretary of the Ministry of National Defense and War when the German armies were knocking at the gates of Paris, and it was by accident that he found himself in contact with the British. This made it easy for him to leave for England and from there to launch his defiant appeal for resistance. In the dark days of June, 1940, when France lay defeated and the British faced the German armies alone, De Gaulle proclaimed his faith in ultimate victory and urged the French army and people to follow him. The situation was desperate for France. De Gaulle had nothing to work from, and even the hope of victory over Germany could not give him relief: France was faced by actual and prospective allies that dwarfed her.

DE GAULLE AS A POLITICAL PHILOSOPHER

The role of the nation-state. To understand De Gaulle as a military and political figure we must understand his unswerving attachment to his country. France in his eyes is more than its

[1]Translated into English under the title, *The Edge of the Sword* (New York: Criterion, 1960).
[2]Translated into English under the title, *The Army of the Future* (New York: Lippincott, 1941).

1

territory and its people and its history. It is a superior way of
life. It is the flowering of the western values of freedom, tolerance, humanism. Nationalism is not a relative standard, therefore: "My country right or wrong" is alien to De Gaulle. In the
best Hegelian terms, he identifies his country with the ideal. The
spirit, after flirting with Prussia, has settled somewhere in
France. For instance, this is the opening paragraph of his
Memoirs:

All my life I have thought of France in a certain way. This is inspired
by sentiment as much as by reason. The emotional side of me tends
to imagine France, like the princess in the fairy stories or the Madonna
in the frescoes, as dedicated to an exalted and exceptional destiny.
Instinctively I have the feeling that Providence has created her either for
complete successes or for exemplary misfortunes. If, in spite of this,
mediocrity shows in her acts and deeds, it strikes me as an absurd
anomaly, to be imputed to the faults of Frenchmen, not to the genius
of the land. But the positive side of my mind also assures me that
France is not really herself unless in the front rank; that only vast
enterprises are capable of counterbalancing the ferments of dispersal
which are inherent in her people; that our country, as it is, surrounded
by the others, as they are, must aim high and hold itself straight, on
pain of mortal danger. In short, to my mind, France cannot be France
without greatness.[3]

He concludes the same volume, which is devoted to an account
of his efforts to create a resistance movement against Germany,
to bring the Empire to rally behind him, and to persuade the
allies to give him recognition and support, in the following
terms:

Poring over the gulf into which the country has fallen, I am her son,
calling her, holding the light for her, showing her the way of rescue.
Many people have joined me already. Others will come, I am sure. I
can hear France now, answering me. In the depths of the abyss she is
rising up again, she is on the march, she is climbing the slope. Ah!
Mother, such as we are, we are here to serve you.[4]

The allusion to the Hegelian spirit was not made irreverently.
De Gaulle taught history at St. Cyr and was familiar with

[3]*The War Memoirs of Charles De Gaulle* (New York: Simon
and Schuster, 1959), Vol. I, p. 3.
[4]*Ibid.*, p. 302.

Hegel. He was also thoroughly conversant with European history. His conviction that France can speak for Europe is due to a genuine belief that France embodies the spirit of western civilization. But the key phrase in the citation above is that he thought of France "in a certain way." De Gaulle's way is vastly different from that of Maurras or Barrès, or from the nationalism of Renan and Gambetta. It is as different from the universalism that followed the French Revolution as it is from the confining and parochial features of the Restoration. The difficulty in defining it is great because the concept is so elusive. It is the France of the Republic, France the bearer of humanistic values, France the cradle of individualism, France Catholic and religious but also tolerant and agnostic; France with the mission to civilize, educate, and assist the new nations, and, finally, France armed with the sword, ready to contribute to the settlement of world problems. This is the paradox that baffles observers. De Gaulle at one and the same time will plead for national power and international order; for France and Europe alike, and for Europe and the Atlantic world.

De Gaulle's attachment to France is based also upon a general outlook on the role of the nation-state in contemporary life. For De Gaulle, the nation-state is the most durable and inclusive form of association. It is not that "soldiers fight only for their country" (his pithy comment when taking issue with the European Defense Community), but that human beings emote, act, work, and obey within a national setting. This is a datum—not a value judgment. It applies to Albanians and Americans, to French and Luxembourgeois alike. Furthermore, it is a fact that may well be regretted. De Gaulle often has evoked the prospect of larger wholes, alluding to the possibility that cooperative arrangements transcending the nation-state might be developed.

It is also an incontrovertible fact for De Gaulle that even if nations are the only centers of human loyalty, some nations are more developed than others. This has particular relevance to his conception of international relations and the role of the United Nations. The new nations have not as yet developed sufficiently to share with the older ones the same attachment to western

civilization that characterizes the European states. The re-
straints that come from the sharing of common moral and political values are missing. Conflicts about different values, interests, and loyalties are projected upon the international community, only to disrupt it.

If the nation is a reality, how does it manifest itself? The
vehicle of national expression is the state. De Gaulle is heir to
Colbert and Richelieu. The state is the supreme organization
that embodies national aspirations for justice, order, freedom,
cooperation, and equality. No association or group can super-
cede the state—not even the army. In the very depths of defeat
in 1940 when the French Commander-in-Chief, Weygand, urged
an armistice unless the government had other "suggestions," to
make, as he put it, De Gaulle, speaking as a Junior Minister on
behalf of the government, snapped back at his superior officer,
"The government . . . has not suggestions to make, but orders
to give. I am sure it will give them."[5]

Time after time, as we shall see, the same theme is repeated.
The state is supreme; it represents the collective interest, and
must implement values and provide for social and economic
services. In the best idealist tradition De Gaulle sees in the
state the embodiment of the collective will of the nation—detached, equitable, humane, and rational. Where it ceases to
exist there is chaos and conflict; where it is strong and active
there is order and justice and freedom. De Gaulle is not an
authoritarian—though authority is indispensable; he is not a
collectivist—though he advocated more reforms in the last
thirty years than the Socialist Party of France; he is not a
traditionalist—though tradition is an important ingredient of
the authority of the state. De Gaulle is a statist in the sense
that he believes that side by side with the individual, parties,
groups, organizations, and interests, the state has an ultimate
and comprehensive role to play. In the years immediately following the Liberation, for instance, he spoke of the "levers of
command" of the economy and argued that they belonged to the
state. After he assumed the Presidency of the Republic in 1958,
his speeches indicate that he had lost none of his interest in

[5]*Ibid.*, p. 62.

state intervention to serve purposes that individual initiative
either fails to serve or serves without regard to principles of
social equity. For example, when De Gaulle heard of Mussolini's
death, these were his thoughts: "Certainly at the time of the
Fascist apogee, his dictatorship had seemed a firm one. But
fundamentally how could it be, when within it subsisted *the
Monarchy, the Church, and the interest of capitalism,* and when
its people, jaded by the centuries, remained what they had always been despite his fetishes and his rituals?"[6] Neither capitalism nor the church should be served by the state since the
duty of the latter is to serve the whole. Appropriately enough
De Gaulle's conception of the Army is, as we shall see, identical.
The Army is an instrument of *la politique*—it is the arm of the
state.

If the state is viewed as the instrument for the implementation
of national values, its role in international relations is to guarantee the independence and the integrity of the nation against
other states. De Gaulle considers international relations to be
relations between nation-states. No other form of cooperation or
interaction at the international plane is conceivable to him. This,
of course, involves the possibility, indeed the ever-present reality,
of conflict. It calls, therefore, for constant readiness to meet
conflict and hence for the imperative of self-defense.

Force and ideology. There is an almost geometric simplicity
in De Gaulle's tactics, which are based upon the postulate that
only nation-states are real; they each and all must protect the
interests they are supposed to safeguard. Each and every state
covets, or at least may endanger in the pursuit of its interests,
the interests of the others. If this is a dismal picture of the
world, as dismal as the one Hobbes portrayed for human societies, De Gaulle's defense is that he is not to be blamed. He is
not God, even if his critics claim that he acts as if he were!
Force is built into human life and history; only force can
counter force. "Only if children cease to be born, only if minds
are sterilized, feelings frozen, men's needs anesthetized, only if
the world is reduced to immobility, can [force] be banished.
Otherwise, in some form or another, it will remain indispensable

[6]*The War Memoirs, op. cit.,* Vol. III, p. 197. (My italics.)

for, without it thought would have no driving power, action no strength. . . . Force has watched over civilization in the cradle; force has ruled empires and dug the grave of decadence; force gives laws to the peoples and controls their destinies." De Gaulle quotes Cardinal de Retz approvingly, "Laws, if they are not backed by force, will soon fall into contempt." France, like all nations, "was made by the sword and must be defended by the sword." [7]

It is then imperative for a nation-state to be strong. De Gaulle's conception of domestic strength is primarily that of order and leadership. Various ideologies, political regimes, institutions fit different peoples to serve best the needs of their particular nations. They are only instruments, often changing to meet new contingencies. Underneath them there is always the reality of the nation they serve. When the ideological "break" between China and the Soviet Union was mentioned in a press conference on July 29, 1963, De Gaulle answered as follows:

The break? Over what ideology? During my lifetime, Communist ideology has been personified by many people. There have been the eras of Lenin and Trotsky and Stalin—whom I knew personally—and of Beria and Malenkov and Khrushchev and Tito and Nagy and Mao Tse-tung. I know as many holders of the Communist ideology as there are fathers of Europe. And that makes quite a few. Each of these holders in his turn condemns, excommunicates, crushes, and at times kills the others. In any event, he firmly fights against the personality cult of the others. I refuse to enter into a valid discussion on the subject of the ideological quarrel between Peking and Moscow. What I want to consider are the deep-rooted realities which are human, national, and consequently international.

The banner of ideology in reality covers only ambitions. And I believe that it has been thus since the world was born.[8]

Communism, he argued, has only given added strength to that which always existed in Russia, and the Chinese adoption of the same ideology hides the perennial drive of the "yellow multitude" to expand and conquer. As for the United States, "liberalism"

[7] *The Edge of the Sword, op. cit.,* p. 9.
[8] *Major Addresses, Statements, and Press Conferences of General Charles De Gaulle,* May 19, 1958–January 31, 1964 (New York: French Embassy, Press and Information Service), pp. 236–237.

is a mask that hides the face of a powerful and industrial nation, determined to establish its hegemony over the world.

Unless and until a given ideology and a given political system attempt directly or indirectly to subvert the other systems, De Gaulle is not interested in evaluating political forms and expressing preferences for ideologies. Except, of course, for France. A devout Catholic and a military man, De Gaulle has never done or said anything to deride the Republic in France. During the thirties, when many officers flirted with extreme right-wing movements, De Gaulle was associated with a progressive Catholic group whose attachment to the Republic was unimpeachable. Upon the liberation of France he proceeded to rebuild the Republic and ultimately to allow it to go its own way. Again in 1958 he reaffirmed his faith in the republican institutions and became the architect of a constitution that, whatever his critics say, preserves the heart of a republican state—free elections, free popular consultations, free parties, free speech, and freedom of assembly. To say this, however, is not necessarily to argue that De Gaulle is a republican by preference or conviction. The Republic appears to him to be the only viable political form for France. A statesman, as a weaver, must work with the material he has. A greater number of Frenchmen can live together under the Republic than under any other system. History and tradition have woven the fabric—to tear it apart is to endanger the nation. The fabric must be rewoven stronger than ever. As we try to show in some of the excerpts we reproduce, De Gaulle has nothing but contempt for institutional arrangements that deprive the nation of leadership; that allow particular interests to entrench themselves; that prevent the people from participating in one form or another in the large national decisions. A republican regime must therefore provide for leadership and popular participation. Neither the Third nor the Fourth Republic managed to do this. The Fifth Republic, established at a time when France seemed to be on the brink of civil war, is what in De Gaulle's mind best reconciles leadership with political participation; representation of interests and government for national interest; freedom and stability; popular control with central direction.

To be precise, a major defect of the Third and especially of the Fourth Republic was to have concentrated all powers in the hands of a divided assembly and thus to have undermined national leadership by creating an "irresponsible" President who had no authority to speak for France when it came to major internal problems and, more particularly, foreign policy and defense. The state, therefore, became so weakened that it could not represent the nation, since the system itself put the premium on local, party, and interest representation from which no national purpose could emerge. De Gaulle's thoughts here probe one of the most critical and unresolved problems of political theory —that of the national will. His resolution of the problem is that political life can be viewed from two planes. The one plane is that of the particular and group interests constantly acting and interacting. They must be given a large degree of latitude since their activity is essential for the release of the mainsprings of individual interest and action. But while De Gaulle maintains that such freedom is essential, he argues that it is not adequate. A system must also provide its citizens with the possibility to contemplate issues that go beyond their specific professions, interests, or roles. A citizen is more than the sum total of the interests he represents or the roles he performs. This is the second plane of discourse and, according to De Gaulle, the Third and Fourth Republics were at fault for not having instituted mechanisms and institutions to provide for leadership and representation on the broader issues that transcended particular ones. While the interests thrived, purpose was at a standstill; while particularisms flourished, the whole slumbered; while each was represented in parliament, the voice of the nation was not heard; while the particular man was solicited in elections, the citizen was ignored. As a result, the political community was reduced to warring and irreconcilable factions and the nation-state was allowed to disintegrate. To provide the institutions through which the interest and purpose of the nation and its citizenry can be tapped without doing away with legitimate spheres of particular interest is then the objective of the Fifth Republic. De Gaulle provided for a strong President, national participation on key national issues through referendums, and a parliament whose functions and role are limited within specified, albeit broad, spheres of action. Thus the Republic, he claimed, is preserved and the state strengthened. Through the President, who is to be elected by the whole nation for a period of seven years, France can communicate with other states; prepare her defense; be ready to meet emergencies that threaten her and, when need be, appeal to the people for consultations on key issues and periodically in elections.

The Army. In addition to his understanding of the role of force in history, one will find in De Gaulle's writings a strong appreciation of the importance of the army. In *The Edge of the Sword* he develops a theme that brings together into a curious synthesis Hegel, Clausewitz, and Bergson. War is a continuing process and a necessity; through force and military power great ideals are realized. Instinct, as much as reason and meditation, is an important attribute of the military leader. He rejects the Tolstoian idea that chance and accident can shape events, and emphasizes design and planning. The will of a leader "capable of giving intense, extended, and indefatigable consideration to a single group of objects" will prevail. Events are likely to bend to his purpose.

But the role of the army for De Gaulle is part and parcel of *la politique*—of state purpose. A commander, if he is to be great, must be capable of more than contemplation; he must also serve the broad designs of statecraft. This is difficult since the spheres of action, the personalities, and the roles of the political and the military leaders differ. The only way out, according to De Gaulle, lies in a common effort between military and political leaders to reach agreement. Despite his numerous jabs at the politician, he nowhere advocates the superior claim of the military, even in time of war. The soldier must obey the state. But which state? This is the rub. When the military in Algeria rose in May, 1958, against the civil authority in Paris, De Gaulle did not condone the revolt, but neither did he condemn it. When Pétain signed the armistice with Nazi Germany, De Gaulle appealed to the army to revolt. The ultimate criterion for obedience is the character of the state. In 1940 and again in 1958, De Gaulle rationalized his intrusion into political life and his assumption of power by claiming that there was no state. In 1940 the State had violated its treaties and "betrayed" France. In 1958 there were strong indications that the State could no longer exact obedience and impose order.

This criterion is a pragmatic one. While disobedience can be entertained (or even encouraged) when the state abdicates its role, it cannot be tolerated when there is a state. Since his return to power, however, De Gaulle has done more than attempt to inculcate obedience where there was disobedience and establish loyalty where there was equivocation. For eighteen years after the end of World War II French soldiers and officers had been fighting and losing. When De Gaulle came to power, Algeria seemed to be the last stand and many had turned against the Fourth Republic because of their unwillingness to face another defeat. De Gaulle after four years of effort put an end to this situation. The army is back in France. The "lost soldiers" are home, even if many had to go to prison first. The army is again a servant of the Republic and colonial adventures and misadventures have given way to the construction of what the Third and Fourth Republics failed to build—an *Armée de Métier*, a professional army.

The colonies. De Gaulle's colonial policy took many by surprise. The man who defied the awesome combination of Roosevelt and Churchill during World War II, when France was weak and the Empire divided and a prey to the actual or putative ambitions of the British and Americans, has liquidated what he fought so hard to preserve. In 1958 he tried to bring the African colonies and Madagascar into the "French Community," a scheme which allowed broad autonomy to the erstwhile colonies while retaining in the hands of France the power to make decisions on major matters. But even then he ventured further than any previous statesman. He promised the colonial peoples that they could become free and independent if they chose to vote against the draft of the new Constitution in the referendum of September 28, 1958. When Sékou Touré of Guinea indicated in August, 1958, that he intended to ask his followers to do just that, De Gaulle was taken by surprise. When Guinea actually rejected the Constitution, he expressed overtly his displeasure. But he proceeded thereafter calmly to accept what was inevitable and to grant the colonies their independence.

It was Algeria that taxed his statecraft, his authority, and perhaps even his understanding. He was caught in a tangle in which at least five groups were involved—part of the French Army, the French *colons* in Algeria, the French in the metropolis, the Algerians in Algeria, and the Algerian rebel forces. Occasionally a sixth group—the Algerians in France—thrust its rebellious head into the open only to be countered by still a seventh group—the French militant nationalists in the metropolis with their conspiratorial organization committed to acts of terror and political assassination. The "game," grim and implacable, was so complex, took so many turns, involved so many alliances and fronts that broke down only to be reformed with different players in different combinations, that we simply cannot discuss it here. But De Gaulle managed to "play" it successfully and, what is more, succeeded in writing what appears to be its definitive epilogue. The solution was one that no French party or political leader, not even De Gaulle, dared openly espouse: direct negotiations with the Algerian rebels, liberation of their leaders from the French prisons, independence of Algeria, and repatriation of the more than 800,000 French men, women, and children to the metropolis, with their consequent resettlement at the expense of the state. The Algerian case is now closed. Unless there are dramatic international developments that bring the Algerian leaders into an alliance with China and Algeria becomes the Cuba of Africa, it is very doubtful that Algeria will again becomes a critical and divisive issue in French politics. Thanks to De Gaulle's policy (no matter what the equivocations) the French political community appears today to have solved the most difficult and dangerous problem it has faced since the end of World War II.

It is interesting to speculate about De Gaulle's motives for his policy of decolonization. Did he really believe in colonial emancipation and independence as a matter of principle, or was it expediency? I think it was rather the latter. Over a period of time, De Gaulle came to the conclusion that military and political control of the colonies would ultimately weaken France, thus detracting from his main purpose of making her again a great power. World conditions had changed radically; to continue to fight for dominion over the African peoples would eventually prove to be debilitating and detrimental to the power of France. To fight guerrilla wars and to deploy forces in the former colonies was to dim the hope of building a strong army equipped with modern weapons. It was preferable to lose Algeria than in effect to lose the French Army. It was also better to lose the adventurous and romantic soldiers who were fighting hopeless battles in the desert and to gain the technicians and the professionals that would fashion the new sword of France. In giving up Algeria, De Gaulle was asking the French, in his words, to "wed the twentieth century."

The nuclear arm. "War is an activity in which the contingent plays an essential part," are the opening words of *The Edge of the Sword*. So is the preparation for war. Though techniques rapidly changed during and after World War II, De Gaulle's general analysis in *The Army of the Future*[9] applies today and provides us with a guideline to his military policy. Defense is the inalienable and ultimate prerogative of a nation. It cannot be delegated nor can it be so implemented as to allow any one but the nation-state the discretion to use force. This is the heart of the Gaullist doctrine. To be sure, alliances and treaties, military agreements, common defensive plans are indispensable. But their scope and the choice of allies is contingent upon the shifting character of the interests of the nation and the existing equilibrium of forces.

New techniques naturally modify geographic considerations, but cannot possibly eliminate them. In the thirties, De Gaulle had predicted that the coming war would be one of great mobility. He pleaded for mechanized units with maneuverability to bring the war if need be to the territory of the enemy, for concentration of mechanized power and for operations far behind the enemy lines. He felt that given her industrial potential and know-how, France could and should have developed a mechanized army. What then applied to his conception of a mechanized army now applies to an atomic force. Without it a country is doomed

[9]*Op. cit., passim.*

to be dependent upon an ally when there is no guarantee that the ally's interests are or rather will remain congruent with those of France. Such dependence puts the country at the mercy of both ally and enemy, each possessing nuclear weapons. Without such weapons France can have no credible force to sustain her interests in Europe and elsewhere, or to deter an enemy from territorial expansion which, even if not directly aimed at France's territory, may finish by isolating her, encircling her, or destroying her allies. "The enemy may appear in many different ways" writes De Gaulle. "Events may lead to an action being fought now in one place, now in another." Besides, a former enemy may be today's friend and the friend of today the enemy of tomorrow.

While the implications of this stand with regard to foreign policy and international relations are complex, from the strict military point of view, they mean one and only one thing. France must have her own nuclear force. De Gaulle founded the French Atomic Commission in 1945, and the Fourth Republic proceeded at a slow but steady pace, at least until about 1955, to allocate credits for the development of fissionable material. After the Suez adventure in 1956, the atomic energy program was stepped up, and when De Gaulle returned to power in 1958 the plans for the manufacturing and testing of atomic weapons had been made. In 1960 and 1961 France tested four atomic weapons and began the production of operational atomic bombs of the magnitude of sixty kilotons—roughly three times the power of the Hiroshima bomb. All preparations have also been made for the testing of hydrogen bombs in the French possessions in the Polynesian islands. Reliance on nuclear weapons has accordingly led to the reduction of the length of military service and of conventional armaments, and to an emphasis upon the development of delivery systems, including ballistic missiles that can launch atomic bombs from the air and the ground or later in the future from submarines.

It is not surprising then that France was the only other great power besides China not to sign the Limited Test Ban Treaty, forbidding atmospheric testing of nuclear weapons. According to De Gaulle, to do so would have deprived the nation of the chance to acquire weapons that its present allies and adversaries already have. It would have allowed a perpetuation of an unequal and dependent status for France. Nor is it surprising that the French position with regard to disarmament has been so uncompromising. France is willing to agree with the United States, the Soviet Union, England, and other powers for gradual and general disarmament to bring about some equality among the large nation-states rather than to consecrate the inequality of all vis-à-vis the two superpowers. Disarmament talks that do not deal with what directly affects the power of the Soviet Union and the United States—nuclear stockpiles and ICBMs—do not affect the existing balance of forces. Rather they perpetuate the superiority of the two rivals. Disarmament talks whose purpose is to freeze the existing balance of nuclear weapons are viewed as a technique to prevent all other powers from acquiring the weapons the Soviet Union and the United States have.

Alliance and the game of balance. According to De Gaulle the nation-state and only the nation-state is real. International relations are relations between independent, sovereign, and armed nation-states. Like human beings, nation-states are driven by the quest for power. Neither ideologies nor governmental institutions matter very much. As far as France is concerned, American ambitions for hegemony, in De Gaulle's eyes, have been just as dangerous as those of the Soviet Union, China, or Germany. Any one of them may subjugate France and reduce her to a state of tutelage. This was the perennial, almost pathological, fear that haunted him during World War II. The "Anglo-Saxons," his allies, were also his potential enemies. And as victory over Germany became inevitable the danger to France increased!

Alliances like ideologies are not necessarily lasting. They are constantly qualified by changing economic, political, and power considerations. De Gaulle was among the very first to predict that, notwithstanding their ideological affinities, China and the Soviet Union would soon find themselves at odds. The most implacable enemies may find new situations in which common interests dictate conditions for peace and ultimately alliance. There is a remarkable passage in De Gaulle's *Memoirs* in which he tells us that shortly before the total collapse of Germany he received a semi-official memorandum from Himmler in which the German leader conceded defeat. "But now what will you do?" he asked. "Rely on the Americans and the British? They will deal with you as a satellite . . . Actually the only road that can lead to greatness and to independence is that of an entente with defeated Germany." De Gaulle admits that there was "certainly an element of truth in the picture it sketched" and adds significantly enough: "But the desperate tempter being what he was received no reply from me . . . *Moreover he had nothing to offer*."[10] The case was different, of course, with West Germany more than a decade later. Bonn had something to offer!

The irresistible drive to power and domination by one or more states can be countered only by the power of another state or a coalition of states. Hence the role of alliances and their ever-changing and shifting character. For a weak state to be allied with a strong one may under certain conditions be the very essence of survival. For the same state to be allied to a strong one may under different conditions be the essence of tutelage. To allow only two powerful states to have nuclear weapons may, in classic Hobbesian terms, suggest to them agreements that will consecrate their hegemony over all the others. Alliance must be made only with an understanding of what they are—temporary expedients to face common dangers for the protection of the interests of a nation-state. They must be carefully distinguished from any integrative schemes that would inevitably subordinate the sovereignty and freedom of a state. In one of his most critical speeches of American policy, De Gaulle said: "The same people with the same intention, wanted our country . . . to be literally dissolved in a Europe described as integrated, which, lacking the incentives of sovereignty of the peoples and responsibility of the States, would automatically be surbordinated to the protector across the ocean."[11]

If Metternich, Castlereagh, and Canning are the names we associate with the balance of power in the nineteenth century, De Gaulle has been its foremost exponent in the shrinking world of the mid-twentieth century. It is in the name of balance that he has opposed the consolidation of the two power blocs in the

[10]*The War Memoirs, op. cit.*, Vol. III, pp. 200–201. (My italics.)
[11]*Address of April 27, 1965.*

world, because he feared a collusion between the two superpowers that would destroy the independence of other states. It
is in the name of balance that he has done all he could to undermine American control within NATO and, if at all possible,
Soviet control over the satellites of Eastern Europe. It is in the
name of balance that he recently saw in a Franco-German alliance
the foundation of a West European bloc, and it may well be that
in the name of balance he may try to come to terms, over the
ghost of German unification, with the Soviet Union *if* the Franco-
German alliance fails to provide him the leverage he wants in
Western Europe. De Gaulle, in the pursuit of France's interest,
as he perceives it, has tried every conceivable scheme of balance
and is likely to continue to experiment with others as the situation changes. If I may quote what I wrote some time ago:

General De Gaulle's conception of a "balance" has been a permanent
trait of his thinking and action ever since he became a public figure.
This conception underlay his belief in a "buffer" Central Europe with a
dismembered Germany. In the third volume of his *Memoirs* he points
out that the only way to have kept Russia out of the heart of Europe
was to dismember Germany. By so doing the threat of a new Germany
would have been eliminated and with it the fears of the Eastern European nations alleviated. There would have been no need for them to
seek Soviet support and correspondingly no compelling urgency on the
part of the Soviet leaders to give it.

A second plan to achieve "balance" was outlined in his offer to
Churchill in November 1944 to combine forces so that the two countries
with their far-flung Empires would be able to act independently of the
Russians or the Americans.

. . . A third scheme that was to lead to an equilibrium involved an
alliance with the Soviet Union. Speculating about his trip to the Soviet
Union in December 1944 and only a few weeks after he had talked with
Churchill, De Gaulle writes wistfully: "Perhaps it might be possible to
renew in some manner the Franco-Russian solidarity, which even if
misunderstood and betrayed in the past, was nonetheless compatible
with the nature of things [*nature des choses*] both with regard to
the German danger and the Anglo-Saxon efforts to assert their hegemony." After the conclusion of the *"belle et bonne alliance"* with
the Soviet Union in December 1944 De Gaulle declared that the pact
of alliance and mutual assistance with Soviet Russia answered a
"natural and traditional" orientation for the two countries.

A fourth and perhaps more persistent effort to recreate a balance is the revival of Europe as a "Third Force." A definition of what "Europe" exactly means for De Gaulle is a difficult matter. In his *Memoirs* he speaks of an organization of the peoples of Europe from "Iceland to Istanbul and from Gibraltar to the Urals." Sometimes Russia is part and sometimes it is not, though emphasis is often put on the European destiny of Russia. Sometimes it is western Europe and sometimes the whole of Europe, sometimes Europe with a dismembered Germany, sometimes a divided Germany, and sometimes a Franco-German rapprochement without qualifications. Two things are certain: Europe, whatever it is, is distinct from the "Anglo-Saxon powers." It is also separate from Soviet Russia, without, however, excluding under certain conditions the European vocation of Russia.

The search for a balance finally has led De Gaulle to examine the role of China. In his November 10, 1959, press conference he declared: "Without any doubt Soviet Russia, though it has helped the establishment of Communism in China, realizes that nothing can change the situation of Russia—white nation of Europe—facing the yellow multitude that is China, innumerable and miserable, ambitious and indestructible, building—thanks to severe sacrifices—a force that cannot be measured, and eyeing the vast areas into which it will have to expand sooner or later." Thus, the Soviet foreign policy may be influenced by the realization on the part of Soviet leaders that their destiny and future lie ultimately with the West against some of the forces of Asia to which Soviet Communism has given leadership and a new vision.[12]

De Gaulle as a Statesman

World War II, despite its victorious progress, was a record of bitterness for De Gaulle. It took long and painful efforts to establish his authority to speak on behalf of France. It is a story that he tells himself in the first two volumes of his *Memoirs*. But it is one that shows him to be a great tactician. By the end of 1944 he had managed to weave the various resistance forces in the interior of France and the Free French Forces into one. He had broadened his Provisional Government to include leaders of various resistance groups and political parties, including the Communists, and had established a con-

[12]"De Gaulle's Foreign Policy and the Fifth Republic," *The Yale Review*, Winter, 1961, pp. 175–179.

sultative assembly representing the various political interests and forces.

From the domestic point of view his position in 1944 was unequivocal. He represented all the forces of France that had rallied against Germany and the remnants of the "Vichy government." The conflicts with the Communist Party and the Communist front organizations were resolved speedily after the Liberation because of De Gaulle's willingness to grant them participation in his government, because the massive presence of allied troops would have made any Communist effort to seize the government impossible, and because of the conciliatory attitude of Moscow which was concerned with a speedy resolution of the war rather than Communist take-overs in western Europe. When Paris was liberated on August 25, 1944, De Gaulle entered it as the new head of France, receiving recognition from all major governments. But at the very moment of victory the military and international problems facing France were stupendous. He realized this only too well in the closing lines of the second volume of his *Memoirs*. "Slowly, severely, unity was forged. Now the people and the leader, helping each other, were to begin the journey to salvation. . . ."[13] Salvation meant reconstruction at home and reaffirmation of France's sovereignty and independence abroad. Above all it meant the return to the status France had occupied before her defeat in 1940.

Internal reconstruction called for comprehensive institutional reforms. During his stay in office between August 1944 and January 1946, De Gaulle proceeded with drastic economic and social reforms. Under his government, credit was nationalized, coal and electricity came under state ownership and control, a new school to train civil servants and a new process of recruiting them was introduced, special legislation provided for benefits to families with more than two children (a measure designed to cope with the population decline in France), and for the relief and rehabilitation of the veterans and the prisoners of war. A commission to plan the economy by providing subsidies and investment to key industrial and agricultural activities was established and undertook the monumental task of taking inventory of

[13]*The War Memoirs, op. cit.*, Vol. II, p. 362.

the French economy, suggesting reforms and recommending investments. De Gaulle's nineteen months in office embrace a period of the most comprehensive social and economic reforms undertaken in the twentieth century in France.

De Gaulle failed, however, to reorganize successfully the political institutions. Unity had been forged and while the war continued it lasted. After V-E Day, however, the political parties were unable to agree with De Gaulle's scheme for a new constitution. But even the institutional difficulties were perhaps less ominous than the pressing international problems. They revolved around the following: the fate of Germany; the settlement of the European peace; the future of the French Empire. Relatedly they affected the role France was to play in the future world settlement and organization for peace. De Gaulle's position on Germany was unequivocal. No settlement could be reached that was not based upon the consent of France. No occupation of enemy territory could be envisaged which did not provide also for French participation. Both before and after Yalta De Gaulle made it clear that he would not accept anything that had been decided there in his absence. He has returned to this theme quite frequently but it was not until 1965 that he began to present forcefully the thesis that European problems could be settled by Europeans (including the Russians), and that even the resolution of the German territorial problems and the signing of a definitive peace settlement could be solved in the same manner.

In his *Memoirs,* De Gaulle wrote of the aftermath of the Yalta Conference in the following terms:

. . . The enormous chunk of Europe which the Yalta agreements had abandoned in advance to the Soviets was now in their hands. Even the American armies, after having overrun the frontiers established for them in Germany during the last days of the fighting had fallen back 150 kilometers. . . . Thus all question of frontiers was decided quite simply by the Soviets. Furthermore, in Warsaw, Budapest, Sofia, Belgrade, and Tirana, the governments that had been installed were at their discretion and almost all at their beck and call. Yet the rapidity of this Sovietization was only the inevitable result of what had been agreed upon at the Crimea conference. The regrets the British and Americans now expressed were quite uncalled for.[14]

[14]*The War Memoirs, op. cit.,* Vol. III, p. 229.

The Potsdam Conference held some five months later was an anticlimax; De Gaulle expected that no good could come of it except to consecrate the mistakes perpetrated at Yalta. "Now that everything had been arranged," he writes, "what could he have done there?"

By the end of 1945 De Gaulle had failed to accomplish his dream:

I intended to assure France primacy in Western Europe by preventing the rise of a new Reich that might again threaten its safety; to co-operate with East and West and, if need be, contract the necessary alliances on one side or the other without ever accepting any kind of dependency; to transform the French Union into a free association in order to avoid the as yet unspecified dangers of upheaval; to persuade the states along the Rhine, the Alps, and the Pyrenees to form a political, economic, and strategic bloc; to establish this organization as one of the three world powers and, should it become necessary, as the arbiter between the Soviet and Anglo-American camps.

The means were poor indeed! Yet if France had not yet taken into her hand the trump of her ultimate power, she still held a number of good cards: first of all, the singular and century-old prestige which her miraculous return from the brink of the abyss had partially restored; then the fact that her cooperation was no longer to be despised amid the disequilibrium that burdened the entire human race; and lastly, the solid units constituted by her territories, her people and her overseas extensions. Even before we had recovered all our strength, these elements put us in a position to act and to make ourselves respected.

On condition we put them to good use. Here, indeed, lay my task. But to compensate for all we lacked, I required bold support from the nation. This granted, I could promise that no one would ignore or defy the will of France. Naturally, our allies expected the situation to be otherwise; whatever their regard for General De Gaulle, they oriented their nostalgia toward the old, political France, so malleable and so convenient, and watched for the inevitable discords to appear between myself and those who anticipated a return to yesterday's regime.[15]

That he was unable to use the means available to him was due primarily to the domestic difficulties that led to his departure in January, 1946. Thereafter, France experienced what the framers of the constitution had professed to avoid: weak cab-

[15]*Ibid.*, pp. 204–205.

inets, a vacillating foreign policy, and a slow erosion of military strength. The alliance with the United States in the form of NATO became France's sole security. But both England and Western Europe were coming increasingly under the control of the United States. In Egypt and again in Algeria this was driven home. But even more serious was the fact that the defense of Europe was virtually in the hands of the United States. Thus when France appeared on the road to recovery after her liberation, world developments underscored her weakness and her dependence upon a friendly but foreign power.

This was the picture De Gaulle saw when he returned to power in 1958. While there was never any doubt that American protection was needed, and that Soviet Communism represented the obvious danger for France, he was determined to break away from American tutelage and assert fully France's independence and freedom of action. The course he had to follow was a difficult one. In essence he had to oppose a friendly but overwhelmingly powerful ally—as long as the potential enemy did not threaten. He had to steer a careful course between the ally's threshold of tolerance (which he knew to be high) and the enemy's potential aggressiveness (which with the emergence of the Sino-Soviet dispute was considerably moderated). The parameters of freedom proved to be greater than De Gaulle had anticipated.

Immediately after his return to power, De Gaulle asserted that it was not the intention of France to limit her foreign policy "within the confines of NATO." On September 23, 1958, he addressed a secret memorandum to Henri Spaak, Prime Minister Macmillan, and President Eisenhower. It is, however, common knowledge that the memorandum was a diagnosis of the problems facing NATO and, in addition, a statement of French policy. De Gaulle indicated his sympathy with the common responsibilities imposed upon the alliance in case of war, but pointed to the inequality in armaments and, what is more, the inequality in the power to make decisions among the allies. Events in Egypt contrasted sharply with those in the Near East and Formosa. He proposed, therefore, the establishment within NATO of a "directorate" of three—England, France, and the United States—with the responsibility for elaborating a global military and political strategy, creating allied commands for all theaters of operation, to say nothing of joint strategy deliberations and decision for the use of atomic weapons. "The European states of the continent," he stated on April 11, 1961, ". . . must know exactly with which weapons and under what conditions their overseas allies would join them in battle." Thus he reminded President Kennedy that "the theaters of war are no longer limited to Europe" and that the North Atlantic Treaty Organization should accordingly be revised in order to meet jointly non-European problems. There was also a threat in the memorandum: France would reconsider its NATO policy in the light of the response of England and the United States.

Though ostensibly addressing himself to problems related to NATO, De Gaulle was actually attempting to place France at a level to which no other European power in NATO could aspire. NATO was to remain a regional organization, but with three of its members—France, England, and the United States—jointly in charge of global strategy. The three great powers were to be in charge at the NATO level of problems of the Atlantic Alliance and jointly in charge of global strategy as well. When his proposal was rejected, De Gaulle withdrew the Mediterranean Fleet from NATO command; he refused to integrate French air defense with NATO; he prevented the building of launching sites and the stockpiling of atomic warheads over which France could have no control. In May 1965, France refused to participate in the NATO military exercises.

Since the allies seemed unwilling to subordinate use of atomic weapons to a "directorate," France proceeded with the explosion of her own atom bomb in 1960 and with preparation for the testing of hydrogen weapons. A number of additional reasons for so doing were then given: the uncertainty about the use of the bomb by the United States except in self-defense; the need for a French deterrent; the injection of a new pride and higher morale in an army that had experienced one frustration after another, and finally, the worldwide commitments of France.

As long as other powers have nuclear weapons, De Gaulle claims that the only policy consistent with French interests is to develop nuclear strength. And at the various disarmament con-

ferences the French continued to favor the liquidation of stockpiles and delivery missiles *before* the suspension of the manufacture and testing of nuclear weapons.

De Gaulle's enthusiasm for the Common Market was motivated
in part by economic reasons and by considerations favoring the
development of a European "whole." The crucial reasons, however, were political. The Common Market gave him a bargaining
position with the British in respect to the demands of the Memorandum of September 23 and a number of other issues, notably
Berlin, atomic weapons, and the agenda of the ill-fated summit
conference of June 1960. In repayment for Adenauer's participation in the Common Market and as a compromise of their disagreements about the extent and nature of military integration
in NATO, De Gaulle became a staunch supporter of the Berlin
status quo.

Thus, while opposing European political integration, De Gaulle
has been quick to use as a political weapon the hopes of his
partners that the Common Market might lead to eventual union.
In 1963 he decided that England, whose ties with the United
States appeared to him too close, should not be permitted to
join the Common Market. He concentrated on establishing special
relations with West Germany and repeatedly stated that political
cooperation in Western Europe should be based upon intimate relations between the two former enemies. When the successor of
Konrad Adenauer, Ludwig Erhard, appeared to hesitate and
then to favor the continuation of close ties with the United
States, De Gaulle opened up the prospect of direct negotiations
between France and the Soviet Union in order to settle the
future of Germany. In the meantime he continued to whittle
down France's participation in NATO. The recognition of China,
his trip to Latin America in 1963, his pronouncements in favor
of the "neutralization" of Southeast Asia, his criticisms of
"military and political intervention in the affairs of other states"
(during the American intervention in Santo Domingo in May
1965), his violent opposition to the American MLF arrangements and to the principle of graduated deterrence, his scornful
rejection of the Moscow Test Ban Treaty, were all part of the
same grand design. France under De Gaulle was an independent

world power. As André Fontaine wrote with justice some years ago:

Everything is aimed to accomplish an objective, however remote. A Europe to its full geographic limits, with African, Near Eastern, and —who knows—South American extensions . . . A Europe that will no longer be divided between American and Soviet zones of influence, a Europe which might even receive Russia the day it becomes "Russian" as it is predestined by history, a Europe that will once more become the nerve center of the world and which might if it were necessary arbitrate between the great empires. De Gaulle, like the other French political leaders, cannot envisage such a Europe except under French leadership, so that France in the name of Europe will have attained the rank of world power and full independence.

Thus the vocation of greatness continues to be the central part of French foreign policy. Relying upon national strength and nuclear weapons, counting upon the development of a modern economy which already begins to compare very favorably with that of Great Britain and Western Germany, De Gaulle believes that France is creating a Third European Force that will ultimately be able to arbitrate between the United States and the Soviet Union.[16]

A strong nation-state; a nation-state interacting with other nation-states; a republican state with leadership and authority in France—these are then the basic presuppositions of De Gaulle. Since 1958 his reform of the institutions; his efforts to invigorate the economy and to bring the Army under control; even his liquidation of the French Empire and the withdrawal from Algeria, have all been part of the great design to provide national strength. If we ignore his tactical mistakes; a certain propensity for pomp and ritual (but De Gaulle would fully agree with Bagehot that the ceremonial is easily understood and appreciated by the people) ; some contradictions and ambiguities which, given the highly contingent character of politics, were often unavoidable; a harsh and intolerant attitude to many of the former leaders of the Fourth Republic; a gift (sometimes more of a contrivance) for making remarks and taking steps almost calculated to wound and antagonize others; a resentment against the strong of yesterday before whom De Gaulle appeared during

[16]*Le Monde,* March 10, 1960.

the years of the war as a suppliant—if we ignore these many frailties and look, as we would say, at the record, we cannot say that De Gaulle has failed. With remarkable political acumen he borrowed what he needed from the much maligned Fourth Republic: he accepted the Common Market; he endorsed and, despite arguments to the contrary, continued economic planning and public investment in the social sector of the economy; he stepped up, as might have been expected, the atomic energy program in order to build nuclear weapons. Where the Republic was unable to act, De Gaulle acted: the Army was brought under control and the institutions were reformed; Algeria became independent; the colonies were allowed to move more rapidly in the same direction; defense was radically reorganized and a new foreign policy was pursued with vigor. In economic, political, and military terms the Fifth Republic appears to be immeasurably stronger than the Fourth. The national patrimony has been preserved and defended. But against whom and for what purpose?

Much criticism has been heaped upon De Gaulle both by American and by European (including French) writers. He has been criticized as a "nationalist" and a "nineteenth-century man." But it is a moot point whether De Gaulle's nationalism is different from American or Russian nationalism, unless we were willing to argue that big nationalisms are better than smaller ones and that small bombs are more dangerous than big ones.

If we are to criticize De Gaulle seriously, we must be prepared to discuss international developments after the Second World War in a somewhat different vein. Very briefly, four models of world developments could be envisaged at that time: the creation of a genuine world government with its own force; an agreement between the two superpowers to divide the world and police it; the development of a few large regional associations of states with institutional, economic, and military arrangements that were genuinely cooperative; and finally a return to state nationalisms. We can quickly dismiss the first and second models. Thus the most likely direction of development lay in a choice between the restoration of a great number of national centers of power or the development of a few genuine regional cooperative wholes. Upon his return to power De Gaulle seemed to accept the second alternative. He had spoken of the necessity of *grands ensembles* and had accepted the European Market. He pleaded for the development of a genuinely cooperative arrangement with NATO so that at least the three great powers within it—England, France, and the United States could assume responsibility for global strategy and its implementation and, by inference at least, for the use of nuclear weapons. He asked in other words to become a member of the Anglo-Saxon club within the Atlantic Alliance on a footing of equality—a relative equality, however, since he constantly reminded his countrymen that the United States was footing the major bill and the major burden for defense and hence was entitled to a greater voice. His position on Western Europe was by and large analogous. He urged a cooperative scheme in which the Franco-German alliance was later to form the axis, with France assuming responsibilities and burdens commensurate with her strength. Within such a cooperative scheme nation-states would continue to act side by side; and from cooperation, political unity and integration might gradually evolve.

Thus within the Atlantic Alliance there might be regional groupings in Europe, North America, and the Mediterranean, with specific duties and obligations and under flexible and varying institutional arrangements. The over-all direction and control would be lodged in the hands of a small NATO committee consisting of France, England, and the United States. This proposition should have merited serious consideration. Yet very little was given to it, until the NATO meeting of the Council of Defense Ministers in May, 1965. American statesmen then preferred to maintain their monopoly within NATO. While we blamed De Gaulle for attempting to speak on behalf of Western Europe we found it only natural to speak and act on behalf of the free world. It was inevitable that a reaction would set in and that another country would raise the flag of independence.

In essence, as Professor Grosser argues,[17] De Gaulle wishes to become in Europe what the United States actually is in the Atlantic Alliance. He assumes that he can speak on behalf of Europe very much as we assume we can speak on behalf of the

[17]"Le Grand Débat Nucléaire," *Sedeis*, February 10, 1965, pp. 33–38.

free world and when his nuclear weapons are ready he expects
to pose as Europe's protector very much as we claim to be the
defender of the Atlantic world. In a real sense all his arguments
against the United States can also be used against him by the
small European countries and particularly by West Germany.
What is more, all his criticisms of American leadership can, if
one were to assume the durability of the nation-state and the
exclusively national character of military preparedness and defense, be turned by other European nations against France's
military and nuclear aspirations.

Criticisms of De Gaulle's policies in France and Europe stem
largely from the reasons alluded to by Professor Grosser. Criticism of De Gaulle, therefore, among many European statesmen
and intellectuals is also tantamount to criticism of the nationalist
policy pursued thus far by the United States. But De Gaulle has
undermined one of the most cherished dreams of post-World
War II Europeans. He has been an obstacle to European union,
refusing to undertake discussions that might lead ultimately to
the establishment of even a loose political union. Thus his passionate desire for independence has led him to reject what he
professed to espouse—a European "whole." His nationalism, as
Maurice Duverger has pointed out, should have been European,
aiming at the creation of Western European independence,
which is feasible and realistic in terms of its power configura-
tion, rather than French national independence, which is an
illusion. Many have also argued that De Gaulle's "no" to Great
Britain, despite legitimate grievances and doubts, was ill-man-
nered, hasty, and unsound. England's entry's into the Common
Market, whatever her special associations with the United States,
might have given her some elbow room to disassociate herself
slowly from her Atlantic cousin and thence to move in concert
with Western Europe; it would also offset Germany's power
within the six—a power whose resurgence the French, especially
the French elites, continue to fear.

But even with a united and independent Europe there would
remain the problem of what De Gaulle has called "Europe's
daughter"—the United States. The majority of the French, even
if they prefer a Western European union independent of the

United States and an independent European Third Force, with
or without England, still see in the Atlantic ties and in the
presence of American troops in Europe the ultimate guarantee of
France's and Europe's security. In some interviews I conducted
in the summer of 1964 two French political leaders told me that
the first soldier to die in Europe in case of Soviet attack must be
an American. The one offered me his apologies and the other
his condolences. Besides, most people in western Europe believe
that the United States will use its nuclear power to retaliate
against any Soviet attack upon Western Europe. A large majority
realize that the American deterrent is France's ultimate defense.
Many would like to see France participate in the MLF arrangements, since by so doing Germany's future claims (in strict accord with Gaullist logic) to accede to atomic weapons may be
avoided and a competition for nuclear weapons among nation-
states may be averted. De Gaulle's defiance of American policies
and the manner in which he has done it; his apparent intention
to break away from NATO; his decision to consider defense
as an exclusively national affair—all may finally bring about a
situation in which France will have made American support to
Western Europe difficult or—even worse—divisive. The alternative policy, according to many critics, was to cooperate within
NATO while trying to build a united Europe with England and
to try within the councils of NATO to press for greater equality,
consultation, and division of labor with regard to theaters of
operation and other matters. France's policy should ultimately
be directed toward an independent Western Europe allied with
the United States. If one were to accept the Gaullist premises,
are not France and history better served in an Atlantic community where American leadership and power are qualified and
tempered by the counsels of a strong and united Western Europe
under the leadership of France? Is not the road to peace and
stability better served, thanks to France's vision and experience,
within the Alliance rather than outside? Such a cooperative approach would also settle once and for all the German plans for
reunification and avert the menace of the proliferation of nuclear
weapons. Thus, according to many, De Gaulle's purpose—the
greatness of France—cannot be realized. What is more, his

objective, however noble, may be imitated by other nations. After his departure his lofty nationalism may become only lip service for lesser men at home, who under changing conditions may misuse the legacy of national military strength. A strong France in a disunited Europe or a strong Europe in a disunited Atlantic community may prove to be a serious liability in the future.

De Gaulle's contribution to such a development will have to be assessed by future historians. His failure to promote the cause of European unity and to improve the prospects of Atlantic co-operation are the two most salient negative aspects of his foreign policy. He has contributed to the resurgence of nationalism when there were prospects for European cooperation and he has sown in Europe the seeds of national rivalries when there was for the first time a genuine hope for political unity. He has undermined the Atlantic community because it was based on American leadership, instead of trying to associate himself with it, thus providing a restraining influence upon what he feared would be the mistakes or the hasty actions of American statesmen. His "isolationism" in the name of the nation-state and the national exclusiveness of defense may in turn revive an American isolationism that many Europeans fear most. Without American power in Europe, German or Italian "Gaullisms" may emerge, using the ready-made arsenal of arguments that De Gaulle has marshalled against American leadership to argue for *their* independence and *their* inalienable right to defend it with the most modern weapons. Then Europe will once more become the *Europe des patries*—the Europe of the nation-states, and the dream of an Atlantic Community and a united Europe will become the nightmare of warring states. De Gaulle's philosophy of political life will then be vindicated again, but only if we forget the other opportunities that lay open before him when he returned to power in 1958.

PART 1

THE CONDITIONS OF INDEPENDENCE

In this part we reproduce De Gaulle's pronouncements on three related issues that may well be considered, in addition to the issue of the Army that we will discuss in Part II, the basic conditions of French recovery and independence. They are (1) the re-establishment of political institutions capable of providing leadership and continuity; (2) economic growth and development, which also includes social reforms to bridge the gap between the poor and the rich and to realize objectives that the free enterprise system could not be expected to bring about; and (3) the fate of the colonies—which became progressively equated in De Gaulle's mind with "decolonization."

De Gaulle's foreign and military policies have been commented upon frequently, and many of his views are familiar, if at times misunderstood. But little attention has been paid to what might be called his political and social philosophy. As for the future of the colonial system, De Gaulle's thinking underwent a significant transformation before he became the champion of independence.

1. THE INSTITUTIONS

❖

During the period of the Resistance and immediately after the Liberation of France, De Gaulle became deeply concerned with the new political institutions. What he called the "disjointedness" of the government had, in his opinion, accounted for a lack of political direction and a failure to develop a coherent military doctrine, thus leading to defeat and national degradation. Very much impressed with the ambiguity of the position of the President of the Republic as a factor in the collapse of 1940, he determined to create a strong Presidency. And, although he complained bitterly of the absence of stability and cohesion, he was convinced that a strong state could be built. This he set out to do.

Between 1940 and 1944 he set up various deliberative and representative bodies which became in 1943 a Consultative Assembly; it was as the head of a Provisional Government, aided by this Assembly, that De Gaulle governed France after the Liberation. However, he felt that a new constitution could be established only by a Constituent Assembly and elections were therefore held in October, 1945. By 1946 it had become apparent that the three political parties that controlled the Constituent Assembly—Communists, Socialists and the MRP—favored a strong parliamentary government and a weak executive. This was incompatible with De Gaulle's conceptions. Sensing that defeat was inevitable, he resigned on January 23, 1946. But he almost immediately re-entered the political scene by presenting his own constitutional views; the Bayeux speech reproduced in this section embodies with the greatest possible clarity his views, and ultimately became the charter of the Constitution of the Fifth Republic.

Could De Gaulle have assumed dictatorial powers in 1945?

33

His prestige was immense; the war was still going on; the Army was for all practical purposes his tool. We reproduce his thoughts on the subject (see pp. 39–41); thoughts, incidentally, that are restated in an answer to a question asked in 1958 when he was about to assume power. De Gaulle felt that neither France nor he was suited for dictatorship!

When the Fourth Republic and its constitution came into being in 1946, De Gaulle moved into active opposition by leading a new political movement (not a party)—the *Ralliament du Peuple Français* (RPF)—whose purpose was constitutional reform along the lines of a stronger executive and a stronger state. When his movement failed after the elections of 1951, he went into retirement and wrote his *Memoirs*. Indeed, from 1953 until 1958 little was heard of him. As he mentions in *The Edge of the Sword*, the great leader often is cast aside and has to tolerate long periods of inaction and contemplation. But the people know that he is there in case disaster strikes and the affairs of the state can no longer be managed. This is, in a sense, what happened in 1958. An insurrection of the generals and the Army in Algeria against the designated government of the Republic, coupled with the inability of the government to cope with it, brought De Gaulle out from his retirement. Quickly the Assembly gave him powers to govern and to prepare a new constitution. His speech of June 1, 1958 (see pp. 43–45), is an explicit statement of what De Gaulle intended to do in this domain. The constitution of the Fifth Republic was prepared during the summer of 1958 and submitted to the people in a referendum held on September 28, 1958. It was overwhelmingly approved— all parties supporting it with the exception of the Communists and some splinter left-wing groups. His supporting speech (pp. 45–48) shows the remarkable continuity of his thought when compared with the Bayeux speech given twelve years earlier. The text of the constitution pertaining to the powers of the President of the Republic (pp. 48–51) also repeats his earlier views.

In 1962 De Gaulle proceeded, through a referendum, to amend the constitution dealing with the manner in which the President of the Republic was to be elected. He now advocated a direct election by the people—a mechanism that had, according to his opponents, a distinct plebiscitary flavor. Both because of the opposition of the parties and because it was generally held that the constitution could not be effectively amended by simple referendum, De Gaulle proceeded to dissolve the legislature, after it had voted a motion of censure against the Government, and to hold a referendum and elections. The situation resembled that of 1946. Again all parties except his own—the UNR—were against his constitutional project. But this time he remained in office and his project was carried (pp. 51–56).

The next two speeches included are the first and last of his major addresses given prior to the October 28, 1962 referendum. In the first he outlines the reform and defends it, but in his fourth speech he asks the people to vote for him *and* the reform. In other words, the referendum assumed a personal element which made it indistinguishable from a plebiscite, especially since De Gaulle went so far as to threaten to resign if his reform did not receive a "good" majority. This personal element became even more noticeable in the elections that followed on November 18. Here De Gaulle, despite his earlier promise to remain above political parties and aloof from political struggles, lashed out against the political parties and their leaders. The speech of November 7, 1962 (pp. 56–59), shows the President actively campaigning; he is no longer an arbiter—he is a political leader. But again the election gave him, or at least the Gaullists, an astounding victory—so much so that the Gaullist party (UNR) alone won almost a majority in the National Assembly.

The Fifth Republic is De Gaulle. The most serious problem facing it is whether the institutions he set up, so inextricably associated with his personality and popularity, can survive him. The Fifth Republic may either become the basis of a stable government with significant presidential overtones, or it may disintegrate once more into a government dominated by a multi-party assembly. It is too early to tell whether the Gaullist institutions have been legitimized in a manner that can survive their founder. But whatever happens, there is little doubt that

the Gaullist structure not only served its historical mission
—providing for stability and economic reconstruction, taming
the Army, and disengaging France from Algeria and the former
Empire—but it has given for the first time to the nation an
opportunity to reconsider presidential government in the context
of republican institutions. Whatever the qualifications, De Gaulle
has lived up to his word and has respected the principles of an
open and free society; Presidential government has not sub-
verted the Republic.

THE STATE AND THE POLITICAL PARTIES

In his *Memoirs* De Gaulle had many an occasion to discourse
on French domestic politics—particularly on the weakness of
the state, the divisions engendered by the institutions, and the
factionalism of the political parties as he saw them after the
Liberation.

As for me, considering France's immediate political realities and the
extent and difficulty of the state's task, I had determined what the
desirable institutions had to be; to realize them, I had naturally taken
into account the lessons of our recent disaster, still so painful, as well
as my experience of men and affairs, and lastly the role which events
enabled me to play in the establishment of the Fourth Republic.

As I saw it, the state must have a head, that is, a leader in whom
the nation could see beyond its own fluctuations, a man in charge of
essential matters and the guarantor of its fate. It was also necessary
that this executive, destined to serve only the national community, not
originate in the parliament which united the delegations of particular
interests. These conditions implied that the chief of state not belong
to a party, that he be designated by the people, that he be empowered
to appoint the Cabinet, that he possess the right to consult the nation,
either by referendum or by election of assemblies, that he receive, finally,
the mandate of insuring the integrity and independence of France in
case of danger. Beyond those circumstances when it would be the
President's duty to intervene publicly, government and parliament would
collaborate, the latter controlling the former and authorized to cause its

SOURCE: *The War Memoirs of Charles De Gaulle,* trans. Richard
Howard (New York: Simon and Schuster, 1960), Vol. III, pp. 116,
272–275, 292–293.

fall, but the national magistrate exercising his arbitration and having recourse to that of the people.

* * *

What particularly struck me about the regrouping parties was their passionate desire to accord themselves all the powers of the Republic in full at the earliest opportunity, and their incapacity, which they revealed in advance, to wield them effectively. In this respect, nothing promised any sort of improvement in regard to the futile maneuvering which comprised the regime's activity before the war and which had led the country to such fearful disaster. Verbally, the politicians jealously emulated each other in denying such practices. "Revolution!" was the watchword that echoed most loudly through their speeches. But no one defined just what this meant, what effective changes were to be made in the previous situation, and particularly what authority, and endowed with what powers, would be in a position to carry them out. As for the Communists, they knew what they wanted, but were careful not to say what it was. The groups which for all their bold phraseology were fundamentally moderate cloaked their circumspection beneath Georges Bidault's formula, "Revolution by law!" As for the groups and men of the Left, or laying claim to be such, they appeared rigorous in criticism and repudiation, but vague and querulous in every constructive issue. Receiving delegations, reading newspapers, listening to speeches, I was inclined to think that for the renascent parties the revolution was not an undertaking with definite goals implying action and risk, but rather an attitude of constant dissatisfaction toward every policy, even those they had advocated themselves.

* * *

To the parties' factional character, which infected them with weakness, was added their own decadence. The latter was still concealed beneath rhetoric, but the doctrinal passion which was once their source, their attraction and their greatness could not be maintained in a period of materialism so indifferent to ideals. No longer inspired by principles, no longer ambitious to proselytize since they found no audiences on these grounds, they were inevitably tending to degradation, shrinking until each became nothing more than the representation of a category of interests. If the government fell into their hands again, it was certain that their leaders, their delegates and their militant members would turn into professionals making a career out of politics. The conquest of public functions, of influential positions, of administrative sinecures would henceforth absorb the parties and limit their activities to what they called tactics, which was nothing more than the practice of compromise and denial. Since all were minority representatives, they would have to share the positions of command with their rivals in order to accede to them at all. As a result they would proceed by giving themselves the lie in relation to the electorate. While the constant juxtaposition, within the government, of conflicting groups and men could result only in impotence.

•   •   •

That the Third Republic had constantly failed to achieve equilibrium, finally collapsing in an abyss of capitulation, gave each party reasons to attack the others in its own behalf, but not the necessity to abjure the same weaknesses. That France could not re-establish herself without the cohesion of her people, the abnegation of factions, and the leadership of a recognized and continuous authority was a principle altogether alien to their universe. For them, on the contrary, it was a matter of opposing all competitors, of provoking those passions and claims by which they could support themselves, of seizing power not so much to serve the entire nation as to fasten their own particular program to it. That De Gaulle, having succeeded in uniting the nation and leading it to salvation, should now be kept at its head was not the way they envisioned the future, though they were careful to lavish their praises upon him now. For tomorrow, they conceded, his withdrawal could not occur without certain transitions. They even attempted to create some sort of decorative position to which he could be relegated. Yet none of them supposed that leadership could long remain in the hands of a person whose mere presence was evidently incompatible with their regime.

Nonetheless, though I did not expect the spontaneous support of the parties, it seemed conceivable to me that the nation's instinct and the confidence it had hitherto accorded me were sufficiently manifest to oblige the "politicians" to swim with the current. It was my task to sound out French opinion as to whether the state should be constructed as I proposed. If they responded affirmatively, the parties would adapt themselves to it, and the new Republic would have my participation. If not, I would not fail to draw the consequences.

But if I had always intended that the people should ultimately make the decision, I felt no less doubt and anxiety as to the result. For was this people, beneath the moving proofs of affection it lavished upon me which nevertheless expressed its distress as much as its affection—was this people not exhausted, discouraged, divided? And as for these enormous enterprises, this vigorous action, these strong institutions which I proposed to its effort, did they not exceed its means and its desires? And I myself—had I the capacity, the skill, the eloquence necessary to galvanize them, when everything was sinking into mediocrity? Yet, whatever the nation's eventual answer to the question which would be put to it, it was my duty, while I waited, to govern with all the authority it had accorded me.

THE TEMPTATION OF DICTATORSHIP

On two occasions—one month immediately following the Liberation and again two weeks before he returned to power—when the question was bluntly put to him, De Gaulle rejected personal dictatorship.

As the champion of France rather than of any class or party, I incited hatred against no one and had no clientele who favored me in order to be favored in return. Even the men of the resistance, if they remained emotionally loyal to the ideal that once united them, had already, to a large degree, abandoned me politically and split into various factions. Only the Army could furnish me the means of controlling the country by constraining the recalcitrant elements. But this military omnipotence, established by force in peacetime, would soon appear unjustifiable to adherents of every tendency.

Fundamentally, what was, what could be dictatorship's resource if not great national ambition or the fear of a people imperiled by foreign powers? France had had two empires. She acclaimed the first when she felt capable of dominating Europe and when she was exhausted by disorder and confusion. She consented to the second in her desire to efface the humiliation of treaties which had sealed her defeat and in the agony recent social upheavals had forced upon her. Yet how had each of these Caesarean regimes ended? Today, no conquest, no revenge tempted our citizens; the mass of the people feared neither invasion nor revolution. Public safety was now a *fait accompli,* and I had no desire to maintain the momentary dictatorship which I had exercised in the course of the storm and which I would not fail to prolong or resume if the nation were in danger. Therefore, as I had promised, I would let the people make their choice in a general election.

Yet even as I dismissed the notion of my own despotism, I was no

SOURCE: *The War Memoirs of Charles De Gaulle,* trans. Richard Howard (New York: Simon and Schuster, 1960), Vol. III, pp. 271–272.

less convinced that the nation required a regime whose power would be strong and continuous. The parties were evidently unqualified to provide such power. Apart from the Communists, who intended to dominate by any means whatever, whose government would ultimately be infiltrated by an alien organization, who would find in France the resolute support of a portion of the population and of the Soviets abroad, but who would bring France to servitude, I observed that no political formation was in a position to assure the leadership of the nation and of the state. Although some among them could obtain the votes of an important fraction of the citizens, not a single one was thought of as representing public interest as a whole. Each would gather only the voices of a minority, and many electors would vote not so much *for* one party as *against* the others. In short, no organization commanded either the power or the credit which would permit it to lay claim to national authority.

· · ·

QUESTION: What would your attitude be toward basic public liberties?

ANSWER: Did I ever make any attempt on basic public liberties? On the contrary, I restored them . . . Why should I, at 67, begin a career as a dictator? . . .

It is not possible to solve the serious national crises of the present time within the limits of everyday routine. As matter of fact, one of the politicians recently charged with untangling the famous crisis, which has really been going on for twelve years, this politician himself admitted that it was necessary to form a government, but a government which would be different from the others.

I find that our country has been extremely weakened and that it is struggling against great difficulties, and even great threats, in a disturbed world. I find that France holds some good cards for the future: the birth rate; an economy that has gone beyond the stage of routine; French technology, which is constantly developing; the oil which has been discovered in large quantities, and so on.

These cards which we hold may lead, in the near future, to the resurgence of France, to great prosperity in which all Frenchmen must share and in which the people who need and ask for our assistance may also be associated. But it is true that, for the moment, we are in a sad plight, and that is why my last word will be: "I thought it would

SOURCE: *Major Addresses, Statements, and Press Conferences of General Charles De Gaulle, May 19, 1958–January 31, 1964* (New York: French Embassy, Press and Information Service), p. 6.

be useful for the country to say what I have said. Now I shall return to my village and I shall remain there at the disposal of the country."

THE GAULLIST CONSTITUTIONAL CHARTER

As we have indicated, the Bayeux speech on June 16, 1946, is the constitutional charter of Gaullism. It was delivered after the first constitutional referendum of May 5, 1946, in which a constitutional draft consecrating legislative supremacy and a weak executive was rejected by the people. However, it did not prevent a modified draft from becoming the Constitution of the Fourth Republic.

During a period of not more than twice the life of a man France was invaded seven times and experienced thirteen different political systems —for everything is connected in the misfortunes of a nation. So many upheavals have injected poisons in our public life that feed our gallic propensity toward divisions and quarrels. The hard misfortunes we have experienced naturally have aggravated this situation. In the present state of the world, opposed ideologies, behind which lurk the powerful states that surround us, do not cease to inject in our own political struggle an element of passionate "controversy." In brief, the rivalry of the parties in our country takes on a fundamental character that sets everything adrift and very often wrecks the superior interests of the country. This is an obvious fact which is due to our national temperament, to the accidents of our history, and to the disturbances of today, but which our institutions must take into consideration in order to preserve the respect for law, the cohesion of governments, the efficiency of administrations, and the prestige and authority of the state.

It is true, as a matter of fact, that the uncertainties about the state alienate the citizen from the institutions. . . . All that is needed then is the right opportunity for the menace of dictatorship to appear. . . . It is sufficient to mention this in order to understand to what extent our new democratic institutions must compensate, by themselves, for our perpetual political effervescence. It is also a matter of life and death for us, in the world and century in which we live, when the position, the independence, and the very existence of our country and our French Union are in peril. No doubt it is the very essence of

SOURCE: *Discours et Messages, 1940–1946* (Paris: Berger-Levrault, 1946), pp. 721–727. (My translation.)

democracy that opinions be expressed and that through the suffrage they influence the public decisions and legislation. But also, both principle and experience require that the state organs—legislative, executive, and judiciary—be firmly balanced and separate, and that above political contingencies a national arbiter be established embodying continuity in the midst of the political game.

Thus it is clear that the final vote on legal and budgetary matters belongs to an Assembly elected by direct and universal suffrage. But the opinion of such an Assembly is not always the wisest or most detached. We must then give to a second Assembly, elected in a different manner, and with a different composition, the duty to examine in public what the first has done, to suggest amendments, and introduce bills. Thus if the major points of view about issues of general policy are expressed in the Chamber of Deputies, local interests also will have their own say and claims. This is true for the metropolis as well as for the overseas territories, which are related to the French Union in many ways. . . . The future of 110 million men and women who live under our flag is in a federative formula that time will determine gradually, but that the new constitution must initiate and slowly help to develop. Everything points therefore to the establishment of a second chamber that should be elected mainly by our municipal and general councils. . . . It is also natural to introduce in it the representatives of economic, family, and intellectual organizations so that the important voices in the country will be heard within the state. . . .

It goes without saying that the executive power should not emanate from a bicameral Parliament that has [the] legislative power. In that case there would be such a mingling of powers that the Government would be merely an assemblage of delegations. . . . How are unity, cohesion, and discipline to be guaranteed if the executive power emanates from the very legislative power that it should balance, and if each member of the government that is collectively responsible to the entire body of representatives of the nation, were, when in the government, merely a delegate of his party?

It is then the chief of State—placed above political parties, elected by an electoral college that includes Parliament but that is much broader and is composed in such a way as to make him the President of the French Union as well as President of the Republic—who should hold executive power. To the chief of State belongs the duty of reconciling the national interest with the general orientation of Parliament when it comes to choosing men to govern; to him the duty of nominating the Ministers and, first of all, of course, the Prime Minister, who must be in charge of the work and direction of the Government; to the chief of State the duty of promulgating the laws and the executive orders; . . . to him the task of presiding over the meetings of the Council of Ministers and to exercise the influence and continuity without which the nation cannot last; to him the task of acting as arbiter above political contingencies, either within the Council of Ministers or in moments of great confusion by inviting the country to express in an election its sovereign decision; to him, if the country is in danger, the obligation to act as guarantor of national independence and of the treaties that bind France.

The Greeks once asked Solon "What is the best Constitution?" He answered "Tell me first for which country and for what time?" Today the question is for France and the French Union in a period that is difficult and dangerous. Let us take ourselves for what we are. Let us take the century for what it is. We have to bring about, despite great difficulties, a drastic reconstruction that will make it possible for each man and woman to lead a life of greater ease, security, and happiness, and that ought to increase our numbers and make us more powerful and united. We must preserve the freedom that we have safeguarded with so much effort. We must assure the destiny of France in the midst of so many obstacles that confront us and endanger peace. We must show ourselves to all other peoples for what we are to aid this poor and old mother of ours—the Earth. Let us be lucid and strong and give to ourselves the rules of national life that will unite us even when all the time we are prone to divide against ourselves! In our whole history, great misfortunes of a divided people alternate with inspiring feats of a free nation grouped together under the aegis of a strong state.

THE CONDITIONS OF A RETURN TO POWER

On May 13, 1958, the Army in Algeria, led by a number of prominent generals, demanded the formation of a government of national unity to pursue the war in Algeria and threatened to impose their will upon the metropolis by force if necessary. Civil war was imminent until, after two hectic weeks of negotiations and maneuvering, De Gaulle was asked to form a government with sweeping powers. On June 1, he outlined his program before he received a vote of confidence. Subsequently he was granted powers to amend the Constitution.

The rapidly accelerating degradation of the State, the immediate danger to French unity, Algeria in the throes of trials and emotions,

SOURCE: *Major Addresses, Statements, and Press Conferences of General Charles De Gaulle, May 19, 1948–January 31, 1964* (New York: French Embassy, Press and Information Service), pp. 7–8.

Corsica suffering from a feverish contagion, opposing movements in Metropolitan France hourly whipping up their passions and, reinforcing their action, the Army, long tried by sanguinary and praiseworthy tasks but shocked by the lack of any real authority, our international position disparaged even within our alliances—such is the situation of our country. At this very moment, when so many opportunities, in so many directions, are offered to France, she finds herself threatened by disruption and perhaps even civil war.

It is in these circumstances that I offered my services to try, once again, to lead the country, the State, and the Republic to safety; and that, designated by the Chief of State, I have been led to ask the National Assembly to invest me with a heavy task.

In order to perform this task, means are necessary.

If you invest this Government, it will propose that you give it these means right away. It will ask you for full powers in order to be in a position to act with all the effectiveness, speed, and responsibility demanded by the circumstances. It will ask you for these powers for a period of six months, hoping that at the end of this time—order having been re-established in the State, hope regained in Algeria, unity restored in the nation—it will be possible for the public powers to resume their normal course.

But what good would be a temporary remedy, a remedy of sorts, for a disastrous state of affairs unless we decided to eradicate the deep-seated cause of our troubles? This cause—the Assembly knows and the nation is convinced of it—is the confusion and, by the same token, the helplessness of constituted authority.

The Government which I shall form, provided I obtain your vote of confidence, will submit to you without delay a bill reforming Article 90 of the Constitution, thus enabling the National Assembly to give a mandate to the Government to formulate and then propose to the country, through a referendum, the indispensable changes. In the explanatory statement which will be submitted to you at the same time as the text, the Government will specify the three principles which must be the basis of the republican regime in France and to which it pledges that its bill will conform: universal suffrage is the source of all power; the executive and the legislative branches must be separate and apart so that the Government and the Parliament can, each for its own part and on its own responsibility, assume its full powers; the Government must be responsible to the Parliament.

Through the same constitutional reform, the country will be given a formal opportunity to organize the relations between the French Republic and the peoples associated with it. The Government will pledge itself to promote this new organization in the draft which it will put to the vote of the women and men of France.

Having received this double mandate, conferred on it by the National Assembly, the Government will be able to undertake the immense task which will have thus been defined. If I am to assume this double mandate, I shall first and foremost need your confidence. Then the Parliament must without delay—for events do not permit of any delay— enact into law the bills which will be submitted to it. These laws once passed, the Assemblies will adjourn until the date set for the opening of their next regular session. Thus the Government of the Republic, having been invested by the elected representatives of the nation and given, with extreme urgency, the means for action, can then be responsible for the unity, integrity, and independence of France.

THE CONSTITUTION OF THE FIFTH REPUBLIC

During the summer of 1958 the new Constitution was prepared by De Gaulle and his associates with the help of a special Constitutional Council. It incorporated the ideas of the Bayeux speech on the Presidency, and those of the then Minister of Justice, Michel Debré, on a parliament with "limited" powers. It was submitted to a referendum on September 28, 1958, and was overwhelmingly endorsed. In this speech, on September 4, De Gaulle defends the new constitutional text and urges its approval.

•   •   •

It was inevitable that the paralysis of the State should bring on a grave national crisis and that, immediately, the Republic should be threatened with collapse.

The necessary steps were taken to prevent the irreparable at the very moment that it was about to occur. The disruption of the State was, by a narrow margin, prevented. They managed to save the last chance of the Republic. It was by legal means that I and my Government assumed the unusual mandate of drafting a new Constitution and of submitting it to the decision of the people.

SOURCE: *Major Addresses, Statements, and Press Conferences of General Charles De Gaulle, May 18, 1958–January 31 1964* (New York: French Embassy, Press and Information Service), pp. 14–16.

We have done this on the basis of the principles laid down at the time of our investiture. We have done this with the collaboration of the Consultative Committee instituted by law. We have done this, taking into account the solemn opinion of the Council of State. We have done this after very frank and very thorough discussion with our own Councils of Ministers. These Councils were formed of men as diversified as possible as to origin and inclination, but resolutely united. We have done this without meanwhile doing violence to any right of the people or any public liberty. The nation, which alone is the judge, will approve or reject our work. But it is in good conscience that we propose this Constitution to them.

Henceforth what is primordial for the public powers is their effectiveness and their continuity. We are living at a time when titanic forces are engaged in transforming the world. Lest we become a people out of date and scorned, we must evolve rapidly in the scientific, economic, and social spheres. Moreover, the taste for progress and the passion for technical achievements that are becoming evident among the French, and especially among our young people, are equal to this imperative need. These are all facts that dominate our national existence and that, consequently, must order our institutions.

The necessity of renovating agriculture and industry; of procuring—for our rejuvenated population—the means of livelihood, of work, of education, of housing; and of associating workers in the functioning of enterprises: the necessity to do all this compels us to be dynamic and expeditious in public affairs. The duty of restoring peace in Algeria, next of developing it, and finally of settling the question of its status and its place in our great whole, impels us to arduous and prolonged efforts. The prospects offered us by the resources of the Sahara are magnificent indeed, but complex. The relations between Metropolitan France and the Overseas Territories require profound adjustment. The world is crossed by currents that threaten the very future of the human race and prompt France to protect herself while playing the role of moderation, peace, and fraternity dictated by her mission. In short, the French nation will flourish again or will perish according to whether the State does or does not have enough strength, constancy, and prestige to lead her along the path she must follow.

Therefore, it is for the people we are, for the century and the world in which we live, that the proposed Constitution was drafted. The country effectively governed by those to whom it gives the mandate and to whom it grants the confidence that makes for lawfulness. A national arbiter—far removed from political bickering—elected by the citizens who hold a public mandate, charged with the task of ensuring the normal functioning of the institutions, possessing the right to resort to the judgment of the sovereign people, accountable, in the case of extreme danger, for the independence, the honor and integrity of France, and for the safety of the Republic. A Government made to govern, which is granted the necessary time and opportunity, which does not turn to anything other than its task and which thereby deserves the country's support. A Parliament intended to represent the political will of the nation, to enact laws, and to control the executive, without venturing to overstep its role. A Government and Parliament that work together but remain separate in their responsibilities, with no member of one being at the same time a member of the other. Such is the balanced structure that power must assume. The rest will depend upon men.

A Social and Economic Council, appointed outside politics by the business, professional, and labor organizations of France and the Overseas Territories, that gives advice to Parliament and to the Government. A Constitutional Committee, free of any attachment, empowered to judge whether the laws that have been passed are constitutional and whether the various elections have been properly held. A judicial authority assured of its independence which remains the guardian of individual liberty. Thus will the competence, the dignity, the impartiality of the State be better guaranteed.

A Community formed between the French nation and those of the Overseas Territories that so desire, within which each Territory will become a State that governs itself, while foreign policy, defense, the currency, economic and financial policies, use of raw materials, the control of justice, higher education, long-distance communications will constitute a common domain over which the organs of the Community —the President, Executive Council, Senate, and Court of Arbitration— will have jurisdiction. Thus, this vast organization will renovate the human complex grouped around France. This will be effected by virtue of the free determination of all. In fact, every Territory will have an opportunity, through its vote in the referendum, either to accept France's proposal or to refuse it and, by so doing, to break every tie with her. Once a member of the Community, it can in the future, after coming to an agreement with the common organs, assume its own destiny independently of the others.

Finally, during the four months following the referendum, the Government will be responsible for the country's affairs and, in particular, will establish the system of elections. In this way, through a mandate from the people, the necessary measures may be taken for the setting up of the new institutions.

Here, women and men of France, is what inspires and what makes up the Constitution which, on September 28, will be submitted to your vote. With all my heart, in the name of France, I ask you to answer "Yes."

If you do not vote thus, we shall return, that very day, to the bad old ways with which you are familiar. But if you do, the result will be to make the Republic strong and effective, provided that those in positions of responsibility know, hereafter, the meaning of determination. But there will also be, in this positive display of the national will, the proof that our country is regaining its unity and, by the same token, its opportunity for grandeur. The world, which understands full well what importance our decision will have for it, will draw the inevitable conclusion. Perhaps it is already drawing the conclusion.

A great hope will arise over France. I think it has already arisen.

Vive la République! Vive la France!

THE POWERS OF THE PRESIDENT

The articles on the Presidency were tailored to De Gaulle's specifications, and nobody had any doubt that the new President would be De Gaulle.

TITLE II
THE PRESIDENT OF THE REPUBLIC

Article 5

The President of the Republic shall see that the Constitution is respected. He shall ensure, by his arbitration, the regular functioning of the governmental authorities, as well as the continuity of the State.

He shall be the guarantor of national independence, of the integrity of the territory, and of respect for Community agreements and treaties.

Article 6

The President of the Republic shall be elected for seven years by an electoral college comprising the members of Parliament, of the General Councils and of the Assemblies of the Overseas Territories, as well as the elected representatives of the municipal councils . . .

Article 7

The President of the Republic shall be elected by an absolute majority on the first ballot. If this is not obtained, the President of the Republic shall be elected on a second ballot by a relative majority.

The voting shall begin at the summons of the Government.

The election of the new President shall take place twenty days at the

SOURCE: Text of the Constitution of the Fifth Republic.

least and fifty days at the most before the expiration of the powers of the President in office . . .

Article 8

The President of the Republic shall appoint the Premier. He shall terminate the functions of the Premier when the latter presents the resignation of the Government.

On the proposal of the Premier, he shall appoint the other members of the Government and shall terminate their functions.

Article 9

The President of the Republic shall preside over the Council of Ministers.

Article 10

The President of the Republic shall promulgate the laws within fifteen days following the transmission to the Government of the finally adopted law.

He may, before the expiration of this time, ask Parliament for a reconsideration of the law or of certain of its articles. This reconsideration may not be refused.

Article 11

The President of the Republic, on the proposal of the Government during parliamentary sessions, or on joint motion of the two assemblies, published in the *Journal Officiel,* may submit to a referendum any bill dealing with the organization of the governmental authorities, entailing approval of a Community agreement, or providing for authorization to ratify a treaty that, without being contrary to the Constitution, might affect the functioning of the institutions.

When the referendum decides in favor of the bill, the President of the Republic shall promulgate it within the time limit stipulated in the preceding article.

Article 12

The President of the Republic may, after consultation with the Premier and the Presidents of the Assemblies, declare the dissolution of the National Assembly.

General elections shall take place twenty days at the least and forty days at the most after the dissolution.

The National Assembly shall convene by right on the second Thursday following its election. If this meeting takes place between the periods provided for ordinary sessions, a session shall, by right, be held for a fifteen-day period.

copy 1

There may be no further dissolution within a year following these elections.

Article 13

The President of the Republic shall sign the ordinances and decrees decided upon in the Council of Ministers.

He shall make appointments to the civil and military posts of the State.

Councillors of State, the Grand Chancellor of the Legion of Honor, Ambassadors and Envoys Extraordinary, Master Councillors of the Audit Office, prefects, representatives of the Government in the Overseas Territories, general officers, rectors of academies [regional divisions of the public educational system], and directors of central administrations shall be appointed in meetings of the Council of Ministers.

An organic law shall determine the other posts to be filled in meetings of the Council of Ministers, as well as the conditions under which the power of the President of the Republic to make appointments to office may be delegated by him and exercised in his name.

Article 14

The President of the Republic shall accredit Ambassadors and Envoys Extraordinary to foreign powers; foreign Ambassadors and Envoys Extraordinary shall be accredited to him.

Article 15

The President of the Republic shall be commander of the armed forces. He shall preside over the Higher Councils and Committees of national defense.

Article 16

When the institutions of the Republic, the independence of the nation, the integrity of its territory or the fulfillment of its international commitments are threatened in a grave and immediate manner and when the regular functioning of the constitutional governmental authorities is interrupted, the President of the Republic shall take the measures commanded by these circumstances, after official consultation with the Premier, the Presidents of the Assemblies and the Constitutional Council.

He shall inform the nation of these measures in a message.

These measures must be prompted by the desire to ensure to the constitutional governmental authorities, in the shortest possible time, the means of fulfilling their assigned functions. The Constitutional Council shall be consulted with regard to such measures.

Parliament shall meet by right.

The National Assembly may not be dissolved during the exercise of emergency powers [by the President].

Article 17

The President of the Republic shall have the right of pardon.

Article 18

The President of the Republic shall communicate with the two assemblies of Parliament by means of messages, which he shall cause to be read, and which shall not be followed by any debate.

Between sessions, Parliament shall be convened especially for this purpose.

Article 19

The acts of the President of the Republic, other than those provided for under Articles 8 (first paragraph), 11, 12, 16, 18, 54, 56, and 61, shall be countersigned by the Premier and, should circumstances so require, by the appropriate ministers.

POPULAR ELECTION OF THE PRESIDENT

The only major amendment to the Constitution undertaken thus far provides for the direct election of the President by universal suffrage. The excerpt below comes from De Gaulle's address on September 20, 1962, when he spoke in defense of his amendment submitted to the people in the referendum of October 28, 1962.

Ever since the French people called me to take my place again officially at the head of the nation, I have of course felt that one day I would have to ask them a question concerning my succession—I mean the question of the method of electing the Head of State. Reasons which each of you knows have recently made me think that the time may have come to do so.

• • •

This Constitution, which was adopted by 80 percent of the votes, has now been in existence for four years. One might therefore say that it has proved itself. Continuity in the action of the State, stability, effectiveness, and balance of powers have replaced, as if by magic, the chronic confusion and perpetual crises that paralyzed the system of yesterday, whatever may have been the worth of the men. Likewise, the great effort and the great upsurge of the French people are now bearing their fruit. France's position both at home and abroad has made

SOURCE: *Major Addresses, Statements, and Press Conferences of General Charles De Gaulle, May 19, 1958–January 31, 1964* (New York: French Embassy, Press and Information Service), pp. 190–193.

striking progress, recognized throughout the world, without this infringing upon the public freedoms. The grave and arduous problem of decolonization has been for the most part settled. Of course, the work that we still have to carry out is vast, because, for a people, to continue to live is to continue to advance. But no one seriously believes that we could do this if we gave up our solid institutions. No one really doubts that our country would quickly find itself flung into the abyss if, by some misfortune, we delivered it over once again to the sterile and ridiculous games of the past.

The keystone of our system is the new institution of a President of the Republic designated by the minds and the hearts of the French people to be the head of the State and the guide of France. Far from the President's being obligated, as in the past, to remain within a role of counsel and representation, the Constitution now vests in him the distinguished responsibility for the destiny of France and of the Republic.

Under the Constitution, the President is in fact the guarantor—do you fully understand—the guarantor of the independence and the integrity of the country, and of the treaties binding upon it. In short, he answers for France. Furthermore, it is his role to assure the continuity of the State and the functioning of the public powers. In short, he answers for the Republic. To fulfill these supreme responsibilities, the Head of State must possess adequate means. The Constitution gives him these means. It is the President who designates the Ministers and, first of all, chooses the Premier. It is the President who convenes and presides over their Councils. It is the President who, on the basis of their reports, takes, in the form of decrees or ordinances, all the important decisions of State. It is the President who appoints the civil servants, officers, and judges. In the vital domains of foreign affairs and national security he is bound to direct action, since under the Constitution he negotiates and concludes treaties, since he is commander of the armed forces, since he presides over defense. Above all, if it should happen that the country and the Republic are immediately threatened, then the President is personally invested with all the duties and all the rights that the public safety involves.

It goes without saying that all these powers, permanent or contingent, lead the President to inspire, guide, and animate national action. It happens that he has to conduct it directly, as I did, for example, throughout the Algerian affair. Of course, the Premier and his colleagues have, along the lines already marked out, to determine policy as the need arises and to direct the government. Of course, Parliament deliberates on and votes the laws, controls the Government and has the right to overturn it, which marks the parliamentary character of the regime. But, in order to be able to maintain, under all circumstances, the action and the balance of the powers and to implement, when necessary, the sovereignty of the people, the President permanently holds the possibility of having recourse to the country, either by means of a referendum, by new elections, or by both of these at the same time.

In fact, as you see, one of the fundamental characteristics of the Constitution of the Fifth Republic is that it gives the State a head. In modern times, when everything is so vital, so harsh, so precipitous, most of the major countries of the world—the United States, Russia, Great Britain, Germany, etc.—are doing the same thing, each in its own way. We shall do it in ours, which is on the one hand democratic and on the other hand in keeping with the lessons and the traditions of our long history.

Nevertheless, in order that the President of the Republic may effectively fulfill and exercise such a responsibility, he must have the explicit confidence of the nation. Allow me to say that on reassuming the leadership of the State in 1958, I thought that, for myself and in this respect, the events of history had already done the necessary. Because of what we have lived and achieved together, through so much difficulty, blood and tears, but also with so much hope, enthusiasm and success, there is between you, women and men of France, and me an extraordinary bond which invests and binds me. I did not, therefore, attach any particular importance to the means that were to surround my nomination, since this was decided in advance by the force of events. Moreover, in view of political susceptibilities, some of which were worthy of respect, I preferred at that time for there not to be a kind of formal plebiscite as far as I was concerned. In short, I at that time agreed that the initial text of our Constitution submit the election of the President to a relatively limited college of about 80,000 elected representatives.

But, although this method of voting was not able, any more than any other method, to fix my responsibilities toward France, or alone express the confidence that the French people are so good as to have in me, the question would be quite different for those who, not necessarily having been given the same national distinction by past events—will come after me, one by one, to assume the post that I now occupy. In order for these men to be totally able and fully bound to bear the supreme responsibility, no matter how heavy it may weigh, so that our Republic may continue to have a good chance of remaining strong, effective, and popular despite the evils of our divisions, it will be necessary for these men to receive their mandate directly from all the citizens, and this without any necessity to modify the respective rights nor the reciprocal relations between the executive, legislative, and judiciary powers, as defined by the Constitution . . . I believe, therefore, that I must put the following proposal before the country: when my own seven-year term of office comes to an end, or if death or sickness should interrupt it before the seven years are up, the President of the Republic shall henceforth be elected by universal suffrage.

On this subject, which affects all the French people, what is the best way for the country to express its decision? My answer is: in the most democratic way—by a referendum. It is also the most justified way, for national sovereignty belongs to the people and clearly it belongs to the people first and foremost with regard to the Constitution. Moreover, it was from the vote of all the citizens that our present Constitution was directly derived. As a matter of fact, the Constitution specifies that 'the people shall exercise their sovereignty either through their representatives or by means of referendums.' Finally, while the text provides for a definite procedure in the event of the revision being made within the parliamentary framework, it also provides, very simply and clearly, that the President of the Republic may present to the country, by means of a referendum, "any bill," I repeat, "any bill concerning the organization of public powers," and this clearly includes the manner in which the President is elected. The bill that I am preparing to submit to the French people will, therefore, respect the Constitution that, on my proposal, they gave themselves.

Women and men of France, in these perilous times and in this difficult world, we must, to the best of our abilities, see to it that France shall live, prosper, and make her future secure. That is why, when I shall propose to you in the near future to perfect the national institutions in respect to a point on which everything may depend tomorrow, I believe, in all good faith, that I shall be serving our country well. But, as always, I cannot and do not wish to do anything without your approval. As always, therefore, I shall soon ask you for that approval. And then, as always, it is you who will decide.

Vive la République! Vive la France!

VOTE FOR DE GAULLE AND MY REFORM!

On October 26, 1962, De Gaulle urged the people to vote for his reform *and* to show their confidence in him.

SOURCE: *Major Addresses, Statements, and Press Conferences of General Charles De Gaulle, May 19, 1958–January 31, 1964* (New York: French Embassy, Press and Information Service), p. 200.

Women and men of France, as for myself, I am sure that you will say "yes." I am sure of this, because you know that in our world which is so dangerous—it can be seen at this very moment—France could not survive if she fell back into the impotence of yesterday; but, to the contrary, her role, her influence, and her prestige are at this time worthy of her and of her human task. I am sure that you will say "yes" because you understand that in our times, the road to progress, to prosperity, and to grandeur does not lie through and will not lie through the absurd games of former times; but, on the contrary, that the continuity, firmness, and effectiveness established at the head of the State are the necessary conditions for the renovation that we have begun, which is firing our youth and astounding the world. I am sure that you will say "yes," because you feel that if the French nation, before itself and before the world, came to the point of rejecting De Gaulle, or even granted him only a vague and doubtful confidence, his historic task would immediately become impossible and, consequently, terminated; but, on the contrary, he will be capable and duty bound to pursue it if you, as a mass, desire it.

Women and men of France, the day after tomorrow each and every one of you will, in the face of his national conscience, decide on the fate of France.

Vive la République! Vive la France!

THE NEW SYSTEM TO ELECT THE PRESIDENT

NEW ARTICLES 6 AND 7
REFERENDUM OF OCTOBER 28, 1962

New Article 6: The President of the Republic shall be elected for seven years by direct universal suffrage.

The procedures implementing the present article shall be determined by an organic law.

New Article 7: The President of the Republic shall be elected by an absolute majority of the votes cast. If this is not obtained on the first ballot, there shall be a second ballot on the second Sunday following. Only the two candidates who have received the greatest number of votes on the first ballot shall present themselves, taking into account the possible withdrawal of more favored candidates.

SOURCE: French Embassy, Press and Information Division, New York.

The voting shall begin at the summons of the Government.

The election of the new President shall take place twenty days at the least and thirty-five days at the most before the expiration of the powers of the President in office.

In the event that the Presidency of the Republic has been vacated for any cause whatsoever, or impeded in its functioning as officially noted by the Constitutional Council, to which the matter has been referred by the Government, and which shall rule by an absolute majority of its members, the functions of the President of the Republic, with the exception of those provided for by Articles 11 and 12 below, shall be temporarily exercised by the President of the Senate and, if the latter is in his turn impeded in the exercise of these functions, by the Government.

In the case of a vacancy, or when the impediment is declared definitive by the Constitutional Council, the voting for the election of a new President shall take place, except in case of *force majeure* officially noted by the Constitutional Council, twenty days at the least and thirty-five days at the most after the beginning of the vacancy or the declaration of the definitive character of the impediment.

There may be no application of either Articles 49 and 50 or of Article 89 of the Constitution during the vacancy of the Presidency of the Republic or during the period that elapses between the declaration of the definitive character of the impediment of the President of the Republic and the election of his successor.

THE ELECTIONS OF NOVEMBER 18, 1962—VOTE FOR DE GAULLE AND MY DEPUTIES!

In the elections that followed, the lines between De Gaulle and the political parties were drawn more sharply than ever before. De Gaulle urged the defeat of the "old" political parties and singled out many of the leaders who had voted against his government. He urged the people to vote for his supporters. This was the first time that the President had openly participated in a legislative election. In this case, the voters ob-

SOURCE: From *Major Addresses, Statements, and Press Conferences of General Charles De Gaulle, May 19, 1958–January 31, 1962* (New York: French Embassy, Press and Information Service), pp. 201–203.

liged and the "Gaullist" candidates emerged in control of the National Assembly. But there is no doubt that in voting for them the people were voting for De Gaulle whose immense popularity had carried the day. At the very moment of victory, however, many observers raised the crucial question —what would have happened if the "Gaullists" had lost? The same question, with or without De Gaulle as President of the Republic, applies for the future as well.

The sovereign decision which the nation took on October 28 and which is incumbent on everyone is of the greatest import for the future of France.

For the constitutional bill, in the form it was voted, means that henceforth the French people will elect their President by universal suffrage. The man on whom our Constitution confers the extremely heavy responsibility of being the real Head of State will, after me, have the obligation and the opportunity of being this head, through the direct mandate that he will receive from the nation. Thus that fundamental element of permanence and solidity that our institutions contain is to remain—I mean the presence at the head of the Republic of a man who can really be its head.

This is especially true since the sovereign vote of October 28 solemnly confirmed the right that our Constitution attributes to the Head of State to submit to the country, by means of a referendum, any bill concerning the organization of the administrative powers. The nation, which is its own and only master, has thus conclusively judged that its future Presidents will have the power of asking it in their turn, as I myself have done five times, to determine directly such problems as are considered essential.

But also, once again, the referendum has brought into the full light a major political feature of our times—that the parties of the past, even when a common professional passion unites them for a moment, do not represent the nation. We became clearly and terribly aware of this when, in 1940, their regime abdicated in disaster. We again observed this in 1958 when it turned everything over to me on the brink of anarchy, bankruptcy, and civil war. We have just seen it come true again in 1962.

•   •   •

To be sure, no one denies that the parties of the past still embrace and serve various trends of public opinion, individual interests, local wishes, and personal merits. To be sure, through patronage, influences, and schemes—which are their tried and tested means—they are still able to secure the election of a number of their members. To be sure, some of their men have capabilities that might still be useful to the Government of the country so long as they themselves are willing to act within a system devoted solely to the national interest; and you know that I, throughout the years in time of war and in time of peace when I was in charge, took my Ministers, suiting the occasion, from all the political groups, each in its turn and without exception. It is a fact that today, to confuse the parties of the past with France and the Republic would be simply ridiculous.

Now, if in voting "yes" outside of these parties and in spite of them, the nation has just given to political renewal a wide majority, I say that it is absolutely necessary, in order that democracy may endure, for this majority to become stronger and grow larger and, firstly, for this majority to establish itself in Parliament. For if Parliament, which holds the legislative power and the control, were to reappear tomorrow dominated by the factions you know about, bent on re-establishing their impotent reign of the the past, placing itself in opposition to the profound will that the country has just expressed—then, in that case having, less than ever, a truly representative character and being divided, moreover, into rival and opposed groups, such a Parliament would not fail, from the outset, to flourish in obstruction, then to plunge the administrative powers into a confusion too well-known, while awaiting the chance, sooner or later, to submerge the State in a new national crisis. On the contrary, what role can Parliament play if, escaping the pretensions and illusions of the factions, it desires the continuation, with its resolute support, of the task of national recovery which has been carried out for more than four years.

Women and men of France, on October 28 you set your seal to the condemnation of the disastrous regime of the parties and marked your determination to see the new Republic pursue its task of progress, of development and of grandeur. But, on November 18 and 25, you are going to elect the Deputies. May you see that this second consultation does not run in contradiction to the first. Despite, as the case may be, of local habits and fragmentary considerations, may you confirm, through the designation of men, the choice that you, in voting "yes," made with regard to our destiny.

Women and men of France, I ask this of you. I ask this of you in seeing things far beyond myself and my present position. I ask this of you in placing myself, once again, on the ground—the only ground important to me—of the good of the State, of the fate of the Republic, and of the future of France.

Vive la République! Vive la France!

THE CONSTITUTION WORKS—DE GAULLE'S INTERPRETATION

On January 21, 1964, De Gaulle indulged in an interpretation of his Constitution. But whatever the merits of his argument, the burning problem for the future—that of succession—remains unresolved.

As far as our own Constitution is concerned, its spirit proceeds from the necessity to assure the government the effectiveness, the stability, and the responsibility which it was fundamentally lacking under the Third and Fourth Republics.

Undoubtedly the launching of the reform in 1958 was determined by the shock that occurred in Algiers, displaying the powerlessness of the regime of that time to overcome a tragedy that was in the act of engulfing our national unity. What is more, in 1940, in very much more tragic circumstances still, we had already witnessed the abdication of a similar regime. But, even outside of these brutal demonstrations, no one had any doubts for a long time that a system which was placing the power at the discretion of the parties, vegetating in compromise, was being absorbed in its own crises, was incapable of conducting the affairs of our country. That is why the spirit of the new Constitution, while retaining a legislative parliament, consists in seeing to it that the power is no longer a thing of partisans, but that it emanates directly from the people, which implies that the Head of State, elected by the nation, is the source and holder of this power. This is what was done, to everyone's knowledge, when I resumed the direction of affairs, then when I assumed the functions of President. This is merely what was clarified by the last referendum. It does not seem that, since it has been applied, this concept has been misunderstood by those holding positions of responsibility, or that it has been rejected by the people, or contradicted by events.

As for the distribution of powers, this has been observed in accordance

SOURCE: *Major Addresses, Statements, and Press Conferences of General Charles De Gaulle, May 19, 1958–January 31, 1964* (New York: French Embassy, Press and Information Service), pp. 246–249.

with the provisions of our Constitution. The roles attributed respectively: to the President, guarantor of the destiny of France and of the Republic, entrusted therefore with heavy duties and possessing extensive rights; to the Cabinet appointed by the Head of State, sitting around him for the determination and application of policy and directing the administration; to the Parliament exercising the legislative power and controlling the action of the Ministers—these roles have been filled as demanded by the will of the country, the conditions we are living in, the obligation to conduct affairs actively, firmly and continuously.

It is true that, alongside the spirit and the text, there was the practice. This naturally depended in part on the men. With regard to the Head of State, it is quite obvious that his personal equation counted and I do not doubt that this was expected from the start. As for the Ministers and first of all the Premiers: M. Michel Debré and then M. Georges Pompidou acted with obvious efficacity, but each in his own way and a way that was not the same. Finally the Parliament impressed on its task and its attitude a different character according to whether, in the present regime, it was in its first or its second legislature. It should also be said that our institutions have had to function for more than five years in very variable conditions, and at times, under the impact of grave subversive attempts. But the trial of the men and of the circumstances has shown that the instruments fulfill their purpose, not only with regard to the ordinary conduct of affairs but even concerning the difficult situations which the present Constitution, as we have seen, offers the means of facing: referendum, Article 16, dissolution of the National Assembly.

Doubtless this success is due basically to the fact that our new institutions meet the demands of the times as much as the nature of the French people and what they really hope for. However, there are some who find the bride perhaps too beautiful and who suggest changes which, in fact, would upset the system from top to bottom.

Thus some recommend a "government of the legislature." The National Assembly, once it had given the government its confidence, could no longer overthrow it without its automatic dissolution ensuing. In this way the Head of State—and this is undoubtedly the principal aim of the project—would not have to intervene. But, by this token, the parties would have their chance to see that the appointment of the Premier and, at the time chosen by them, his replacement by maneuver, the composition of the Cabinet, then its divisions provoked from outside and its modifications, the policy ostensibly adopted, then its fluctuations, would once again be the object of their games and combinations, while they would shrewdly manage to prevent a crisis to occur that would legally empower the government to dissolve the Assembly. Thus we would come back to the Assembly system.

Others, making the best of a bad situation, profess to accept the existence of a Chief of State who is one, but on condition that the Parliament, on its side, be set up as an impregnable citadel in which the parties would find their empire and their security. Those testify to a preference, quite new on their part, for a system known as "Presidential" which would be similar to that of the United States. "Let the President," they say, "be elected by the people at the same time as the National Assembly and assume in person the executive power, but, on the other hand, let Parliament exercise the legislative power in its entirety. Especially, let each of the two, tightly enclosed in its own domain, have no hold over the other: the President not being able to dissolve, nor the Parliament to overthrow." Thus, allege these neophytes, the government would be concentrated in the hands of a single person, which would obviate the inconveniences of an authority divided between a President and a Premier, while Parliament, finding itself untouchable, would or would not vote the laws and the budget as it would see fit.

One could not fail to recognize that a Constitution of this sort has been able, up to now, to get along in the United States, that is, in a country, which, owing to its ethnic composition, its economic wealth, its geographic position, has known no invasion, nor even, for a century, any revolution; in a country which has only two political parties which are not in opposition on anything essential in any area—national, social, moral or international; in a federal country, lastly, in which the government assumes only general tasks—defense, diplomacy, finances—while it is up to the 50 States of the Union to provide for all the rest. But, how could this system suit the French nation, very highly centralized through the long effort of centuries, victim of all the internal and external jolts for seven generations, always threatened by others, and in which the numerous political parties, with the exception of that which advocates upheavals, are divided and inconsistent?

First of all, because France is what she is, the President must not be elected simultaneously with the Deputies, which would mix up his designation with the direct struggle of the parties, would alter the character and shorten the duration of his office as Chief of State. Moreover, it is normal in our country that the President of the Republic and the Premier not be one and the same man. Certainly, it could not be accepted that a diarchy exist at the top. But, rightly, it is nothing of the sort. In effect, the President, who, in accordance wih our Constitution, is the man of the nation, put in position by the nation itself in order to answer for its destiny; the President, who selects the Premier, who also names the other members of the Cabinet, who has the right to change the Premier, either because the task which he conferred upon him has been fulfilled and he wishes to keep him in reserve for a later stage, or because he would no longer approve of him; the President, who sanctions the decisions taken in the councils, promulgates the laws, negotiates and signs the treaties, enacts into law or not the measures proposed to him, is the chief of the armed forces, appoints the public officials; the President, who, in the case of danger, should take it upon himself to do all that is necessary—the President is obviously the only one to hold and to delegate the authority of the State. But, precisely, the nature, extent and duration of his task imply that he not be absorbed, ceaselessly and limitlessly, by the political, parliamentary, economic and administrative combination of circumstances. On the contrary, this is the job, as complete and praiseworthy as it is essential, of the French Premier.

Indeed, there could be no watertight separation between the two levels at which, on the one hand the President, on the other he who seconds him, daily exercise their respective functions. Furthermore, the councils and meetings exist to permit the Head of State to define step by step the orientation of national policy and to permit the members of the Cabinet, starting with the Premier, to make known their viewpoints, to specify their action and to give an account of their acts. Sometimes the two levels merge, when it is a matter of a subject whose importance involves everything and, in this case, the President distributes the responsibilities as he deems necessary. But, while it should obviously be understood that the indivisibly authority of the State is entrusted completely to the President by the people who elected him, that there is no other authority—either ministerial, civilian, military or judicial —which is not entrusted and maintained by him, finally that it is his duty to adjust the high office which is his own with those whose management he entrusts to others—everything commands, in ordinary times, the maintenance of the distinction between the office and field of action of the Head of State and those of the Premier.

However, sometimes those who are not yet rid of the concept of the past put forward the objection that the Government, which is that of the President, is at the same time responsible to Parliament. How can this be reconciled? Let us answer that the sovereign people, in electing the President, invests him with its confidence. That is, moreover, the heart of the matter, and the basic factor of the change brought about. Thereby the Cabinet, appointed by the Head of State and of which, in addition, the members cannot be members of Parliament, is no longer, with regard to the [two] chambers, what it used to be, when it was only the product of combinations of groups. Also, relations between the Cabinet and Parliament, as they are regulated by the Constitution, provide for censure only in conditions which give this rupture an extraordinarily serious nature. In this extreme case, the President, who is responsible for assuring the continuity of the State, also has the means to do so, since he can have recourse to the nation in order to make it the judge of the dispute by means of new elections, or by that of a referendum, or by both. Thus, there is always a democratic way out. On the contrary, if we were to adopt the American system, there would not be one. In a country like ours, the fact that the Head of State would also be the Premier and the impossibility for him—in the event of a legislative and budgetary obstruction—to appeal to the electorate, while the Parliament could not overthrow him, would inevitably result in chronic opposition between the two untouchable powers. The result would be either general paralysis or situations which would be settled only by pronunciamentos, or lastly the acquiescence of an insecure President who, under the pretext of avoiding the worst, would choose to give way to it, in submitting, as in the past, to the wills of partisans. One can think that it is this hypothesis which is enertained the most willingly by the unexpected champions of the "Presidential system."

Our Constitution is good. It has given proof of itself for more than five years, in times threatening to the Republic as well as in periods of calm. Doubtless, other circumstances and other men later on will give its application a turn, a style that are more or less different. Doubtless, the evolution of French society will lead us, in our times of progress, development, and planning, to reconsider one of its provisions. I mean the one which concerns the role and composition of the Economic and Social Council. But, with the exception of this specific point, which will not upset the balance of the Constitution, let us keep it as it is. Assuredly, it is understandable that neither those who sigh, openly or not, for the confusion of the past, nor that enterprise which aims at a totalitarian regime and which would like to create in our country a political disturbance which would result in its dictatorship—neither of these can willingly accept the Constitution. But the country has chosen and I believe, for my part, that it has done so once and for all.

❧

De Gaulle has been portrayed as an anachronistic and napoleonic figure. A devout Catholic and a general, he has been assumed to be a conservative in social and economic matters. Yet reading over his speeches, one finds a remarkable awareness of modern social and economic questions and an astounding reformist spirit.

Like most educated Frenchmen who read St. Simon and who marveled at the exploits of de Lesseps, De Gaulle is passionately interested in technology, productivity, and construction. In this sense he is part of a French dream that is both old and new—rapid industrialization and the rational exploitation of resources. "Technology dominates the universe," he writes, and he wants to make sure that France will not miss her opportunity. But neither technology nor industrialization are enough. As with the Army, the economy must serve *la politique*—the state.

The state therefore, as we pointed out in the General Introduction, must intervene to guarantee both the production of what is needed and, what is more, its equitable distribution. In the parts of his *Memoirs* reprinted here and also in the speech he gave to the Consultative Assembly two months before the end of the war, De Gaulle lays down his plans for social and economic reform. Had similar plans been openly advanced by Roosevelt at that time, they would have provoked a furor in the United States. De Gaulle therefore appears as the architect of a welfare state—neither more nor less than the Labor Party claimed to be in England a few months later!

When he returned to power in 1958 his concern with economic revival was just as great. The Fourth Republic had continued the mechanism of planning he had instituted—thanks to which investments had been routed to key economic activities; it had

64

benefited from the Marshall plan and was on the eve of entering
the Common Market. Despite the expenditures wasted on colonial
wars, the economic situation was much brighter than it had
been since the end of the war. Indeed, France was on the verge
of economic independence and able to compete with her European partners. De Gaulle accepted the Common Market as an
economic mechanism, introduced some monetary and other reforms to improve the position of the franc, and proceeded by
and large with economic planning. No major reforms have been
introduced since 1958, but the principles of a welfare state
have been implemented if not expanded. In the following
sections we have reproduced some of his major addresses and
thoughts on economic reforms, planning, welfare measures, and
on the economic growth and technological development of the
country.

ECONOMIC RENOVATION AND SOCIAL REFORM

The thoughts expressed here and the reforms outlines were
reiterated in a speech delivered by General De Gaulle before the
Provisional Consultative Assembly on March 2, 1945—only two
months before the end of the war in Europe. They represent
the clearest expression of the gaullist doctrine of state intervention in economic matters, of the imperative need of social
reform to effect an equitable distribution of the national resources, and of the urgent need of integrating the working
classes in the political and economic system. While the Communists found the measures inadequate, the speech alienated
powerful interests among the French middle classes and higher
bourgeoisie.

Like everyone else, I remarked that in our time technology dominated
the universe. This was the source of the century's great debate. Would
the working classes be the victim or the beneficiary of technical progress?
This was the source of those recently formed huge movements—socialism, communism, fascism—which dominated several great peoples and

SOURCE: *The War Memoirs of Charles De Gaulle* (New York: Simon
and Schuster, 1960), Vol. III, pp. 105–112.

divided all the rest. This was the reason that various banners—Liberal, Marxist, Hitlerian—were now hovering over the battlefields and that so many men and women, swept on by cataclysm, were haunted by fears of what would become of themselves and their children. How unquestionable the evidence that the flood of passions, hopes, and griefs that now broke over the belligerent powers, the enormous human mass to which they found themselves subject, the effort required by reconstruction, placed the social question first among all those the government had to resolve. I was convinced that without profound and rapid changes in this realm, there would be no lasting order.

How true this was for France! The war had fallen upon her at the height of the class struggle, the latter all the more intense in that our economy, desperately out of date, rejected changes and our political regime, lacking vigor and faith, could not impose them. Doubtless there were unavoidable causes for such stagnation. Unlike other nations, we were not fortunate enough to possess sufficiently abundant sources of coal and petroleum to develop our heavy industries. Before World War I, the armed peace had obliged us to devote a large part of our resources to the military establishment; after it, since we did not obtain reparations, we had been overwhelmed by the burden of reconstruction. Lastly, before the renascent German threat, we had had to resume the effort of armament. Under such conditions, productive enterprises remained too often neglected, the manufacture of equipment was rarely converted to civilian needs, wealth remained inert while public budgets were balanced with difficulty and the currency lost its value. So many delays and hardships, so many sacrosanct routines and egotisms, had a bad effect on the economy and also on the powers willing to undertake the reforms which might have given the workers their share. It is true that in 1936 popular pressure imposed a few concessions, but the impulse was soon sucked under by the parliamentary quicksands. When France entered the war, an ominous social unrest divided her citizens.

During the catastrophe, beneath the burden of defeat, a great change had occurred in men's minds. To many, the disaster of 1940 seemed the failure of the ruling class and system in every realm. There was therefore a tendency to seek their replacement. Particularly since the collaboration of certain business circles with the occupiers and the contrast between the almost universal penury and the immense prosperity of a small group exasperated the mass of the French people. Then too, a war in which Hitler was simultaneously opposing democrats and Soviets threw the entire working class on the side of the resistance. The nation saw its workers reappear as patriots and revolutionaries too, which had been the case during the Revolution, in 1830, in 1848, and under the Commune. But this time, it was against the enemy that French workers were striking or joining the maquis, and the idea that they might again withdraw from the national community was distasteful to the country at large. In short, to renew the economy so that it served the collectivity before furnishing profits to private interests, and, at the same time, to raise the condition of the laboring classes—that is what was on the nation's mind.

The Vichy regime had attempted to accomplish these goals. If, in the financial and economic realm, its technocrats had despite all setbacks shown incontestable skill, it was also true that the social doctrines of "national revolution"—corporate organization, a labor charter, family allowances—embodied ideas which were not without their attractions. But the fact that this enterprise was identified with the capitulation could only influence the masses toward an entirely different mystique.

That of Communism offered itself to their rage, and to their hopes. Their aversion for the structure of the past was exasperated by poverty, concentrated in the resistance, exalted with the liberation. Here, then, was an extraordinary opportunity for the "party." Deliberately confusing resistance with the class struggle and posing as the champion of both varieties of revolt, the Communist party had every likelihood of seizing control of the country, even when it could not do so by means of the Council of the Resistance, the committees, and the militias—unless De Gaulle, assuming the initiative, realized a number of reforms by which he could regroup allegiances, obtain worker support and assure economic recovery on a new basis.

This was the immediate task on which I set the government to work. The program had long since been determined. For I had prepared the realization of my original intent at the start, while the resistance fighters, of whatever tendency, were unanimous in their intentions. The various movements had taken up their positions. The study committees working clandestinely in France, or openly in London and in Africa, had prepared the drafts. The delegates, particularly those sitting in the Consultative Assembly in Algiers, had approved the main outline of these drafts. It could be said that an essential characteristic of the French resistance was its desire for social reform. But this desire had to be translated into acts. Now, by virtue of my powers and the credit public opinion had granted me, I had the means to do so. In the course of one year, the decrees and laws passed under my responsibility involved changes of an enormous significance for the structure of the French economy and the condition of the workers, changes the prewar regimes had vainly deliberated for more than half a century. The new edifice was apparently a solid one, since nothing subsequently was either added or taken away.

Thus the principal sources of energy were put in the state's hands. In 1944 the National Coal Group of the Nord and Pas-de-Calais departments was instituted, to which the Loire group was added soon afterward. A short while later, the government determined to put the production and distribution of electricity and gas under its control. This decision was carried out as soon as the terms could be specified. In 1945 the "Petroleum Bureau" was created, its object being to encourage, regulate and coordinate all matters concerning the fuel and oil industry. At the year's end, the High Commission on Atomic Energy was created. Given the fact that the country's activity depended on coal, electricity, gas, and petroleum, and would eventually depend on atomic fission; that in order to bring France's economy to the level that progress demanded, these resources must be developed on the largest scale; that expenditures and efforts were necessary which only the collectivity was in a position to realize—nationalization was a necessity.

Proceeding on the same principles, credit regulation also was arrogated to the state. As a matter of fact, once the state had assumed the responsibility of financing large-scale projects itself, it would need to receive the means directly. This would be accomplished by the nationalization of the Bank of France and the major credit establishments. Since the development of the territories within the French Union had become one of France's chief and perhaps supreme opportunities, the old "Caisse centrale de la France Libre" was converted into the "Caisse centrale de la France d'outre-mer," providing for state participation in the development of these new countries. A similar intention inspired the decision to group into a single network—Air France—the airlines operated on state subsidies before the war. By the end of 1945, our transport planes were flying over all the continents of the world. As for the transformation of the Renault works into a national trust, its consequence, not on principle but as a sanction, was to place this "pilot factory par excellence" under state control. Finally, to encourage the new economy to invest, that is to levy on the present in order to build the future, the "High Commission on Plans for Equipment and Modernization" was created during this same year.

But true progress can be made only if those who create it with their own hands find their reward within it. The government of the liberation intended to bring this about, not only by wage increases, but more particularly by institutions which profoundly modified working conditions. During 1945 the social security program was entirely recast and extended to many areas it had not previously covered. Every wage earner would be obligatorily covered. Thus vanished the fear, as old as the human race, that sickness, accident, old age, or unemployment would fall with crushing weight upon the workers. The poor are always with us, but not the wretched, the starving, the hopeless. Further, a complete system of family allowances was implemented. The nation supported its families in proportion to the number of their children, the support lasting from the day of the child's birth until the day he became capable of providing for his own needs. This provision was to revive the French birth rate, once so high it had nourished the spirit of enterprise and the greatness of our nation, but which, in a hundred years, had declined until France was no more than a static and sparsely populated country. At the same time, tenant-farming status was entirely revised; henceforth, a man working a rented farm was assured he could stay on the land as long as he wished, provided that he filled the conditions of his lease. Furthermore, he had right of preemption, if the land should be offered for sale. In this way a remedy was provided for one virulent cause of farm agitation and the desertion of our countrysides.

Furthermore, the program I had drawn up proceeded far beyond these material reforms. It aimed at granting the workers in the national economy responsibilities which raised them far above the role of instruments to which they had hitherto been confined. That they should be associated with the progress of industry, or their labor enjoy the same rights as those accorded to capital, or their remuneration be linked, like the revenue of stockholders, to the results of the industry's developments was the goal I proposed to realize. In order to prepare this promotion of labor, the Committees of Enterprise were created in February 1945. Each committee included the director of the establishment, the workers' representatives, the employees, and the executives. It was kept informed of the common activity. It formulated advice in all matters concerning production. It administered its own funds which were devoted, over and above wages and salaries, to the material and social life of the personnel. By more closely uniting all who, in whatever capacity, participated in the same concern, by encouraging them to study together the functioning, progress and inadequacies of their enterprise, by inspiring the consciousness and organizing the practice of their solidarity, I intended to take a major step toward the association of capital, labor, and technology; in this I saw the human structure of tomorrow's economy.

These metamorphoses, extensive as they might be, were realized without serious upheavals. Of course those in positions of privilege received them sullenly enough. Some nursed their grievances in secret, planning to air them later. But at the moment, all recognized the force of the current and resigned themselves to it at once, particularly since they had feared much worse. As for the Communists, they naturally preferred to regard what was being done as inadequate and to allege that the government was prevented from going any further by its reactionary connections. Nevertheless there was no opposition to our measures. As for the "politicians," they lost no time, in accordance with the rules of their art, in formulating reservations in one direction or another, though on the whole they approved the work being done and granted it overwhelming majorities in the Assembly. Many of them favored these measures because they corresponded, generally, to old and familiar demands. Others accepted them as a concession to social harmony. All intended to take credit for them tomorrow, before the electorate. Once again I remarked that if the goal was perhaps the same for them as for myself, the motives guiding them were not identical with my own. Though they adjusted their attitudes to accord with the prejudices of their respective tendencies, such considerations did not affect me. On the other hand, I perceived that they were scarcely aware of the motive inspiring me, which was the power of France.

For today, as ever, it was incumbent upon the state to create the national power, which henceforth would depend on the economy. The latter must therefore be directed, particularly since it was deficient, since it must be renovated, and since it would not be renovated unless the state determined to do so. This was, in my eyes, the chief motive of the nationalization, control, and modernization measures adopted by my government. But this conception of a government armed to act powerfully in the economic domain was directly linked to my conception of the state itself. I regarded the state not as it was yesterday and as the parties wished it to become once more, a juxtaposition of private interests which could never produce anything but weak compromise, but instead an institution of decision, action, and ambition, expressing and serving the national interest alone. In order to make decisions and determine measures, it must have a qualified arbitrator at its head. In order to execute them, it must have servants recruited and trained so as to constitute a valid and homogeneous corps in all public functions. Of these two conditions, the first was fulfilled today, and I was ready to make certain it would be so tomorrow as well; the second led me to establish the National School of Administration in August 1945. If the structure thus outlined became definitive, the new levers in the hands of the state would give it sufficient control over French activity for it to be able to make the nation stronger and happier.

Independently of the spirit of justice and opportunity, it was this same intention that led me to promote our workers to the rank of responsible associates. The unity of France demanded that her workers morally reintegrate the national community, from which, either out of direct opposition or out of discouragement, many tended to withdraw. If, further, the working class applied itself of its own accord to the development of its capacities, what resources would be added to the nation's productive activity and thereby to the power of France!

HOW TO GET THE COUNTRY'S ECONOMY MOVING

On December 28, 1958, only a few days after his election as President of the Republic, De Gaulle addressed the French on the economic and monetary problems facing them, and suggested stringent measures before the entry of France into the Common Market.

Above all else, women and men of France, I want to tell you that I accept the mandate which you have entrusted to me. Your decision was made known at the time of the national crisis in May; it was reaffirmed by the referendum, reiterated by the elections and made more specific by the vote of the people's elected representatives last Sunday. The national task that has been mine for eighteen years is, by this fact, confirmed. As France's guide and Chief of the Republican State, I shall exercise the supreme power to the full extent henceforth implied by this power and in accordance with the new spirit that has conferred it upon me.

The call made upon me by the country expresses its instinct for self-preservation. If the country looks to me for leadership, that is because it wishes to move, certainly not toward the easy way out, but toward effort and renewal. For seven busy months we have indeed been

SOURCE: *Major Addresses, Statements, and Press Conferences of General Charles De Gaulle, May 19, 1958–January 31, 1964* (New York: French Embassy, Press and Information Service), pp. 30–33.

going in that direction, and we have already made several great strides along the road to recovery. It was certainly high time to do so. For, just before we got under way, French unity was at the breaking point, dragging everything down with it.

Of course, the danger extended to finances and the economy. In the last days of May, we were, in this regard, headed toward disaster. The balance of payments between what we had to buy abroad and what we could sell there was reaching an apparently irreducible deficit, while foreign loans were almost exhausted. Moreover, we could no longer see how to meet all the expenses of the State in a normal manner, taxes being inadequate for that purpose and credit seeming on the point of vanishing. Finally, prices were continuing to rise and social unrest also. To cap the climax, a certain degree of recession was already making itself felt. The agitation in May, although it appeared first in Algeria, in reality proceeded from the general conviction that governmental authority was powerless before the tide of threats, including, naturally, those that were encumbering our economy.

The country's confidence made it possible, in this domain as in the others, for us to reverse the trend and to deal with the most urgent matters first. The situation, however, remains precarious, or in other words, dangerous. When one considers the hopes held out to us by the many young people born since the war, by the petroleum, gas, and uranium that have been discovered, by our growing capital equipment, by our new elites coming forth from among the people, by our association with the Community, and by the imminent enlargement of the European Common Market, then one is seized at one and the same time with impatience and with resolution.

With my Government, I therefore decided to put our affairs really and basically in order. The budget is the occasion for this—perhaps the final opportunity, but in any case a very good one; we have adopted and shall put into effect tomorrow a complete program of financial, economic, and social measures that places the nation on a foundation of truth and austerity—which is the only foundation on which it can build its prosperity. I make no secret of the fact that for some time our country will be put to the test. But the recovery a which we are aiming is such that it can repay us for everything.

With regard to public expenditures, there can be no question of anything that would end in inflation. But, at the same time, everything must be done to continue and even to increase the investments which control our future, whether in the social field—housing, schools, hospitals—or in the economic field—energy, equipment, communications. Moreover, we have undertaken to transform Algeria while its pacification moves forward. Furthermore, we must cooperate in the development of the countries of the Community. Finally, we cannot, in the present state of the world, do without a considerable military force. But all these obligations, together with the normal expenditures of the State, would entail, if we let things go, a deficit of $2.5 billion or twice as much as the country's credit structure could provide. Short of resorting to ruinous inflation or of failing France, there is nothing else to do but to reduce the impending deficit by one half. This is what has been decided upon.

M. Pinay, Minister of Finance and Economic Affairs, will shortly announce in detail what measures have been taken. Here are the salient features:

—increase in taxes on corporations and high incomes, taxes on wine, liquor and tobacco;

—withdrawal of many subsidies granted by the Treasury, especially those covering consumer goods;

—reduction of the part played by the national budget in financing nationalized enterprises, especially the railroads;

—making up the deficit arising from the operation of social insurance, the cost of which must be borne by public funds;

—asking the war veterans who have what they need and who are not crippled to give up their pensions; pensions for widows, orphans, disabled servicemen naturally remaining the same;

—abolition of a series of those escalator clauses which are really only proclamations of distrust of the currency;

—on the other hand, an increase of $496 million, that is to say, of 25 percent, in the total amount of investments, which are the source of our future wealth and which open up opportunities for our youth.

These are harsh measures. I know only too well what they will cost many in the immediate future, but I believe them to be effective, I consider them necessary, and I am sure that, in the long run, everyone will benefit from the stability achieved thereby.

Since we can expect some rise in prices, at least temporarily, as a result of these measures, the Government is also making provisions relative to purchasing power, especially that of the French people with the lowest incomes. Accordingly, on February 1, the minimum guaranteed wage for all occupations will be increased, while, beginning January 1, old people will see a $10.53 increase in their pensions. I might add that, through cooperation between employers and organized labor, a special fund will be created which is designed to maintain employment, and which will assure unemployed workers of an additional payment bringing their benefits almost up to the level of the minimum wage. As for personnel employed directly by the State, in the civil service, the public services and nationalized enterprises, it is provided that, beginning February 1, their remuneration will be increased by a flat 4 percent.

In the present-day world, values are all comparative. Compared with foreign countries, we are now in an unfavorable economic position. Unable to import and export enough, in debt, lacking credit—although our products, our techniques, and our abilities are on a par with all competitors—we are far from attaining the high level of foreign trade that would cause our economy to expand. The artificial factor in the value of our currency stems unmistakably from the disequilibrium of our affairs, but it is not, on that account, any the less a permanent cause of difficulties.

That is why, while we are engaged in curing the fundamental disorder, we must place our franc on a foundation that will be unshakable. So we are doing this, regretting that we must lower the rate, but taking the consequences of prolonged negligence. By the same action, our currency becomes convertible outside France into all foreign currencies, at the same time and on the same basis as a number of our European partners are making their pound, mark, lira, florin, etc., convertible. In addition, we want the old French franc—so often mutilated in proportion to our vicissitudes—to have a substance commensurate with the respect that is its due. Before the end of 1959, the new franc will be issued, which will be worth one hundred present-day francs. As far as foreign trade is concerned, we have decided to free it to the extent of 90 percent, thus opening the flood gates to the tide and emphatically restoring France to her international rank in the economic domain.

This whole policy, all the components of which are related and compliment each other, this entire policy is grave but essential. If this effort to put things in order again is not made with the sacrifices it requires and the hopes it engenders, we shall remain a country in tow, swinging perpetually between tragedy and mediocrity. If, on the contrary, we succeed in the great national undertaking of financial and economic recovery, what a step that will be along the road that will lead us to the top. This is my wish for all the women and men to whom I am speaking as the New Year approaches.

People of France, great people, have pride, courage, and hope.
Vive la République! Vive la France!

INDUSTRIAL GREATNESS

On June 14, 1960, in an address on French, African, and Algerian problems, De Gaulle spoke with confidence of France's
economic recovery.

Once upon a time there was an old country all hemmed in by habits
and circumspection. At one time the richest, the mightiest people
among those in the center of the world stage, after great misfortunes
it came, as it were, to withdraw within itself. While other peoples were
growing around it, it remained immobile. In an era when the power of
States depended upon thir industrial might, the great sources of power
were stingily meted out to it. It had little coal. It had no petroleum.
Furthermore, its population was no longer growing as, in some years,
it numbered fewer births than deaths. In the doubt and the bitterness
which it came to have about itself as a result of this situation, political,
social and religious struggles did not cease to divide it. Finally, after
two world wars had decimated, ruined, and torn it, many in the world
were wondering whether it would succeed in getting back on its feet.

Now, this country, France, is back on her feet again. Already a national movement, which was embodied in the Resistance, had shown a
determined will for renewal. Immediately following the Liberation, a
great impulse was given. Afterwards, in spite of many rough stretches,
the trend did not cease to turn toward expansion. But the difficult
aftermath of a stagnant past continued to bear down upon the nation.
Above all, the inconsistency of the State, whatever might have been the
worth of individual men, condemned the constituted authorities always
to be in a precarious position and always to be contested. Two years
ago, we suddenly found ourselves on the brink of civil war. Doubtless,
the occasion of this crisis was the Algerian question, which followed
upon the humiliating outcome in Indochina, and called for new action.
But, at the same time, we found ourselves, in our territories of Black
Africa, in the presence of a great movement which was stirring that
continent. Finally, and as everything is interrelated, the halting of

SOURCE: *Major Addresses, Statements, and Press Conferences of
General Charles De Gaulle, May 19, 1958–January 31, 1964* (New
York: French Embassy, Press and Information Service), pp. 79–81.

foreign trade, the exhaustion of our credit, the ruin of our currency—all consequences of an inflation that it had been impossible to stem— were threatening, from one moment to the next, to hurl us into the abyss. That is when the country recognized the necessity of a great and strong policy.

But to accomplish what? To accomplish a great deal. For our purpose is to transform our old France into a new country and to enable her to fall in step with her time. From this policy, she must draw prosperity, power and worldwide influence. This change must be our great national ambition.

Since we are the French people, we must accede to the rank of a great industrial State or be resigned to our decline. Our choice is made. Our development is under way. Its aim is both the progress of French power and that of the human condition. Our plans provide that it will be accomplished, in the next few years, at a rate of 5 percent or 6 percent a year, raising the average purchasing power by 4 percent annually. This means that, in twenty years, France—short of a catastrophe— will be twice as prosperous as she is today. This also means that a young couple, to whom a child is born this morning, has every chance that their small son, when it is his turn to be a father, will find himself twice as well off as his parents are today. What is more, it may readily be supposed that the Common Market of the Six is hastening this development. But the fact that we are living in the industrial era does not keep agriculture from remaining an essential branch of France's economic life. Since we have the advantage of being able to feed ourselves from the products of our soil, since we have all that is needed to be the country of fine wheat, choice meat, pure milk, good wine, we will not allow this great economic, social, and national potential to be exhausted.

Women and men of France, you can see with your own eyes what is being done for France. Naturally, first of all, we are bending our efforts to give her the sources of power that she lacks. The point we have reached proves that our efforts were justified: coal in plentiful supply; French or African petroleum, which in five years will cover our needs; gas from Lacq which, little by little, is being distributed; soon, gas from the Sahara, whose inexhaustible reserves may transform the existence of Algeria and influence that of Europe; electricity produced by hydroelectric power in quantities twice as large as those which were produced ten years ago; atomic energy which model installations have begun to supply. This accession of France to the rank of a people, which will find within its boundaries energy, electricity, oil, and gas, and will furnish them to others, is one of the most striking facts of world evolution, which, from the point of view of our independence, will have immeasurable consequences.

On condition, of course, that our country is at the same time given the necessary equipment. I will certainly not assert that all is for the best in this respect. However, look at what changes are being made, day after day, in France's industrial plant; what an effort is constantly being exerted to reconvert it; what a proportion of the profits are being reinvested with a view to development; what an improvement there is in the social atmosphere of our corporations, while awaiting the association of workers in the enterprises. And, in agriculture, the reorganization of the whole structure, of production, of equipment, of marketing and purchasing—a movement which alone can raise agriculture to the level of realities and which will increase under the impetus of law. Finally, note the rate of transformation of our infrastructure: the highway system, railroads, ports, airports, and water supply. There is not a traveler, a tourist, a camper who does not notice this from season to season.

But what would this development of material resources amount to, were it not coupled with the development of human resources? Now, we know that the French birth rate has made a striking comeback, that there are nearly 300,000 more cradles than graves a year and that this human investment will have a powerful influence on the country's economy. What social insurance is providing in the way of security for Frenchmen, and thereby for our economy, is well known. It is also well known that 300,000 dwelling units are being built each year and that this contributes directly to the productivity of the national labor force. It is well known what strides are being made in the country's hospitals, and to what an extent suffering and anxiety are relieved thereby, to the benefit of the whole community. But it is also and especially well known what a tremendous transformation is being achieved in education. While, I must note, the law is trying to organize cooperation between public and private institutions, we intend to give all our youth a level of knowledge commensurate with modern times, to enlarge the field from which the nation's activity draws the values which are necessary to it and to give to each child every chance at the beginning of his life in the community. As facts and figures are more eloquent than words, I shall state, for example, that secondary education will soon enroll three million students, or fifteen times as many as at the beginning of the century, and that our universities will enroll, in the next ten years, 600,000 students, whereas only 30,000 were registered in 1900.

In truth, in order to have an idea what an enormous burden the French nation is imposing upon its present gains with a view to build-

ing the future, one need only consider the use of public funds. Out of
the entire State budget, while barely one fourth is absorbed by the
functioning of the administrative services and another fourth goes for
defense, the remainder, or half, is assigned to the material and human
investments which all go, in the long run, to the national and social
development of France.

PROGRESS AND ITS INFANTILE DISEASES

Again a year later, on July 12, 1961, De Gaulle reminds the
French of the role of progress and economic expansion. An "old"
man reminds his "old" country that they are wedded to the
youthful spirit of the twentieth century! And also warns them
against the inevitable resentments and oppositions that modernization produces.

France has become wedded to her century. This means that, while
living in a difficult world, she is engaged in a vast transformation.
Naturally, there are many habits that do not adjust overnight to so
many new conditions. The six-inch ruler that measured the tiny advances of former days is now worthless. Certain old political refrains
borne out by past times no longer awake an echo. The little representative, administrative and labor game that used to be played not
so long ago is no longer on the scale of our present activities. Worse
luck for the six-inch ruler, the old refrains and the little games; the
undertaking to which France is now bending her energies is immense.

In an industrial era, we must first of all develop our industry. Whether
it is the existence of families and individuals, or of the urban, village,
school, sports, or hospital equipment that social life requires, or of
the basic infrastructure necessary for France as a whole—our needs and
our wants call for constantly increasing production. Furthermore we
must invest in order to be ready for what comes next, export in order to
pay for what we get from abroad, create so that all the young people
who have been born since the war may be able to find jobs.

Well, although the vast process which we have set in motion may
suffer certain jolts, although the very difficult operation which we
carried out nearly three years ago to put an end to inflation did jar
the mechanism, although on entering the Common Market we plunged

SOURCE: *Major Addresses, Statements, and Press Conferences of
General Charles De Gaulle, May 19, 1958–January 31, 1964* (New
York: French Embassy, Press and Information Service), pp. 135–
136.

ourselves of our own accord into the risks of competition—here we are in the midst of a definite upswing. During 1960 alone our production increased by 11.4 percent, which makes us one of the front runners on a world basis. Our country is becoming, before our eyes, a great industrial power, in other words a great power.

France is, therefore, factories, mines, construction sites, and research bodies. But France is also our fields. We must make our agriculture into a modern and balanced factor in our national economy. This means that large numbers of too-small properties must be grouped together to form profitable farms, that our farmers must devote themselves to quality; that they must organize their joint markets in order to sell, buy, preserve, condition, and process while cutting down on the middlemen; that they must take charge themselves of a large portion of the trade and industry dealing with the products of the soil. The delays which have occurred, either in the initiatives of the growers or in the assistance of the administration, are certainly regrettable. The attacks made on law and order during various demonstrations are greatly to be deplored. To arouse among farmers, particularly young farmers, an interest worthy of this great task, or for France to see in her agriculture one of the essential bases of her economic, social, and national future does not prevent the necessary development from occurring.

It is not only machinery and credit which spell progress. It is, above all, the capability of men. We have therefore undertaken a gigantic task of instruction and, at the same time, carried out basic reforms in the national educational system. Since all young French people must be able to rise, according to their abilities, to all levels of knowledge; since the desire to advance is urgent and widespread; since the high birth rate in France after the war is causing a considerable increase in the number of school-age children—we are led to increase, to expand, to re-equip our universities, secondary schools, and elementary schools and to recruit teachers for them. In 1962 we shall spend approximately $2 billion for this purpose, without including what is provided for scientific research, the fine arts, various youth programs, etc. France's young people are going to school in order to become—in culture, science, and technology—leaders of their times.

Such a renovation upsets the old balance. Economic activity and the population are concentrated in certain regions, while in others the upswing is being slowed down or hindered by distances, the lack of resources, an inadequate communications system. Therefore it is necessary to distribute things as much as possible in order to limit the number of excessive differences. On the other hand, the major economic currents which animate our country and link it with the outside world set us

tasks, as regards our railroads, highways, ports, and airports, in proportion to our progress and to the stakes. Finally, the war damage, the
tremendous increase in the number of city-dwellers—in Paris especially—
the steady growth of the population make construction and, at the same
time, urban planning inescapable imperatives. In 1961 we shall have
built 322,000 housing units, more than we have ever built before in one
year's time. In short, we must, as they say, plan on a national scale,
that is, remodel the structure and face of France.

WE ARE ON OUR WAY

Finally, on February 4, 1965, returning to the same theme, he
can assure the French that the country is on its way to rapid
progress and growth.

Under the impetus of the machine, the modern economy is in perpetual
motion. This is true of its structure, since certain branches are created
at a rapid pace, support one another, and make progress, while others
regress or disappear, and thus the distribution of efforts, capital, and
people is continually being renewed. This is true of the country's total
productive activity. This is true of how individuals use their own incomes,
whether they consume, save, or invest in business, housing, or equipment. This is true of what the State levies on the country's productive
activity through taxes, of what it borrows, of what it earmarks its
resources for. Yet, the connections between foreign countries are such
that what happens abroad inevitably influences what goes on at home.
And what is to be said of the wars or the catastrophes that exhaust
the human and material means of production in certain countries, while
they offer other countries a sudden opportunity to increase theirs? In
short, it is the very nature of our mechanized civilization that the
aggregate profits accruing from advances in science, technology, productive capacity, or from progress in structural frameworks, machinery and
trade, are essentially variable in their total and in their distribution.

Doubtless, the growth rate—thanks to the means our era is employing—
has a general tendency to increase rather than to decrease, because
new results are added to those which have already been achieved. But
this advancement is itself exposed to many vicissitudes. Sometimes rapid
and sometimes slow, at times carried away by "overheating" or halted

SOURCE: Press Conference, February 4, 1965 (New York: French
Embassy, Press and Information Service).

by crisis, excessive in various branches and insufficient in others, it entails all kinds of fits and starts and inequalities, unfair profits, and unwarranted setbacks. Hence, many subjects of dispute and difficulties in the material, social, political and moral life of societies. The states are therefore increasingly inclined to frame and to guide their national economies.

Before deciding on them, they can theoretically see before them two contradictory doctrines, one of which is simple and terrible. The "laissez-faire, laissez-passer" applied to economics since the dawn of the machine age has often, thanks to profit, the spirit of enterprise and free competition, given a powerful impetus to development. But it has unmistakably resulted in violent shocks and an enormous amount of injustice. On the other hand, the communist system, enforced in certain countries in which national disasters had swept away their structures and which, although endowed with great natural resources, vegetated under selfish and archaic methods, has succeeded, by using implacable constraint and frenzied propaganda, in building a massive productive apparatus, particularly in mining and heavy industry. But this is at the cost of vast ordeals, enormous waste, and the crushing of individuals, who are left neither their choice nor their freedom. Furthermore, those activities which call for spontaneous effort by the people and adjustment to manifold and changing demands, such as the manufacture of consumer goods, farming, distribution channels, are, under such a regime, constantly inadequate for want of rewarding initiative. The result, apart from compulsory and spectacular mass gatherings and movements, is a life which is ceaselessly threatened, or at least, tedious, colorless, and without flavor.

It was possible to believe once, and there are still those who sometimes believe, that these excessive systems find a wide audience in our country and that it is conceivable that one or another might one day impose itself on the State and on the nation. These are only figments of the imagination. Undoubtedly, it suits the traditional adherents of a theory formerly approved to extoll the illusion of an economy without rules. Undoubtedly, on the contrary, it appears expedient to the champions of subversion to evoke the song of tomorrow which would lull to sleep a society divested of profit and of competition. But everyone knows that, barring a cataclysm which would put everything in question again, we will no longer deliver ourselves to the unbridled discretion of liberal capitalism, and no one believes that we will ever submit to the crushing tyranny of totalitarian communism. No, the path that we have chosen is neither the former nor the latter.

We have made the choice of driving, yes, of driving our effort and our progress toward the greatest yields, the greatest continuity, the greatest justice. Which means that, while giving free rein to the individual and collective spirit of enterprise which involves the risk of gain or loss, we are applying public action to guide our economy, to advance the nation in all domains, and to improve the lot of the French people in proportion to the increase in France's wealth. To do this, our framework is the Plan, through which we determine the goals to reach, the stages, the conditions. Our means are laws, regulations, information, as well as credit, taxes, tariffs, subsidies. Our policy is an action which progressively adapts the national income to the needs and advances of the whole nation, of each of its economic branches and of each of its social categories.

The income policy—Monsieur Jourdain was using "prose" without knowing it. It has been a long time since, without saying so, we began to implement the income policy. We were already doing so when, more than half a century ago, we adopted the graduated income tax; when, at the time of the Liberation, we set up the social security system, family allowances, the minimum guaranteed wage. We are doing so right now when we implement the agricultural orientation laws; when, by taxing the gains of the nation, we give massive assistance to research, education, health, agriculture; when each year we build houses by the hundreds of thousands; when we develop the territory's infrastructure as a whole or by region; when we raise, in proportion to the growth of the national product, the salaries for State civil servants and public service employees. But there is no stopping in our era. Each day that passes makes it more necessary to push further ahead along the path we have chosen.

First of all, according to our goals for collective development, the increased national income must be distributed among consumption, investments, government operating expenses, the country's equipment, settlement of domestic and foreign debts, foreign aid, and so on, in order that the nation's income be distributed as rationally as possible among the various sectors which determine both its present life and its future progress. It is also necessary, of course, that the expected increase in the total wealth—the rate of expansion, in other words—be determined in accordance with our resources, our needs, our own development, and the development of those States with which we are the most closely linked. It is equally necessary that the total resources thus distributed do not exceed what the country has earned, otherwise there would be inflation, which means, sooner or later, bankruptcy.

But it is also necessary that this "programing," which is expressed in percentages, increase its social significance by applying to the totals of various kinds of income: industrial and commercial profits, wages and salaries, farm incomes, earnings from services, and social benefits, with the respective increases henceforth being calculated in real value. Of course, parity in progress is impossible because the facts relevant to the different cases are never identical. Indeed, this kind of parity is undesirable because it would be disastrous to suppress emulation. But, at the risk of imbalance, it is at least important that all categories advance at the same time as the whole in order that each one have its share. This basic harmony that the plan must provide is all the more necessary since the French economy is henceforth developing on the basis of stability, and since in so doing we have eliminated the dangerously easy terms which inflation was offering in order to compensate artificially and temporarily for setbacks and disparities, until that day when everyone would have been engulfed in the same abyss.

It is true that, at first sight, such a policy is apt to antagonize, on the one hand, various groups which are completely absorbed by their own affairs and interests and which distrust government intervention in the working of the economy on principle, and on the other hand, certain occupational organizations accustomed to concentrating their action on claims and which fear, in this form, the reduction of their role as the country's economic and social life would be made more regular, less disparate, and consequently more equitable. But the income policy corresponds too profoundly to the trend of our epoch not to belong to everyone. Besides, if it is up to the powers of the Republic, the Government and Parliament, to decide what it is, the opinions and discussions from which it will be elaborated imply the cooperation of the elements responsible for the areas of production, labor, and technology. The Planning Commissions, the Economic and Social Council, the Economic Development Commissions created recently in the Regions provide, through their respective attributes, the appropriate frameworks for these consultations.

In the midst of the immense dislocations which have taken place or are going on from one end of the earth to the other since the machine has begun to change society, France has now decided upon the ways and means for her own transformation. Of course, we know that we still have far to go, for there are no limits to progress. But, in France, the revolution goes on regularly, day after day, because it is accepted by the public and inscribed in law.

✤

Since his return to power in 1958 De Gaulle has identified himself with decolonization and movements for national emancipation. Algeria received its independence on July 4, 1962; all the former colonies have become full-fledged republics with which France continues to have friendly relations, and to which France provides massive economic aid estimated at about 1.2 billion dollars a year. This is the clear and unequivocal record, but the motives behind De Gaulle's actions and policies are not equally clear.

Throughout the war he was haunted by the fear that either the British or the Americans would lay their hands upon the choicest morsels of the French Empire; he often resisted this with a sensitivity and petulance that bordered on the absurd. Time after time he talked of 100, 110, 150 million people under the French flag, and when insurrection erupted in Indochina he made it clear that the whole issue was the re-establishment of French sovereignty there. How to explain this paradox? I think it likely that De Gaulle was determined that if reforms were to take place within the Empire they were to be made or given by France, acting in a paternal, benevolent role.

But when? This is another moot point. "How could I doubt," he writes in his *Memoirs,* "that on the morrow of the conflict that now enflamed the world, the passion of freedom would rise and swell universally." He then recounts with pride the famous Brazzaville conference held early in 1944—the gaullist charter of colonial emancipation. Yet the question of self-determination for the African colonies was discussed at Brazzaville and ruled out. In Washington, on August 24, 1945, De Gaulle said: "France plans to re-establish her sovereignty in

Indochina. Without doubt this will be accompanied with a new
regime, but for us this sovereignty is a capital matter."[1] Subsequently, he supported the continuation of French military
efforts in Indochina and he seemed equally eager for France to
maintain control over Tunisia and Morocco. In his trip to
Africa in the summer of 1958 he asked the former colonies
that had just been granted a degree of autonomy to become
parts of the French Community and cooperative structure in
which the President of the Republic and metropolitan France controlled decisions on major policies. He promised independence to
those who did not wish to become parts of the Community, as was
the case later with Guinea. The turning point, however, may have
come at this juncture. Within a year, speaking in Dakar in December, 1959, he promised independence to all those who wished
it, thus putting an end to the Community. Three years later he
granted independence to Algeria.

As with economic development, De Gaulle thus appears to be
far ahead of his contemporaries in his understanding of the
new forces released and the new dimensions revealed by the
so-called revolution of rising expectations—economic, political,
and cultural. Force was no longer an antidote—if one were
sought. It was time for the former children of the West to
grow on their own, and all they needed was understanding and
help.

THE FUTURE OF THE COLONIES—THE BRAZZAVILLE CONFERENCE

The Brazzaville Conference, held on February 1, 1944, brought
together top French officials and colonial administrators. Despite
De Gaulle's assertions in the *Memoirs*, the Conference agreed
simply to consider the gradual transformation of the empire in
the direction of increased autonomy. There was no question of
self-government.

But the same profound reasons that required great and immediate
reforms in metropolitan France also demanded the transformation of

[1]*Discours et Messages, 1940–1946* (Paris: Berger-Levrault, 1946),
p. 654.
SOURCE: *The War Memoirs of Charles De Gaulle* (New York: Simon
and Schuster, 1959), Vol. II, pp. 205–209.

the status of the overseas territories and the rights of their inhabitants. I was as convinced of this as anyone while I was fighting the war with the cooperation of the Empire's men and resources. How could I doubt, moreover, that on the morrow of the conflict that now enflamed the world, the passion for freedom would rise and swell universally? What was happening or heralded in Asia, in Africa, in Australasia, would have its repercussions everywhere. Now if in our overseas territories our misfortunes had not destroyed the loyalty of the people, the latter had nevertheless witnessed events that were cruelly prejudicial to our prestige: the collapse of 1940, the abasement of Vichy beneath the enemy's heel, the arrival of the Americans speaking as masters following the ridiculous battles of November 1942. On the other hand, throughout all of French Africa the native populations had been aware of the example of Fighting France; they recognized, on their own soil, the beginning of the French recovery; they participated in it with high hopes. Indeed this was the point where everything must begin again, but on the formal condition of not maintaining these states and these territories at their former level. And since, in such matters, it is never too soon to begin, I intended that my government take the initiative without delay.

•   •   •

With deliberate solemnity, I left for Brazzaville. From Morocco I reached Dakar, where the authorities, the Army, the fleet, the *colons,* and the population as a whole displayed an indescribable enthusiasm. Yet only three years ago it was here that I had been forbidden access to Senegal by cannon shots! Conakry, Abidjan, Lomé, Cotonou, Douala, and Libreville received my visit in their turn and burst into demonstrations that revealed the vibrant certainty of victory. Brazzaville gave me a moving welcome that marked its pride at having served as a refuge for French sovereignty in its worst years. I took up quarters in the "Case De Gaulle," the official residence which the territory, in its generous devotion, had built for my use on the magnificent bank of the Congo.

On January 30, I opened the conference. After Pleven's speech to me, I indicated why the government had decided to convene it: "Without wishing," I said, "to exaggerate the urgency of the reasons impelling us to broach these African questions all at once, we believe that the events now sweeping the world oblige us not to delay." Having hailed France's effort in Africa, I noted that even before the war "had appeared the necessity of establishing here on new foundations the conditions of Africa's development, those of the progress of its inhabitants and those of the exercise of its sovereignty." How much more urgent this was today, "since the war, which will have been, in a large share, an African war, is being fought to determine the nature of man's condition and since, beneath the action of the psychic forces it has everywhere unleashed, every population looks ahead and questions itself as to its destiny!" Yes, France, I declared, had chosen to lead down the road to the future "the sixty million men associated with her own forty-two million sons." Why? "First of all, because she is France. . . . Second, because it is in her overseas territories and in their loyalty that she has found her refuge and the starting point for her liberation. . . . And lastly, because, today, France is animated . . . with an ardent will for renewal."

The conference then began its work which was to result in propositions of an administrative, social and cultural nature. For a meeting of governors obviously could not decide the constitutional questions posed by the Empire's transformation into the French Union. But the route was traced and needed only to be followed. The spirit had blown which had the possibility of making this reform a national undertaking on a universal scale. No one was deceived about this in the rest of the world, where attention was suddenly fixed on Brazzaville. This conference had taken place by France's own choice at the moment when her reviving power and her reanimated confidence put her in a position to bestow what no one would yet dare claim to tear from her. Having accoladed Éboué, who, exhausted by too many efforts, was to die three months later without having seen the liberation, I left the capital of Equatorial Africa by way of Bangui, Fort-Lamy, Zinder, Niamey, Gao, returning to Algiers, where the legitimacy of the banner floating over my roof was no longer questioned by anyone.

COMMUNITY AND INDEPENDENCE

On November 10, 1959, in his second Press Conference, De Gaulle seems to be considering the connection between the colonial drive for independence and the maintenance of the French Community. He believed then that the two were compatible.

With regard to the peoples which France had linked to herself, there are, underlying her policy, two facts which I believe are as large as the earth itself.

SOURCE: *Major Addresses, Statements, and Press Conferences of General Charles De Gaulle, May 19, 1958–January 31, 1964* (New York: French Embassy, Press and Information Service), pp. 65–67.

The first fact is the idea of self-determination, of these people being free to decide their own destiny and, in their eyes, of independence, which stirs these peoples. It is the kind of elementary psychological state of mind which is all the more active as it finds the support of the entire world, including the countries that yesterday were colonizers.

It is true that, for a long time, mankind agreed—and I believe that it was perfectly right—mankind agreed that, in order to open the way to civilization for the peoples who had remained apart from it as a result of natural obstacles or of their own characters, it was necessary that Western Europe penetrate these lands, in spite of some annoying vicissitudes.

Where would North America, South America, Africa, Oceania, a large part of Asia be today if the explorers, settlers, soldiers, missionaries, engineers, and doctors of the West had not gone there bringing ideas, action, organization, and Western technology? Yes, these countries were conquered, revealed, and awakened. Now then, this has been done, and from one end of the earth to the other, each people is becoming aware of itself and wants to determine its own fate.

The second fact which is world-wide—this fact too—is that these people put in contact with progress are assailed with a growing desire to see their own living standards rise; in a world where some live in full prosperity, people resign themselves, with more and more difficulty, to not satisfying their hunger, to being exposed to the weather, to dying in epidemics, to vegetating in ignorance, and these people want, in their turn, to have well cultivated land, mines, factories, roads, railroads and bridges, airplanes, ships, schools, universities. And how can they have them without the administrative, financial, economic, and technical assistance of those who have the means for it? As a people becomes independent, it needs the help of others. This is something which is only human, that is to say, very natural and which may be acknowledge freely.

Therefore, this being the case, what is France's attitude toward the peoples who were under her rule a short while ago, and even more toward those who do not want to be a part of France—which is true for some?

There are some among us—they are not lacking—who are adverse to development, either from nostalgia for a past which, furthermore, did have in it many fine efforts and worthy accomplishments, or from misunderstanding of present realities, or for reasons of personal interest which are often perfectly respectable.

Those people would like us to act as if that which exists did not. They would like us to continue acting in the terms of an empire over peoples who are carried away by the excitement of liberty. If this attitude were that of France, there is no doubt—taking into account current trends— there is no doubt that this would lead her, and all the world, into greater and greater difficulties. Moreover, the inescapable changes would happen all the same, and they would happen badly under undesirable human conditions, and they would happen against France.

On the other hand, there are other people who think that we not only ought not to hinder the separation when it occurs, but also, on the contrary, that we ought to be happy about it. These territories cost us a great deal more than they bring in. If they wish to leave us, let them do so. Our resources, our capacities would find much better use at home than in those countries. I do not think that those people agree with the idea that France has of herself, nor with the idea that the world has of France. We have always had a humane mission, and we still have it, and it is necessary that our policy conform to our spirit. It is quite true that, in the case where some do not want our assistance, there would be no advantage for us in wanting to impose it on them. In this case, it is we who would profit by secession. But, with regard to the peoples who want her assistance, to whom she is attached and who, one day perhaps, will reward her for her efforts—with regard to these, France is resolved to furnish them with the aid which they desire, to the extent that she is able. In other words, France's policy with regard to these countries is to respect and to recognize their free disposal of themselves and, at the same time, to offer them an opportunity to form with her a whole in which they will have her support and in which she will have their participation in her world-wide activity.

THE ADDRESS AT DAKAR: YOU CAN HAVE YOUR INDEPENDENCE

The speech of December 13, 1959, at Dakar is, in my opinion, the dividing line in De Gaulle's "colonial policy." Whatever reservations he may have harbored or whatever nostalgias about the Empire may have haunted him, were abandoned.

Yes, in a few days France, the Federation of Mali, and the states that compose it will begin negotiations to modify the status of their relations. This was implicitly and even explicitly provided for by the Constitution of the Community that we all have voted. It is nonetheless true that

SOURCE: *Le Monde*, December 31, 1959. (My translation.)

this will lead the federal state of Mali, and the member states of Sudan and Senegal that compose it, to a new position. The one they occupied last year was new. And it will be even more so in the immediate future. In other words, this state of Mali will assume what some call a "position of independence" and which I prefer to call that of "international sovereignty." I say that I prefer it, without contesting the attraction and the significance that the term independence may have and ought to have for all peoples and in particular for this one. I prefer, nevertheless, international sovereignty because it appears to me to correspond better to enduring necessities and more particularly to present-day necessities. Independence is a term which signifies an intention, but the world being what it is—so small, so cramped, so interfering with itself—that real independence, total independence does not truly belong to anybody. . . .

When, therefore, a country like yours will assume the international responsibility that I mentioned the whole world is looking to see in which direction it will move of its own accord. Will it choose the camp of freedom, will it choose the other camp? . . . But again, things being what they are and the world being what it is, Mali must choose the direction that it will take. In order to choose it and to follow it there is something essential. . . . What is essential for a country to play its international role is for it to exist by itself, through itself and in itself. There is no international reality which is not at the same time a national reality; for a country in order to play its role in the world must follow the paths permitting it to do so; the first of these paths is that it constitutes itself as a State. A country has never been known to exist and even more important exist internationally without a State. That is to say, an organization which directs the whole of the citizenry, which is accepted and recognized by all the inhabitants, and which leads the entire country toward a better life. . . .

This is a technical epoch in which we are living. There is no state with any weight which does not contribute something to the technical progress of the world. This I must recommend since I have the honor of finding myself among you. You are taking the responsibility and France accepts it with all her heart. I promise that she is ready to help you. She is ready first because of her humane nature. There have been vicissitudes in the history of France but the continuity of this history exists and goes back before the Revolution. . . . From its very inception the vocation of France, the purpose of France, have been a humane vocation and a humane purpose. She is faithful to this purpose when she offers you her loyal and friendly cooperation in the creation, establishment, and progress of your state. . . .

That is why you may count on France. In the world in which we are and in which we are going to be, no longer only linked together, but side by side—in this world let us stay together. This is the best service that we can render to ourselves, and in any case it is, in the last resort, what humanity requires of us.

DECOLONIZATION IS . . . INEVITABLE

On April 11, 1961, De Gaulle emerges as the champion of decolonization, and he retrospectively asserts that he had always favored it.

Since Brazzaville, I have not ceased to affirm that the populations dependent on us should have the right to self-determination. In 1941, I granted independence to the mandated States of Syria and Lebanon. In 1945, I gave all Africans, including Algerian Moslems, the right to vote. In 1947, I approved the Statute of Algeria which, if it had been applied, would probably have led to the progressive institution of an Algerian State associated with France. At that time, I agreed that the protectorate treaties concerning Tunisia and Morocco should come to an end. In 1958, having resumed leadership, I, along with my Government, created the Community and later recognized and aided the independence of the young States in Black Africa and Madagascar. Not having returned to power in time to prevent the Algerian insurrection, immediately upon my return I proposed to its leaders to conclude the peace of the brave and to open political talks. In 1959, I proclaimed the right of the Algerian populations to self-determination as well as the determination of France to accept the solution, whatever it might be, which would result from this. In 1960, I affirmed many times over that Algeria would be Algerian. I spoke of the birth of its future republic and renewed our offer of discussions. It was not our fault that the Melun contacts did not have any results; at the same time I broke the plots intended to force me to support integration. In 1961, I asked the French people to give me their approval, which was done through a massive "Yes" vote in the referendum, and, once again, I invited the men of the rebellion to get in touch with our representatives.

· · ·

SOURCE: *Major Addresses, Statements, and Press Conferences of General Charles De Gaulle, May 19, 1958–January 31, 1964* (New York: French Embassy, Press and Information Service), pp. 114–117.

In conclusion what does this add up to: to decolonization. But if I have undertaken and pursued this task for a long time, it is not only because we could foresee and later because we witnessed the vast movement toward freedom which the world war and its aftermath unleashed in every corner of the globe, and which the rival bids of the Soviet Union and America did not fail to emphasize. I have done it also, and especially, because it seemed to me contrary to France's present interests and new ambition to remain bound by obligations and burdens which are no longer in keeping with the requirements of her strength and influence.

Moreover, this is true for others as well. It must be recognized that in the great transformation which is taking place from one end of the universe to the other, the itching for independence of erstwhile dominated peoples and also the incitements thrown out by all the demagogies of the world are not the only motivating forces. There is another which is not always very clearly perceived because of habits of mind, but which is nonetheless a very positive factor, one that is growing and tending to become the predominant one, especially in France. I mean that the reasons which once led certain civilized peoples to take under their direct control certain other peoples which were not—these reasons are disappearing even from the minds of the ex-colonizers. It now seems to the most powerful nations that their future, their welfare, and the potentialities of their world action depend on their own development and on the cooperation of the formerly colonized countries, much more than on domination imposed on dissimilar peoples.

It was not always like that. We French built our empire at a time when our internal activities had reached a sort of ceiling—an industry which was not breaking any new ground, an agriculture which was not making any changes, trade channels which were fixed, salaries and wages unchanged, practically stereotyped budgets, gold currency, interest rates at 3 percent, etc. On the other hand, our old ambitions of European hegemony and natural frontiers were countered by the treaties of 1815 and, after 1870, by the unity and strength of a threatening Germany. Then we sought in distant extensions a new role for the surplus of our enterprising abilities, a complement to our prestige and soldiers for our defense.

France does not have to be at all sorry for what she has achieved overseas in this capacity and in this form. I have said it often and I repeat: it constitutes a great human accomplishment which—notwithstanding certain abuses and errors and despite all the endless spouting of all sorts of worthless demagogues—will forever be a credit to France. But how many things have changed today.

Now our great national ambition is our own national progress constituting a real source of power and influence. Now the modern era permits us, compels us, to undertake a vast development. Now for this development to succeed we must first of all employ the means and resources at our disposal on our own behalf, in our own country. All the more so as we need these means and resources to ensure our own defense and that of our neighbors against the greatest imperialism that the world has ever known—the imperialism of the Soviet Union. We also need these means to win out in the tremendous economic, technical and social struggle now under way between the forces of humanity and the forces of slavery.

It is a fact: our interest, and consequently our policy, lies in decolonization. Why should we continue to cling to costly, bloody, and fruitless domination when our country has to undergo complete renovation, when all the underdeveloped countries, beginning with those which yesterday were our dependencies and which today are our favorite friends, ask for our aid and our assistance? But this aid and this assistance—why should we extend them if it is not worthwhile, if there is no cooperation, if what we give finds no return? Yes, it is a matter of exchange, because of what is due us, but also because of the dignity of those with whom we are dealing.

This is the basis of France's policy with regard to her future relations with Algeria. If in the final analysis the Algerian populations are willing to let themselves be led to a break with France, such that we will no longer have any part to play in their destiny, we shall not oppose this in any way. Naturally, we shall cease immediately to sink in a henceforth hopeless enterprise our resources, our men, and our money. We shall invite those of our nationals who are there and who truly run too many risks to leave the territories concerned. On the other hand, we shall send back home those Algerians living in France who would cease to be French. In that case we shall draw the consequences of the will which will very probably be expressed by certain populations to belong to France—populations whose location, moreover, is already fairly well known. These people too have the right to self-determination, just like the others, and they would not owe anything at the outset to a national Algerian unity of which they would not be a part, to an Algerian sovereignty which has never existed, to an Algerian State still unborn. Therefore these populations would first of all have to be relocated by us and their protection assured. And what then? Then, we shall see.

Some people say, "What would happen to these territories if France withdrew? They would straightaway fall into misery and chaos, until

Communism took over." That is, no doubt, what would happen to them; but then we would no longer have any duty toward them other than to pity them.

THE END OF THE COMMUNITY

The French Community therefore is virtually extinct, he will say on the same occasion.

We have followed the work of the Yaoundé conference with the greatest interest. We consider it very important for Africa, for our relations with Africa, and for the world that the French-speaking African States and Madagascar join their efforts—economic, political, and undoubtedly even military. We consider this to be very useful, and France naturally has no objection to this—quite the contrary.

As regards relations between these States and ourselves, you know that they are not as yet fully defined. Some States belong to the remodeled Community; the others—which do not—are working, however, toward a form of cooperation, and we believe that the agreements establishing this cooperation will be signed shortly. In any case, the spirit in which France views these young States, and, I believe, the spirit in which these young States view France, is as friendly and gratifying as it could be. I am happy that you have given me the opportunity to say so.

With regard to the Senate of the Community, it is true that since a certain number of States are no longer explicitly a part of this Community, its Senate—in the form previously provided—no longer has any reason to exist. But I believe that everyone, or almost everyone, feels the need to establish on the parliamentary level an organized system of contact between France and these States. And I believe that this is one of the points on which it will not be difficult, for France at any rate, to come to complete agreement.

SOURCE: *Major Addresses, Statements, and Press Conferences of General Charles De Gaulle, May 19, 1958–January 31, 1964* (New York: French Embassy, Press and Information Service), pp. 122–123.

PART II

THE MARGIN OF INDEPENDENCE

In Part II are contained some of De Gaulle's major pronouncements on the role of France in the world. We have called it "The Margin of Independence" because international relations and the balance of world power are looked upon by De Gaulle with an eye to the role France can play. To do so France must be independent. She must be free to pick and drop her allies; to defend herself with her own weapons; to threaten the potential enemy with reprisals; to defend her European and world interests; to develop her own resources and, in the ultimate sense, to make her own war.

The margin of independence naturally changes. Vanquished by a powerful enemy, France was befriended and supported by an even more powerful ally—an ally that was immensely rich, who emerged from the war unscathed, flexing its muscles for what some called the "American century." De Gaulle quickly realized that the American isolationist posture of 1919 was unlikely to be repeated. Faced with the inevitable clash of power and ideology with the Soviet Union, the United States would probably be forced into global commitments that would allow little freedom and power to the other members of the so-called free world. In the form of NATO, SEATO, CENTO, and numerous other ways, the United States was to influence and, thanks to its powerful weapons, attempt to control its partners. This was De Gaulle's perception of the course events were likely to

95

follow, and this is what he set out to defeat. Hence, "anti-Americanism" is not a matter of personal antipathy to American leaders, nor a matter of doubt about the nature of American leadership and policy or the American way of life—though undoubtedly all these elements are present—but a simple and realistic policy aimed at increasing France's margin of independence.

De Gaulle has consistently assumed the necessity of American protection and support as long as France was unarmed and the Soviet Union appeared to have further European ambitions. A powerful ally was preferable to a powerful enemy. But even then he refused to forsake the principle of France's freedom of action within or outside of the alliance. As the Soviet attitude changed and France grew stronger, the burdens of the alliance appeared at times to be greater than its advantages. By 1964 France could afford to assert her own course of action in Europe and elsewhere. She was "independent"—and the period of tutelage was over.

Three major sections are devoted to this theme of French independence. First we reproduce some of De Gaulle's over-all views on world events and the role of France. Second, there follow some extremely telling excerpts on the techniques De Gaulle used to seek alliances that strengthened France; this of course is the classic game of balance of power he has played and continues to play with consummate skill. Finally, we examine his views on the role of the army and military weapons—an essential ingredient of French independence.

4. THE CLAIMS OF FRANCE

❧

Throughout World War II De Gaulle never ceased to assert that France must assume a primary role—the "primacy," as he put it—in Europe, and he never relinquished his claims to maintain the full integrity of the French Empire. Despite defeat, France was to re-emerge as the first European power and to continue its former world-wide interests and involvements. France, with Europe, was also to play an important role in East-West relations on a footing of equality with the two superpowers.

From the moment De Gaulle launched his defiant appeal for the continuation of the French war effort against Germany on June 18, 1940, his course of action was clearly delineated. He was the custodian of all French interests that he presumed would be safeguarded during the war and fully reaffirmed after its termination. As a result France was to be treated as an ally on equal terms during the war; France was to be consulted on all matters of common concern and allied strategy; the Free French Forces were to be generously supported and provisioned by the allies; top French officers were expected to assume high level positions both within the Joint Chiefs of Staff and in the theater commands; and last and most especially France should be fully consulted on all matters of postwar settlement, particularly though not exclusively with regard to Europe.

As we shall see in more detail in the third part, these claims unfulfilled during the greater part of the war and in the years immediately following the Liberation, were restated in more pressing terms after 1958. However, De Gaulle's thoughts during the period of World War II are revealing of his subsequent stand, and we therefore have reproduced some of the most significant excerpts from his *Memoirs,* wherein can be found the groundwork for his conceptions of a new balance based upon the emergence of French national power and a strong Europe.

THE FIRST APPEAL

The first defiant appeal for French independence was made by De Gaulle on June 18, 1940—when the French army lay defeated and Germany occupied most of France.

The leaders who, for many years past, have been at the head of the French armed forces, have set up a government.

Alleging the defeat of our armies, this government has entered into negotiations with the enemy with a view to bringing about a cessation of hostilities. It is quite true that we were, and still are, overwhelmed by enemy mechanized forces, both on the ground and in the air. It was the tanks, the planes, and the tactics of the Germans, far more than the fact that we were outnumbered, that forced our armies to retreat. It was the German tanks, planes, and tactics that provided the element of surprise which brought our leaders to their present plight.

But has the last word been said? Must we abandon all hope? Is our defeat final and irremediable? To those questions I answer—No!

Speaking in full knowledge of the facts, I ask you to believe me when I say that the cause of France is not lost. The very factors that brought about our defeat may one day lead us to victory.

For, remember this, France does not stand alone. She is not isolated. Behind her is a vast Empire, and she can make common cause with the British Empire, which commands the seas and is continuing the struggle. Like England, she can draw unreservedly on the immense industrial resources of the United States.

This war is not limited to our unfortunate country. The outcome of the struggle has not been decided by the Battle of France. This is a world war. Mistakes have been made, there have been delays and untold suffering, but the fact remains that there still exists in the world everything we need to crush our enemies some day. Today we are crushed by the sheer weight of mechanized force hurled against us, but we can still look to a future in which even greater mechanized force will bring us victory. The destiny of the world is at stake.

I, General De Gaulle, now in London, call on all French officers and

SOURCE: *The War Memoirs of Charles De Gaulle* (New York: Simon and Schuster, 1959), Vol. I, pp. 83–84.

men who are at present on British soil, or may be in the future, with
or without their arms; I call on all engineers and skilled workmen from
the armaments factories who are at present on British soil, or may be
in the future, to get in touch with me.

Whatever happens, the flame of French resistance must not and shall
not die.

THE DARK YEARS: VISION AND ANXIETIES

The *Memoirs* are replete with reflections and speculations on the
position of France, her claims, her expectations, and the dangers
that she faced in the hands of friend and foe alike.

• • •

What would happen to Europe after the defeat of Germany, and what
would be the latter's fate? These were the chief dilemmas which events
proposed from one day to the next and by which, of course, I was
particularly concerned.

In one man's lifetime, France had survived three wars instigated by
her neighbor across the Rhine. The first had terminated in the mutila-
tion of the national territory and crushing humiliation. Victorious in
the second, France had recovered Alsace and Lorraine, but at a cost of
men and material that left her bloodless and ruined. Furthermore, the
ill will of the Anglo-American powers, taking advantage of the inconsistency of our regime, led us, subsequently, to renounce the guarantees
and reparations which had been granted us in exchange for control
of the Reich and the Rhine frontier. The third war had seen our army
fall to pieces at the first encounter, the government rush to capitulate,
the nation endure occupation, organized pillage, forced labor, and the
detention of two million men. By virtue of a kind of miracle, independence and sovereignty had been maintained in the remotest parts
of the Empire. Gradually an army had been reconstituted, while the
resistance grew in Metropolitan France. France contributed to her own
liberation with important military forces, a solid government, a united
public opinion. She had, henceforth, the assurance of being present
at the victory. But it was all too obvious she would then find herself
reduced to such a weakened condition that her world situation, the
adherence of her overseas territories, and the very sources of her life
would be compromised for a long time. Unless by this very occasion

SOURCE: *The War Memoirs of Charles De Gaulle* (New York: Simon
and Schuster, 1960), Vol. III, pp. 7, 50–54, 204–205.

—perhaps the last—she could reconstruct her power. This is what I wished to effect.

To make France's recovery possible, the German collectivity must lose its capacity for aggression. In the dangerous world already looming before us, existence under the threat of war from a neighboring state which had so often demonstrated its taste and its talent for conquest would be incompatible with France's economic recovery, her political stability, and the moral equilibrium without which all efforts would remain futile. It is true that the exhaustion of Germany, the Allied occupation, the annexation of her eastern territories, would prevent the worst for years to come. But afterward? What would become of the German people, what changes would they undergo after their imminent defeat? Perhaps they would choose wisdom and peace? Perhaps this transformation would prove to be a lasting one? Obviously the conditions of our security would vary accordingly. But as long as we did not know the answer, we had to proceed as if Germany might remain a threat. What guarantees, what pledges would reassure us, while granting the great German people an opportunity to live, advance and cooperate with us and the rest of the world?

The abolition of a centralized Reich! This, in my opinion, was the first condition necessary to prevent Germany from returning to its bad ways. Each time a dominating and ambitious state had seized the German polities, obliterating their diversity, imperialism had been the result. This had been only too evident under Wilhelm II and under Hitler. Conversely, if each of the states within the German federation could exist by itself, govern itself in its own way, handle its own interests, there would be every likelihood that the federation as a whole would not be led to subjugate its neighbors. This would be even more likely if the Ruhr, that arsenal of strategic matériel, were given a special status under international control. Further, the Rhineland would, of course, be occupied by French, British, Belgian, and Dutch armies. But if its economy were moreover linked to a grouping of the Western powers—and with no opposition to other German units joining this alliance as well—and if the Rhine itself became an international freeway, then cooperation between complementary nations could be instituted forthwith. Lastly, there was every reason to suppose that the Saar, retaining its German character, would be transformed into a separate state and united to France by trade agreements which would settle the question of our reparations in terms of coal. Thus the German federation, recovering its diversity and turning its eyes toward the west, would lose the means of war but not those of its own development. In addition, none of its fragments would be annexed by the French, thus leaving the door to reconciliation open.

This conception of tomorrow's Germany was closely related to my image of Europe. After the terrible lacerations she had undergone in the last thirty years, and the vast changes which had occurred the world over, Europe could find equilibrium and peace only by an association among Slavs, Germans, Gauls, and Latins. Doubtless she must take into account what was momentarily tyrannical and aggrandizing in the Russian regime. Utilizing the procedures of totalitarian oppression and, on the other hand, invoking the solidarity of the Central and Eastern European peoples against the German peril, Communism was apparently trying to gain control of the Vistula, the Danube, and the Balkans. But once Germany ceased to be a threat, this subjection, for lack of a *raison d'être,* would sooner or later appear unacceptable to the vassal states, while the Russians themselves would lose all desire to exceed their own boundaries. If the Kremlin persisted in its enterprise of domination, it would be against the will of the nations subject to its government. Yet in the long run there is no regime that can hold out against the will of nations. I believed, moreover, that timely action by the western Allies with regard to the masters of the Kremlin, on condition that such action be concerted and categorical, would safeguard the independence of the Poles, the Czechs, the Hungarians, and the Balkan peoples. After which the unity of Europe could be established in the form of an association including its peoples from Iceland to Instanbul, from Gibraltar to the Urals.

This was the plan I had conceived, knowing perfectly well that in such matters nothing turns out exactly as one has hoped. I sounded the weaknesses in our policy of credit abroad and support at home, yet I remained convinced that France could undertake great actions, assume great proportions, and greatly serve her own interest and that of the human race as well. But to begin with, we would have to insinuate ourselves into the dissimulated and discordant argument by which America, Russia, and England were determining what was at issue without us.

No sooner had the sound of gunfire faded than the world's appearance changed. The strength and spirit of the peoples mobilized for the war suddenly lost their unifying object, while the ambition of states reappeared in all its virulence. The Allies revoked those considerations and concessions they had necessarily granted each other in time of peril, when they were confronting a common enemy. Yesterday was the time for battle; the hour for settling accounts had come.

This moment of truth revealed France's continuing weakness in relation to her own goals and to the partisan calculations of other states. The latter, of course, would take advantage of the situation to try to force our hand on those issues still undecided, or else to relegate us to a secondary place among nations responsible for constructing the peace. But I had no intention of letting this happen. Considering, in fact, that Germany's collapse, Europe's laceration, and Anglo-American friction offered a miraculously saved France exceptional opportunities for action, it seemed likely that the new period would permit me to achieve the great plan I had conceived for my country.

I intended to assure France primacy in western Europe by preventing the rise of a new Reich that might again threaten its safety; to cooperate with East and West and, if need be, contract the necessary alliances on one side or the other without ever accepting any kind of dependency; to transform the French Union into a free association in order to avoid the as yet unspecified dangers of upheaval; to persuade the states along the Rhine, the Alps, and the Pyrenees to form a political, economic, and strategic bloc; to establish this organization as one of the three world powers and, should it become necessary, as the arbiter between the Soviet and Anglo-American camps. Since 1940, my every word and act had been dedicated to establishing these possibilities; now that France was on her feet again, I would try to realize them.

The means were poor indeed! Yet if France had not yet taken into her hand the trump of her ultimate power, she still held a number of good cards: first of all, the singular and century-old prestige which her miraculous return from the brink of the abyss had partially restored; then the fact that her cooperation was no longer to be despised amid the disequilibrium that burdened the entire human race; and lastly, the solid units constituted by her territories, her people and her overseas extensions. Even before we had recovered all our strength, these elements put us in a position to act and to make ourselves respected.

On condition we put them to good use. Here, indeed, lay my task. But to compensate for all we lacked, I required bold support from the nation. This granted, I could promise that one would ignore or defy the will of France. Naturally, our allies expected the situation to be otherwise; whatever their regard for General De Gaulle, they oriented their nostalgia toward the old, political France, so malleable and so

THE CLAIMS OF FRANCE

103

convenient, and watched for the inevitable discords to appear between
myself and those who anticipated a return to yesterday's regime.

THE MEMORANDUM OF SEPTEMBER 23, 1958

The Memorandum of September 23, 1958, remains technically
secret. Here we give the version that one of the most knowledge-
able French analysts of foreign policy, André Fontaine, gives
in his book.

The Memorandum consisted of three parts—a diagnosis of the situation generally conceded by all to be correct, a prescription that was
bound to provoke much less enthusiasm, and last, a menace, whose
advisability appears highly contestable. What was the diagnosis? It
was in the paradox of opposing the global threat of communism by frag-
mented and dispersed alliances. The contrast between the equality of
the risks assumed (by all members of NATO) in case of thermonuclear wars and the inequality of the responsibilities undertaken by
each in the decisions that might lead to the possibility of the
use of such weapons . . . was great. The remedy: The establishment of
a political and military organization consisting of the United States,
Britain, and France to:
  a. elaborate a common military and political strategy for our planet.
  b. set up for each possible theater of operations allied commands.
  c. decide, when the occasion arose, on the utilization of the weapons
     of massive destruction . . .
And the menace? . . . "France would subordinate her participation in
NATO to the consideration of the above proposals."

THE EAST-WEST CONFLICT AND CONDITIONS FOR
A SUMMIT MEETING

In his second press conference, on November 10, 1959, De Gaulle
spoke about the role of France in the East-West conflict and in
the negotiations between the Soviet Union and the United
States.

SOURCE: André Fontaine, *L'Alliance Atlantique à l'Heure du Dégel*
(Paris: Calmann-Levy, 1959), pp. 91–93. (My translation.)
SOURCE: *Major Addresses, Statements, and Press Conferences of
General Charles De Gaulle, May 19, 1958–January 31, 1964* (New
York: French Embassy, Press and Information Service), pp. 57–59.

After years of international tension, it seems that on the Soviet side of the world a few indications or relaxation are beginning to appear.

What can be the reasons for this first appearance of change? We are free to make suppositions concerning them. Doubtless Russia —having provided itself with colossal power and knowing that the West possesses power of the same order—doubtless Russia accepts the fact that conflict—regardless of which side it comes from—would lead to general annihilation and that, failing war, it is necessary to make peace.

Doubtless the Communist regime in power in Russia for the past 42 years, which with all its ideology opposes the free world—doubtless the Communist regime is losing some of its virulence under the strong pressure of the people toward that which man, by nature, desires: a better life and freedom. Doubtless this same regime which Russia has made use of in order to govern by force, through fraudulent intermediaries, the territory of its neighbors in Europe—doubtless it recognizes that, while it may be ruling over Poland, Czechoslovakia, Hungary, Rumania, Bulgaria, Albania, Yugoslavia, Prussia, and Saxony, it has not won the people over, and that there is no doubt that if the populations of these countries could express themselves freely, they would reject this regime by a tremendous majority.

Doubtless, Soviet Russia, although having helped Communism become established in China, realizes that nothing can happen to prevent it, Russia, a white European nation which has conquered part of Asia and, in short, is quite well endowed with land, mines, factories, and wealth —nothing can happen to prevent it from having to reckon with the yellow multitude which is China—numberless and wretchedly poor, indestructible and ambitious, building by dint of violent efforts a power which cannot be kept within limits and looking around at the expanses over which it must one day spread. Doubtless—last and perhaps above all—the personality of the present head of Soviet Russia—discerning that at the highest level of responsibilities, the service rendered to man, to his living conditions, to his peace, is the most realistic realism, the most politic policy—doubtless this personality play a determining role in the appearance of a new direction for Russian policy.

From all these factors has come the idea of a conference of the Chiefs of State who have world-wide responsibilities. There is no opposition from any side to the principle of such a meeting. France is in favor of it. But precisely because she hopes that the proposed gathering will lead to something positive, she believes it is necessary not to rush into conversations that might be superficial, that is, without outcome, or that would end in some hastily patched-up agreement which would be regretted by the next day and which would become the source of new misunderstandings. Precedents give food for thought. In our time, there have been five meetings of this kind. One, that of Munich, was disastrous for peace. Three others—at Teheran, Yalta, and Potsdam—did not serve the balance of the world. Finally, that of Geneva in no way led to the hoped-for détente.

If it were simply a matter of organizing, between four or five Presidents, a chorus of mutual assurances of goodwill and of effusive statements on both sides, alternating with criticisms addressed to the regimes of the others, and the presentation of the reasons which each has for fearing no one, the East-West summit conference would offer few advantages to offset the disadvantages of ending in disappointment.

If one believes, on the contrary, that such a forum ought to open the way to the practical settlement of the problems that are fettering the world—the armaments race, the poverty of the underdeveloped countries, unwarranted interference in the affairs of others, the fate of Germany, the dangerous situation in the Orient, in Africa, in Asia— if one believes this, then, before meeting, there are three conditions which must be fulfilled.

The first is that international relations continue to improve during the coming months, so that the Chiefs of State can hold talks in an atmosphere of a détente and not in that of a crisis. Opportunities will not be lacking. Right now, the session of the United Nations offers a certain number of them. France is setting the example, for she is refraining from attacking anyone. May others do as much where she is concerned.

The second condition is this: that the Western Chiefs of State who are to participate in the future East-West conference come to an understanding beforehand as to the questions to be discussed and as to the common position which they will take on each of the subjects. The visit of the Secretary of State for Foreign Affairs, and later that of the German Chancellor, are going to be very useful toward this end. On the other hand, I am quite pleased by the fact that four-power meetings have been set for December.

President Eisenhower, Prime Minister Macmillan, and Chancellor Adenauer are all three men whom I admire and to whom I am bound by friendship, regardless of such political divergencies as there may be, in some cases, between our States. I believe that the beginning of spring will be a suitable time for a further meeting, when our

Governments will have worked on the bases which, I hope, we are going to set, and when they will have had leisure to consult the Atlantic allies, particularly Italy. After this we shall be able to begin the conversations with the Chairman of the Soviet Council.

The third condition is Mr. Khrushchev's personal contact with myself, M. Debré, and our Government.

For our part, we attribute great importance to this meeting and to the explanations which Russia and France will thus be able to furnish each other regarding the world problems that are of concern to both countries.

Moreover, it may be good for the person in the supreme position of responsibility in Russia to gain first-hand knowledge of France.

Fortunately, this third precondition to a large summit conference seems to be presenting itself very nicely. Mr. Khrushchev will be in France on March 15 and we are counting on his staying here until around the end of that month.

It seems therefore that, owing as much to the imponderables as to the desires of the leaders, the modern world is getting ready, as it were, to take stock of itself. We approach this day of reckoning with faith and hope, albeit not without caution and modesty.

I am now at your disposal and shall answer the questions you wish to ask me.

REFLECTIONS ON THE FAILURE OF THE SUMMIT CONFERENCE

The failure of the Summit Conference of May, 1960, is another indication to De Gaulle that France must seek a new balance of power.

Man "limited by his nature" is "infinite in his desires." The world is thus full of opposing forces. Of course, human wisdom has often succeeded in preventing these rivalries from degenerating into murderous conflicts. But the competition of efforts is the condition of life. Our country finds itself confronted today with this law of the species, as it has been for 2,000 years.

The division of the peoples that inhabit Europe and North America is the main fact and the worst evil of our time. Two camps are set

SOURCE: *Major Addresses, Statements, and Press Conferences of General Charles De Gaulle, May 19, 1958–January 31, 1964* (New York: French Embassy, Press and Information Service), pp. 75–78.

up, face to face, under conditions such that it depends solely on Moscow or Washington whether or not a large part of humanity is wiped out in a few hours.

In the face of such a situation, France deems that there is no territorial disagreement or ideological dispute that has any importance in comparison with the necessity of exorcising this monstrous peril. In France's view, this situation implies three conditions.

The first is a détente, in other words, the bettering of international relations, putting a stop to provocative actions and speeches and increasing trade, cultural exchanges and the visits of tourists in order that a more peaceful atmosphere might be created; failing this, the dizziness of desperation would afflict discouraged men, to such an extent that one day and all of a sudden, for any reason at all, the world would find itself at war, as it was, twice in my lifetime, because the Archduke was dead or because someone wanted Danzig.

The second condition is a specific degree of controlled disarmament, preferably aimed at the devices capable of carrying bombs strategic distances, in order that the possibility—and, at the same time, the temptation—suddenly to provoke general destruction might vanish.

The third condition is a beginning of organized cooperation between East and West devoted to the service of man, either by helping in the progress of underdeveloped peoples or by collaborating in the great projects of scientific research, on which depends the future of all.

France is all the more disposed toward this détente, this disarmament, and this cooperation in that no direct dispute sets her in opposition to Russia, in that she feels a traditional attraction for the people of that country, in that she hopes to see lifted the iron curtain which separates her from the nations of central Europe and of the Balkans, of which she is the natural friend and ally. She believes, moreover, that by reason of modern activities, man's condition tends to become alike everywhere and that the virulent opposition of the various regimes is destined to diminish.

Now, it recently seemed that certain prospects were about to open up. In the East, as in the West, it was recognized that nuclear war would, whatever happened, spell disaster for the whole world, since the risk would be that after the conflict, on both sides, there would no longer be any constituted authorities, or laws, or cities, or cultures, or cradles, or graves. It was then that a new tune was heard in Soviet Russia. A statesman, who had reached the top, proclaimed the necessity of peaceful coexistence, declared that the competition between the Communist system and the capitalist system should have as its goal men's standard of living, affirmed that the ambition of his country was to ensure its own development and let it be understood that the meeting of those in the positions of supreme responsibility in the Soviet Union, the United States, Great Britain, and France would open the way to peace.

Doubtless Mr. Krushchev was laying down a condition contradictory to the détente, in claiming that a treaty called a "peace treaty," were it to be concluded by him alone, would consecrate forever the present division of Germany and would establish in West Berlin such a status that this city, which is free and intends to remain so, would be doomed, sooner or later, to submit to the totalitarian yoke. But later, this demand seemed to be accompanied, in the mind of its author, by certain delays and compromises. On the other hand, the trips that the Chairman of the Soviet Council of Ministers made to the United States, and then to France, seemed to be the preludes to a new orientation. Beginning then, it seemed that a Summit Conference could offer an opportunity for improving the international atmosphere. For my part, having the Premier and the Minister of Foreign Affairs at my side, I was ready and willing.

Everyone knows what happened. I will not hold a post-mortem of the underlying reasons which succeeded in preventing the conference from being held. But I must state that if the overflight of Soviet territory by an American photography plane two weeks before the meeting, was certainly and, to say the least, ill-timed, which, in fact, the President of the United States recognized when he ordered that no further flights of this nature were to take place—I must state that this was not sufficient reasons for refusing to open the discussion of the affairs of the world at the summit.

In an age when the sky is streaked with satellites, missiles, and planes equipped for taking pictures of any region of the globe and of firing projectiles capable of terrible destruction, what must be done is to organize reciprocal control of these devices, as France has proposed and as the four Chiefs of State or of Government could have decided. At the very moment when Moscow had launched a new space vehicle passing over the West 18 times a day, it seemed excessive to require public apologies and reparations from Washington because a single-engine plane, equipped with a camera, had attempted to cross Soviet territory, considering that the plane had been shot down and its films were being held, and that the guarantee that the act would not be repeated had been received. Finally, if the Chairman of the Soviet Council of Ministers intended to set as a condition for the opening of the conference that the incident of May 1 be settled as he wished, would it not have been better for him to have stayed in his capital until this previous matter was settled definitely in one way or another?

In any case, France took note of this outcome with composure. But, in her eyes, what was necessary yesterday will still be necessary to-morrow. The détente, the controlled disarmament of strategic weapons, the cooperation of well-provided States in the development of those which are not remain, as much as ever, the goals that the other world powers owe it to themselves and to the universe to accomplish together. As for ourselves, we are disposed to return to this course. But also, we believe that in order to follow this course, methodical steps of diplomacy are worth more than tumultuous exchanges of public speeches or the passionate debates of the delegates in the United Nations, which, alas, are not united. On the bases, which a reasonable preparation will enable us perhaps to lay down, France could, when the time comes, consider the reopening of this Paris Conference which we had decided to hold and which could not take place.

Yet, until we achieve an organized peace, if that is at all possible, France intends, as far as she is concerned, to be ready to defend herself. This means, first of all, that she shall remain an integral part of the Atlantic Alliance. Moreover, the recent trial has shown the deep-seated solidarity which exists among the Western powers. Of course, President Eisenhower, Prime Minister Macmillan, and I each have our own problems and our own temperament. But, when faced with recent events, we three, in view of the friendship which unites us, did not have much trouble in reaching agreement, in wisdom and in firmness. Our alliance appeared a living reality. In order for it to become even more so, France must have her own role in it, and her own personality. This implies that she too must acquire a nuclear armament, since others have one; that she must be sole mistress of her resources and her territory; in short, that her destiny, although associated with that of her allies, must remain in her own hands. It goes without saying that such autonomy must be coupled with ever closer coordination among the Western world powers in their policy and their strategy.

But if the Atlantic Alliance is necessary at present for the security of France and of the other free peoples of our old continent, they must, behind this shield, organize to achieve their joint power and development. The trials they have gone through showed them how much their divisions and conflicts had cost them. Neither the Rhine, nor the Low Countries, nor the Alps, nor the Pyrenees, nor the English

Channel, nor the Mediterranean, for which they fought so long and so bitterly, any longer set them one against the other. No feeling of hatred remains between them. On the contrary, the nostalgia inspired in each of these lands by their relative downfall in relation to the great new empires has drawn them closer in the feeling that together they would regain this grandeur for which past centuries had given them the talent and the habit. To this must be added the fact that they constitute an incomparable whole, precisely when our time, which abolishes distances and obstacles, demands large ensembles.

To contribute to building Western Europe into a political, economic, cultural, and human group, organized for action, progress and defense —that is what France wants to work toward. Already West Germany, Italy, the Netherlands, Belgium, and Luxembourg are cooperating directly with her in several fields. In particular, the Common Market of the Six will, on December 31, become a practical reality. Of course, the participants do not want this organization to injure the other countries of Europe, and we must expect a way to be found of accommodating interests. Also, of course, the nations which are becoming associated must not cease to be themselves, and the path to be followed must be that of organized cooperation between States, while waiting to achieve, perhaps, an imposing conferation. But France, as far as she is concerned, has recognized the necessity of this Western Europe, which in former times was the dream of the wise and the ambition of the powerful and which appears today as the indispensible condition of the equilibrium of the world.

Now, in the last analysis and as always, it is only in equilibrium that the world will find peace. On our old continent, the organization of a western group, at the very least equivalent to that which exists in the east, may one day, without risk to the independence and the freedom of each nation and taking into account the probable evolution of political regimes, establish a European entente from the Atlantic to the Urals. Then Europe, no longer split in two by ambitions and ideologies that would become out-of-date, would again be the heart of civilization. The accession to progress of the masses of Asia, Africa and Latin America would certainly be hastened and facilitated. But also, the cohesion of this great and strong European community would lead vast countries in other continents, which are advancing toward power, also to take the way of cooperation, rather than to yield to the temptation of war.

Yes, international life, like life in general, is a battle. The battle which our country is waging tends to unite and not to divide, to honor and not to debase, to liberate and not to dominate. Thus it is faithful to its mission, which always was and which remains human and universal. The purpose is great. The task is hard. But in the midst of world alarms you can see, women and men of France, what weight France's will can have again.

ASSERTION OF FRENCH LEADERSHIP

In 1962 a strong France is ready to assume leadership and direction in matters of foreign policy and defense.

Who can dispute in good faith that our country, in the world of today, could, without rapidly deteriorating, dispense with being a major industrial, agricultural, and commercial power, a country that is making constant social progress, whose population is ever increasing, who is instructing its large population of young people with a view to achieving ever greater and more complex activity, and who has, in addition, a stable currency and balanced finances? Assuredly, while France is remolding her structure, one can see certain private interests disregarding the general interest and staging objections and demonstrations that are more or less loud and more or less valid. But, if one compares what has been accomplished during the last four years with the fact that our political and social life has never actually been so calm as during this period, one can have no doubts as to the reasoned soundness of the country in its very foundations.

Indeed, no one in the world, except some blind partisans, denies the powerful development of France. All of us are struck by this when we travel around the country, even if it be only by looking at pictures. Never before has there been so much production, construction and instruction in France. Never before has the average standard of living of the French people been so high as it is today. Never before, anywhere, has there been so little unemployment as there is now. Never before have our currency and our credit been stronger than they are now, to such a degree that instead of borrowing, we are making loans to the wealthiest countries. And now we are about to implement the great Plan which, in four years, is due to increase our power and our prosperity by one fourth. Admittedly, there are still many gaps and

SOURCE: Address on February 5, 1962, in Algeria. *Major Addresses, Statements, and Press Conferences of General Charles De Gaulle, May 19, 1958–January 31, 1964* (New York: French Embassy, Press and Information Service), pp. 158–160.

many shortcomings in this plan. We are not yet at the end of our troubles. We know what the world around us is like and how outside events can influence our domestic affairs. But why, at the very moment when our success is becoming visible, should we lose heart, like the fisherman in Shakespeare who, finding a pearl and frightened by its beauty, throws it back into the sea?

Who in good faith can dispute the fact that France, directly threatened as she is and seeing that other nations have the means to destroy her in a second, should also be armed, so that no State can contemplate killing her without itself risking death; the fact that, in order to preserve freedom in the world, France ought today to be a true ally of America just as America should be hers; and, finally, that France, owing to the fact that, for the first time in history, the major grievances between her and her European neighbors are removed, must help to build Western Europe into an organized union of States, so that gradually there may be established on both sides of the Rhine, of the Alps, and perhaps of the Channel, the most powerful, prosperous and influential political, economic, cultural, and military complex in the world? No doubt because we are now displaying a determination, building up a force and unfolding a policy that are our own, this new course does not fail to run counter to the network of former conventions that assigned us the role of a so-called integrated nation, in other words, a backseat nation. This inevitably causes astonishment and even bitter feelings. But, as the action of the new France is both inevitable and beneficial to all, it is a fact that will have to be accepted until the time comes when the fact is recognized to be a fortunate one.

And so our national defense comes onto the scene again. Before the end of this year the major part of our Army will be stationed in Europe and undergoing complete reorganization. Before the end of next year we shall have the first operational unit of the French atomic force. After that, we shall continue with the development of this deterrent force unless no other power possesses one. We believe that the material and moral possibilities of the free world will derive great benefit from the rebuilding of the French armed forces.

Moreover, by taking the stand of refusing to negotiate on Berlin or Germany so long as the Soviet Union does not put a stop to its threats and its injunctions and bring about an actual easing of the international situation, we believe that we have spared our allies and ourselves the catastrophic retreat, dramatic rupture, or tragi-comical engulfment, in which the conference would obviously have ended.

Finally, we are actively applying ourselves to lifting the union of

Europe out of the ideological and technocratic plane onto the plane of realities, in other words, onto the political plane. For instance, despite the urging of a mystical faith and of somewhat artificial dates, we refused to accept the development of a Common Market that did not include agriculture and in which France, a country that is both agricultural and industrial, would have ever seen her economic, social, and financial equilibrium thoroughly upset. On the contrary, we on our side acted in such a way that the serious omission in the Treaty of Rome in regard to this sector was, for the most part, rectified and that the necessary provisions and safeguards were decided upon by the six contracting States. But, in addition, we have proposed and we are proposing to our partners an over-all organization for cooperation between the States, without which there cannot be a united Europe, except in dreams, parades, and stories.

THE BURDENS OF INDEPENDENCE

But the burden of independence is heavy, De Gaulle will caution his countrymen, on April 19, 1963.

In order to be prosperous, to be masters of ourselves, and to be powerful, we French have done a great deal. Much remains for us to do. For progress demands effort. Independence is not free. Security is costly. That is of course why the State, whose role and raison d'être is to serve the general interest, has no right to let things go.

Nor can there be any facility outside. After the last world war, our country saw, in fact, its power and its influence terribly diminished in relation to those of the two world giants. And again, until last year, it was divided and paralyzed by the aftereffects of a colonization that had its merits and its glories but that, in our time, was nothing more than vain and outdated. Thus, imbued once more with the spirit of renovation, in the full flush of invention, production, and demographic growth, provided with solid institutions, released from colonial bonds, France finds itself, for the first time in half a century, with a free spirit and free hands. And thus it can and must play throughout the world the role that belongs to it.

This policy is not an easy one. The world abounds with sirens that

SOURCE: *Major Addresses, Statements, and Press Conferences of General Charles De Gaulle, May 19, 1958–January 31, 1964* (New York: French Embassy, Press and Information Service), pp. 223–226.

sing to us the sweetness of renunciation, unless, annoyed at seeing us indifferent to their seduction, they raise toward us a noisy chorus of invectives. But without our being cocksure, in the interest of everyone as much as in our own, our ship is pursuing its course. There is absolutely no chance that, giving in to facility, we would allow France to be pushed into the background.

That is why, if the union of Western Europe—Germany, Italy, the Netherlands, Belgium, Luxembourg, France—is a capital aim in our action outside, we have no desire to be dissolved within it. Any system that would consist of handing over our sovereignty to august international assemblies would be incompatible with the rights and the duties of the French Republic. But also, such a system would undoubtedly find itself powerless to sweep along and lead the peoples and, to begin with, our own people, in the domains where their souls and their flesh are in question. This abdication of the European States, of France in particular, would inevitably lead to subjection from without. It is, moreover, in order to avoid such an inconsistency and, as its consequence, such a dependence that we are bent on seeing the union of Europe constituted by nations which can and really wish to belong to it. While retaining the hope that one day, perhaps, the great British people, freeing themselves from that which keeps them out of our community, will come to join it in accordance with the conditions which are those of the institution, we consider that our community must develop as it is and without delay. In short, it appears essential to us that Europe be Europe and that France be France.

In addition, within the Atlantic Alliance—indispensable so long as the ambitions and the threats of the Soviets are raised—our country, while combining its defense with that of its allies, intends to remain the master and, if necessary, contribute to the common effort something quite different from the soulless and powerless assistance of a people that would no longer be responsible for themselves. This leads us to provide ourselves with the modern means of ensuring our security, in other words, with the means of deterring any country whatsoever from attacking ours, at the risk of subjecting itself to frightful destruction. I mean, of course, atomic weapons. It is true that our American allies possess in this respect a collosal power, capable of throwing into chaos all or part of the Soviet empire, that they are resolved, as we know, to fight if necessary to prevent Europe from falling, dead or alive, into the other camp, that they are our good allies as we are theirs. But that is not the entire question.

Indeed, the possible adversary is himself equipped with enormous means of the same kind. This being the case, no one, nowhere, can know in advance whether, in the event of a conflict, the atomic bombs would or would not be used at the start by the two principal champions; whether, if they did use them, they would use them in Central and Western Europe only, without striking each other directly and immediately; or whether, on the contrary, they would be led right away to hurl death at each other's vitals. Anyhow, and in light of this enormous and inevitable uncertainty, France must itself have the means of directly reaching any State that would be its aggressor, that is, the means of deterring it from being so and, according to the circumstances, the means of assisting in the defense of its allies, including —who knows—America.

In sum, our country, perpetually threatened, finds itself once again faced with the necessity of possessing the most powerful weapons of the era unless, of course, the others cease to possess them. However, to dissuade us, the voices of immobility and demagogy are as always simultaneously raised. "It is useless," say some. "It is too costly," say others. These voices France listened to, sometimes and to its misfortune, notably on the eve of the two world wars. "No heavy artillery," they exclaimed in concert, until 1914. "No armored corps, no fighter aircraft," the same backward and brainless groups cried in unison before 1939. But this time we shall not allow routine and illusion to invite invasion of our country. Moreover, in the midst of the strained and dangerous world in which we live, our chief duty is to be strong and to be ourselves.

Women and men of France, after may trials, we had to decide in favor of progress or decline. The choice has been made. We are going forward. But there must be order and effort. Let us leave facility to others.

Vive la République! Vive la France!

5. THE GAME OF BALANCE

⚜

Nothing better illustrates De Gaulle's determination to create a balance of power favorable to French independence than the alliances he contemplated during World War II. We reproduce here his thoughts and acts in approaching England, the Soviet Union and the Vatican. When he returned to office in 1958, De Gaulle continued to use the same tactics to strengthen his position. The archenemy in 1940—Germany—became in 1962 the axis of a new Europe, while the chief wartime ally—Great Britain—was excluded. When Communist China emerged unmistakably as a new power, De Gaulle insisted on French recognition of the regime; a recognition whose chief purpose seemed to be to underscore French world-wide interests and potentially to create an Asian balance favorable to France. Another illustration of his commitment to the balance of power is in his relations with the United States, which shift and change as world conditions vary.

In this part, we give only the historical background: De Gaulle's appeal to Churchill for a privileged alliance with England; his efforts in 1944 to establish relations with the Soviet Union independently of his western allies; and finally his blatant appeal to the Vatican for support. But his efforts were of no avail. The allies proceeded at Yalta to destroy, in De Gaulle's eyes, the balance of Europe. This De Gaulle set out to rebuild after his return to power in 1958.

FLIRTATIONS WITH ENGLAND

In November 1944, De Gaulle saw in a Franco-British pact the best guarantee for the maintenance of the equilibrium of Europe and indirectly the world, and seemed sure that America and Rus-

SOURCE: *The War Memoirs of Charles De Gaulle* (New York: Simon and Schuster, 1960), Vol. III, pp. 58–60.

sia, "hobbled by their rivalries," could not raise objections. But
both Churchill and Eden seemed more attached than ever to
American leadership. It is interesting to compare De Gaulle's
passionate appeal to Churchill in 1944 with his haughty dismissal,
almost twenty years later, of England's plea to enter the Common
Market.

During the entire day of November 13, under ceaselessly falling
snow, Mr. Churchill saw the renascent French Army, its major units
in position, its services functioning, its general staffs at their work, its
generals confident; all were prepared for the offensive which was, in
fact, to be launched the next day. Churchill appeared deeply impressed,
and declared that he felt more justified than ever in placing his confidence in France.

Churchill's confidence, however, was insufficient for him to adopt,
in our regard, that policy of frank solidarity which might have re-
established Europe and maintained Western prestige in the Middle
East, in Asia, and in Africa. The visit he paid us was perhaps the last
possible occasion to bring him to a change of heart. I took every
opportunity to do so during the conversations we had together.

I repeated to Churchill: "You see that France is making a recovery.
But whatever my faith in her, I know that she will not regain her
former power all at once. You English, of course, will emerge from this
was covered with glory. Yet to what a degree—unfair though it may
be—your relative situation risks being diminished, given your losses
and expenditures, by the centrifugal forces at work within the Commonwealth, and, particularly, the rise of America and Russia, not to mention China! Confronting a new world, then, our two old nations find
themselves simultaneously weakened. If they remain divided as well,
how much influence will either of them wield? On the other hand,
should England and France act in accord on tomorrow's peace settle-
ments, they will weigh heavily enough in the world's scales so that
nothing will be done which they themselves have not consented to or
determined. It is this mutual resolve which should be the basis of
the alliance you offer us. Otherwise what is the good of signing a
document which would be, at best, ambiguous?

"The equilibrium of Europe," I added, "the guarantee of peace
along the Rhine, the independence of the Vistula, Danube, and Balkan
states, the creation of some form of association with the peoples all
over the world to whom we have opened the doors of Western civilization, an organization of nations which will be something more than an
arena for disputes between America and Russia, and lastly the pri-

macy accorded in world politics to a certain conception of man despite the progressive mechanization of society—these, surely, are our great interests in tomorrow's world. Let us come to an agreement in order to uphold these interests together. If you are willing to do so, I am ready. Our two nations will follow us. America and Russia, hobbled by their rivalry, will not be able to raise any objection. Moreover, we shall have the support of many states and of world-wide public opinion, which instinctively shies away from giants. Thus England and France will together create peace, as twice in thirty years they have together confronted war."

Winston Churchill answered: "Certainly I do not foresee a Franco-British schism. You are the witness and the proof of what I have done to prevent such a thing when it was most likely. Even today, I offer you an alliance in principle. But in politics as in strategy, it is better to persuade the stronger than to pit yourself against him. That is what I am trying to do. The Americans have immense resources. They do not always use them to the best advantage. I am trying to enlighten them, without forgetting, of course, to benefit my country. I have formed a close personal tie with Roosevelt. With him, I proceed by suggestion in order to influence matters in the right direction. At present, Russia is a great beast which has been starved for a long time. It is not possible to keep her from eating, especially since she now lies in the middle of the herd of her victims. The question is whether she can be kept from devouring all of them. I am trying to restrain Stalin, who, if he has an enormous appetite, also has a great deal of good sense. And after the meal comes the digestion period. When it is time to digest, the surfeited Russians will have their difficult moments. Then, perhaps, Saint Nicholas can bring back to to life the poor children the ogre has put in the salting tub. Meanwhile, I attend every meeting, yield nothing for nothing, and manage to secure a few dividends.

"As for France," Churchill repeated, "thanks to you, she is reappearing in the eyes of the world. Don't be impatient! Already, the doors are ajar. Soon they will be open to you. It will be only natural for you to sit at the table of the Administration Council. Nothing, then, will keep us from working together. Until then, leave matters in my hands!"

The Prime Minister took his departure on November 14 to inspect the British sector of the front. Eden had already returned to London. From the statements both had made, it was apparent that England favored France's political reappearance, that she would continue to do so for reasons of equilibrium, tradition, and security, that she desired a

formal alliance with us, but would not consent to link her strategy
with ours, believing herself in a position to function independently
between Moscow and Washington, to limit their demands, but also
to take advantage of them. The peace we French hoped to build in
accord with what we regarded as logic and justice, the British found
it expedient to approach with formulas of empiricism and compromise.
Furthermore, they were pursuing certain precise goals which, in areas
where the positions of states and the balance of power were not yet
determined, offered British ambitions numerous possibilities of manipu-
lation and aggrandizement.

THE FRANCO-SOVIET PACT: LA BELLE ET BONNE ALLIANCE

France had hardly been liberated when De Gaulle envisaged the
new equilibrium of Europe in classic terms, involving an alliance
with the Russians that the French had sought in the years before World War I and again in the thirties. He insisted that
a Franco-Soviet pact was to be negotiated and signed exclusively
by France and the Soviet Union—the two most powerful states
in Europe. In his negotiations with Stalin in December 1944,
De Gaulle displayed an intransigence and concern with the fate
of Eastern Europe and the independence of the Eastern European states that he had found lacking in Roosevelt. Nevertheless,
in thinking that the Russians would ever permit a return to the
European status quo as it existed before World War II, he was
perhaps deluding himself as much as was Roosevelt, who thought
that the Russians would abide by the obligations they undertook
at Yalta!

I began by remarking how France envisaged the settlement of Germany's fate: no further sovereignty of the central German State on
the left bank of the Rhine; the territories thus seperated retaining
their German character but receiving their autonomy and consistency,
economically speaking, from the western zone; the Ruhr placed under
international control; the eastern German frontier marked by the Oder
and the Neisse. We regretted that Russia was unwilling to conclude,
with regard to these conditions, an immediate agreement with France

SOURCE: *The War Memoirs of Charles De Gaulle* (New York: Simon
and Schuster, 1960), Vol. III, pp. 77–79, 90.

which would then be proposed to England and the United States. But our position would not be modified.

As for alliances, we considered that they must be constructed "in three stages": first a Franco-Russian treaty providing for initial security; the Anglo-Soviet pact and an agreement still to be made between France and Great Britain constituting a second degree; the future United Nations pact, in which America would play a decisive role, crowning the entire edifice and serving as an ultimate recourse. I repeated the reasons which determined us not to adopt Churchill's proposition of a single Anglo-Franco-Russian pact. Finally, I confirmed the fact that we would be leaving Moscow on the morning of December 10, as previously arranged.

Stalin challenged nothing of what I once again formulated in regard to German frontiers. He emphasized the advantages which he believed a tripartite pact would have. But suddenly, shifting the direction of his interests, he exclaimed, "After all, you're right! I don't see why the two of us shouldn't make a pact. But you must understand that Russia has a fundamental interest in the matter of Poland. We want Poland to be friendly to the Allies and resolutely anti-German. This is not possible with the government in London, which represents an anti-Russian spirit as virulent as ever. On the contrary, we could come to an understanding with another Poland, a Poland great, strong, and democratic. If you share this view, recognize the Lublin Committee publicly and make an official arrangement with it. Then we can sign a pact with you. Notice, furthermore, that we Russians have recognized the Polish Committee of National Liberation, that this Committee is governing and administering Poland as the enemy is driven out by our troops, and that consequently it is to Lublin that you should address yourself for everything that concerns your interests in the country, particularly the fate of prisoners and French deportees whom the retreating Germans are leaving on the spot. As for Churchill, I shall telegraph him that his project has not been accepted. He will be offended, of course. Once again. But he's offended me often enough."

Henceforth, everything was clear. I declared openly to Stalin that France was ready to conclude a security pact with Russia, that she bore no ill will toward the Lublin Committee, but that she had no intention of recognizing it as the government of Poland or dealing with it officially. The practical questions relative to the French prisoners could be settled, as they came up, by a delegate we would send to Lublin without his having the character of a diplomatic representative. I added: "France and Russia have a common interest in seeing an independent, united, and genuine Poland on the scene, not an artificial Poland in which France, for her part, would have no confidence. In our eyes, the question of the future Polish government can be settled only by the Poles themselves, after the nation's liberation and with the agreement of the four Allies."

• • •

The general reaction to the signing of the pact was indeed satisfactory. The public saw in the occasion a sign of our return to the concert of great powers. Political circles appreciated it as a reassuring link in the chain that held the United Nations together. Certain professionals—or fanatics—of faction whispered that the treaty had been effected only by concessions to the French Communist party, allowing it to moderate in the political and social struggle and participate in the nation's recovery. But on the whole, for various reasons, response to the Moscow agreement was distinctly favorable. The Consultative Assembly, too, expressed its approbation. Bidault opened the session on December 21 by discussing the stipulations the pact actually involved; I closed it by explaining "what had been, what was, and what would be the philosophy of the Franco-Russian alliance we had just concluded."

Nevertheless the general euphoria did not distract my attention from the disturbing probabilities revealed by the Moscow discussions. We must expect that Russia, America, and England would conclude a series of bargains from which the rights of France, the liberty of peoples, and the equilibrium of Europe had everything to lose.

THE APPEAL TO THE VATICAN

At the Vatican I first made contact with Cardinal Maglione, Secretary of State, who though ill and near death insisted on getting up to converse with me. Even as Rome, from the height of her serenity, watches from one century to the next while the tides of men and events flow by beneath her walls, ceaselessly attentive to all, so the Church, impavid but compassionate and well informed besides, observed the war's ebb and flow. Monsignor Maglione, convinced of the Allied victory, was especially concerned as to its consequences. In the case of France, he counted on Vichy's disappearance and declared

SOURCE: *The War Memoirs of Charles De Gaulle* (New York: Simon and Schuster, 1959), Vol. II, p. 263.

that he saw in my person, in fact, the head of the French government. He hoped that the change of regime could be effected without serious shocks, particularly with regard to the French Church. I indicated to the Cardinal that the Government of the Republic intended this should be the case, although certain French ecclesiastical circles had adopted an attitude that would not make things easier for the Republic tomorrow. As for the future of Europe after the Reich's defeat and Russia's ascendancy, I declared that France's recovery, at home and abroad, would be the condition of a new equilibrium. I asked the Vatican to aid in this task by its immense influence.

THE CRIME OF CRIMEA . . .

While he was busy negotiating the Franco-Soviet pact, De Gaulle was fully aware that the Americans, British, and Russians were about to meet to settle the basic issues of postwar Europe without him. He remained convinced that his participation was vetoed by Roosevelt. His thoughts on the Yalta settlement and on Potsdam throw light upon his own conception of Europe, as well as his deep personal resentment for his—and France's—exclusion.

As a matter of fact, since the beginning of January, without any diplomatic communication having been made to us, the Anglo-American press announced that Messrs. Roosevelt, Stalin, and Churchill were to have a conference. The "Big Three" would decide what was to be done in Germany after the Reich's "unconditional surrender." They would determine their behavior with regard to the people of Central and Balkan Europe. They would, finally, prepare the convocation of an assembly with a view toward organizing the United Nations.

Naturally I was offended that we were not invited, but I was not at all surprised. Whatever the progress we had made along the road that would lead France to her place, I knew the starting point too well to believe we had reached our goal already. Moreover, there was every evidence that our present exclusion would provoke a demonstration greatly to our advantage. For matters had ripened sufficiently so that we could not be kept out of what was to be done. Although Messrs.

SOURCE: *The War Memoirs of Charles De Gaulle* (New York: Simon and Schuster, 1960), Vol. III, pp. 90–91, 95–99.

Roosevelt, Stalin, and Churchill could reach decisions regarding Germany and Italy, they would be obliged, in order to apply them, to ask for General De Gaulle's cooperation. As for the Vistula, the Danube, and the Balkan States, America and England would doubtless abandon them to the discretion of the Soviets. But in that case the world would discover that there was a correlation between France's absence and Europe's new laceration. Finally, judging that the time was ripe to indicate that France did not sanction the way she was being treated, I decided to take this exceptional occasion to do so.

Actually, among the "Big Three," only one state was opposed to our presence. To emphasize this fact, the British and Russians immediately had recourse to semiofficial informants. Naturally I had no illusions that Marshal Stalin, who knew my position with regard to Poland, and Mr. Churchill, who expected to obtain carte blanche in the Middle East from his partners, had stipulated that De Gaulle sit beside them at the council table. But I could not doubt that the explicit refusal came from President Roosevelt. Moreover, he himself felt he must make his attitude explicit. For this purpose, he delegated his closest adviser and intimate friend, Harry Hopkins, as his "special envoy" to Paris.

•   •   •

On February 12, the "Big Three," concluding the conference, published a communiqué which proclaimed the principles on which they had agreed. They declared that the war would be continued until the Reich surrendered unconditionally; that the three great powers would occupy its territory, each in a different region; that the control and administration of Germany would be exercised by a military commission formed of the commanders in chief, with headquarters in Berlin. But in the terms of the communiqué, France was invited to join America, England, and Russia in occupying a zone of German territory and in being the fourth member of the German government. Further, the communiqué declared the intention of the "Big Three" to dissolve all German armed forces, to destroy forever the German general staff, to punish the war criminals, and lastly to make Germany pay reparations, to whatever degree possible, for the damages she had caused.

To maintain peace and security throughout the world, a "General International Organization" was to be set up. For this purpose, a conference of all the states which had signed the Atlantic Charter would be held in San Francisco on April 25 and would take as the basis of the "Organization" those principles which had been defined at the Dumbarton Oaks Conference. Although France had not taken part in this last, it was specified that she would be consulted immediately by the three "great powers" in order to determine all final arrangements with them, which obviously meant that she would sit with them on the "Security Council."

The communiqué also included a "Declaration Regarding Liberated Europe." This actually concerned Hungary, Rumania, and Bulgaria, who had marched with Germany and were now occupied by Russia. The declaration proclaimed the right of all peoples to settle for themselves the re-establishment of democracy, the freedom of the elections which would create their governments, but remained vague as to the practical measures to be applied, which came down to leaving the Soviets to their own devices. The three great powers expressed their hope that "the government of the French Republic would associate itself with them in regard to the proposed procedure."

The "Big Three" lastly announced that they had "come to an agreement" regarding the Polish question. They decided that Poland would be bounded, on the east, by the Curzon line and would receive, in the north and west, "a substantial increase of territory." As for the political regime, no allusion was made to free elections. A government, referred to as one of "national unity," was to be formed "starting from the provisional government already functioning in the country," that is, the the Polish Committee of Liberation, known as the "Lublin Committee." Doubtless, it was indicated, the latter would be enlarged "to include democratic leaders residing in Poland and abroad." But since there was no reference to the London government-in-exile, since the composition of the new government remained quite unspecified, since no control on the part of the western powers was provided for, there could be no doubt as to the kind of government Poland would receive. Nor as to the authority that would be established in Yugoslavia. Although in regard to this country the Yalta communiqué referred to the ratification by a future "National Assembly," as a matter of fact Tito's dictatorship was recognized unconditionally. Thus Stalin was granted all he demanded in regard to Warsaw and Belgrade. To this, and this only, France was not—and for good reason—invited to accede.

• • •

In other words, if it remained inadmissible, from our point of view, that our three allies should have held their Crimean conference without us, the steps they were now taking in our behalf were in no way offensive. Certainly several of their conclusions might seem irritating to us, and the propositions by which they sought to attract us would have to be studied carefully before we accepted them. But on certain essential points, their communications included important satisfactions for us.

. . . IS UNACCEPTABLE

As for the arrangements of the future peace settlement or of any decisions related to it we have made it known to our allies and we have declared publicly that France would not be naturally bound by absolutely anything that had not been discussed and approved by her on the same footing with others. A fortiori France will not accept anything except what is in accord with her own objectives to ensure that no future aggression from Germany, either against France or against any other state allied to France, can ever take place again. I must specify again that the presence of France from one end of the Rhine to the other—the separation of the territories east of the Rhine and of the Ruhr basin from Germany—the independence of the Polish, Czech, Austrian, and Balkan nations in the friendship of their peoples who will have to bear the major burden of the maintenance of peace in Europe, are conditions that France deems essential. We hope very much that they will be considered to be so by our allies. We are not very concerned, of course, about the likelihood of realizing the greater part of these objectives, because we are one hundred and six million strong, rallied under the French flag in close proximity to what concerns us directly.

Of course, we do not have the temerity to believe that we can alone assure the security of Europe. We need alliances. For this purpose we have concluded a good and sound treaty with the strong and brave Soviet Russia. In the same spirit we shall conclude another with the old and courageous England, as soon as she agrees to adhere to what our vital concerns regarding Germany are and as soon as we manage to eliminate certain traces of outdated rivalries in some parts of the world. We are also planning to be in a position to establish practical agreements of cooperation and security with our neighbors —the Dutch, the Belgians, and the Luxemburgians. We hope that time, a gentle and generous friend, for those who know how to use it, will permit us to reestablish good relations with a new Italy. Finally we shall hold ourselves ready, when the fury of the battles in Europe and in the Far East have ended and we have recovered our freedom of

SOURCE: "Speech of February 5, 1945," *Discours et Messages*, 1940–1946 (Paris: Berger-Levrault, 1946), pp. 561–563.

action and the freedom in our own territories, to participate in the studies and negotiations from which will emerge without a doubt a world organization for peace. This will entail first the participation of the United States and will guarantee to each state its life and development in the human society.

POTSDAM: THE DESTRUCTION OF THE EUROPEAN BALANCE

According to De Gaulle, Potsdam simply confirmed the destruction of the European balance. And again, De Gaulle was not invited to the meeting that brought together Truman, Churchill (to be replaced during the conference by Attlee), and Stalin.

That our allies of yesterday should convene yet again in our absence —for the last time, moreover—could only cause us renewed irritation. Yet fundamentally we considered it preferable not to be introduced into discussions which could henceforth be nothing but supererogatory.

For the facts were decided. The enormous chunk of Europe which the Yalta agreements had abandoned in advance to the Soviets was now in their hands. Even the American armies, after having overrun the frontiers established for them in Germany during the last days of the fighting, had fallen back 150 kilometers. The Russians alone occupied Prussia and Saxony. Without further delay they had annexed all of Poland east of the "Curzon line," transferred the inhabitants along the Oder and western Neisse, and driven the German population of Silesia, Poznan, and Pomerania west. Thus all question of frontiers was decided quite simply by the Soviets. Furthermore, in Warsaw, Budapest, Sofia, Belgrade, and Tirana, the governments that had been installed were at their discretion and almost all at their beck and call. Yet the rapidity of this Sovietization was only the inevitable result of what had been agreed upon at the Crimea conference. The regrets the British and Americans now expressed were quite uncalled for.

As for the Soviet intervention in the Pacific theater, what purpose could it serve? The atom bombs were ready. Arriving in Potsdam, Truman and Churchill announced the success of the New Mexico experiments. From one day to the next, Japan was to suffer the terrible explosions and consequently surrender. Any commitments the

SOURCE: *The War Memoirs of Charles De Gaulle* (New York: Simon and Schuster, 1960), Vol. III, pp. 229–231.

Russians now made as to the war in the Pacific would involve no consequences from the military point of view, but result in the Kremlin's recognized right to participate as a victor in Far Eastern affairs. For Asia and for Europe, there was every reason to foresee that on no issue would the Potsdam conference realize any durable entente, but instead provoke unlimited friction between the Soviet and the Anglo-American participants.

This prospect convinced me that it was wiser not to climb on the bandwagon at this point. Naturally I regretted that I had not been present at Teheran. There, as a matter of fact, I would have defended the equilibrium of Europe when there would still have been some point in doing so. Subsequently, I was sorry not to have been permitted to take part in the Yalta Conference, since there still remained some opportunities of preventing the iron curtain from cutting Europe in two. But now everything had been arranged—what could I have done at Potsdam?

Once the communiqué published by the conference appeared, we learned that it had concluded in a kind of uproar. Despite the wealth of conciliation lavished by Mr. Truman, despite Mr. Churchill's vehement protest, Generalissimo Stalin had agreed to no compromises of any kind. In Poland particularly, the appearance of Messrs. Mikolajczyk, Grabski, Witos, and Stanczyk in the cabinet formed on the basis of the Lublin Committee had induced Washington and London, and obliged Paris as well, to recognize the government directed by Messrs. Bierut and Osuska-Morawski, but it was soon apparent that the totalitarian character of the Warsaw government was in no way diminished thereby. In regard to Asia, Stalin, in exchange for his promise to declare war on Japan, managed to obtain for Russia the Kurile Archipelago and half of Sakhalin, induced the Allies to accord Korea to the Soviets north of the 38th parallel, and forced Chiang Kai-shek to withdraw from Outer Mongolia. The latter became a "People's Republic." For this price the Generalissimo promised not to intervene in China's internal affairs, but he was nonetheless to furnish the support and arms to Mao Tse-tung's Communists which were soon to permit them to seize the country. On the whole, far from consecrating the world-wide cooperation of America and Russia, to which Roosevelt had sacrificed the equilibrium of Europe, the Potsdam conference whetted their opposition.

6. THE FRENCH ARMY
AND THE NUCLEAR SWORD

❧

Today's French Army has been shaped as an instrument of *la politique* by the man who led it into revolt against the state —such is the irony of events that span less than a generation! No other "rebel" except perhaps Luther preached obedience and loyalty to the very forces he had earlier incited to rebellion as eloquently as De Gaulle. His life covers two periods—the first one dedicated to the fashioning of a new army that, side by side with the allies, was to liberate France—even if French had to fight against French. This was a period of frantic appeals and also of a shrewd, careful build-up of a small but effective fighting force. De Gaulle worked constantly for its growth so that by the time France was liberated his military force would be an instrument that the allies could no longer ignore.

The second period began in 1958 when a demoralized army rose against the civil authorities in Paris. De Gaulle hastily became the head of the state and his role thereby changed radically. He proceeded to counsel obedience to the state against the many insurrectionalist army groups. But again he provided the army with new techniques of combat in order to weld it into a modern and well-equipped force. Preaching unity and loyalty, he managed to reconcile what appeared to be irreconcilable, to lead a pacified army from the Algerian wilderness back into France, and to transform it into an instrument of a great national design. In 1960 he cries "Hurrah for France" when the first atomic device is successfully exploded in the Sahara.

After the declaration of Algerian independence in July, 1962, De Gaulle could devote himself to the modernization and re-

organization of the army and to the healing of the wounds that
he himself had first opened by inciting the army to rebel against
the state. Outside of the state, De Gaulle proclaimed, there are
but "lost soldiers." But many who had studied his own career
could not help having legitimate doubts.

We reproduce here De Gaulle's pronouncements on the state
of the French Army after the defeat of France and some of his
most significant addresses to the officer corps in which he proclaims French military independence and counsels loyalty to
the state. There can be no defense and independence without
the nuclear sword, he argues. A national army must have national weapons; the only weapons that guarantee national defense are those that will be respected by the enemy. Therefore,
these must be atomic weapons, since they alone can inflict upon
any potential enemy destruction that will deter him from attacking. To have atomic weapons France must conduct tests;
to use them she must be free to have a finger on the atomic
trigger. Thus, at least for the time being, De Gaulle will not
accept any treaty that bans testing—not unless or until their
own tests have provided the French with the proper know-how;
in order to maintain a free finger on the trigger he rejects any
integrative scheme like the MLF, which in one form or another
would subordinate a national decision to an entity other than
the French government or which would deprive France of the
ultimate power to use an atomic weapon at her own discretion.
"Our glass is small," he says, "but we shall drink from it."

Finally, De Gaulle will accept no disarmament proposals whose
purpose is to freeze the existing status quo—that is to say, proposals that provide for the destruction of weapons in such a
way that the military potentials of the Soviet Union and the
United States are not seriously affected, but that would prevent
France from closing the gap that separates her from the two
superpowers. He will accept the destruction of the ICBMs and
other missiles that he does not have; he will accept massive
destruction of nuclear weapons—he has very few. In other words,
disarmament can be considered only in the context of the French
national interest, and this can be served only if the two superpowers disarm down to the level of France. Otherwise, the

Geneva Disarmament Conference is a pretense and a sham, he claims, and France will have little to do with it.

REFLECTIONS ON THE WEAKNESS OF FRANCE

On the day of the opening of the second front on the beaches of Normandy, De Gaulle reflects on the relationship between military power and policy . . .

But how short France found her sword to be, at the moment the Allies launched their attack upon Europe! Never had our country, on so crucial an occasion, been reduced to forces relatively so limited. Those who struggled for her liberation were often embittered to recall the might of her great past. But never before had her army been of better quality—a recovery all the more remarkable in that it had taken its start in an abyss of submission.

For fourteen centuries, military power had been second nature to France. If our country had on many occasions neglected her defense, misprized her soldiers, lost her battles, she had nonetheless appeared at all times eminently capable of the greatest military actions. The vicissitudes of the contemporary period had not proved an exception to this rule. Whatever our weakness after the Napoleonic conquests, however cruel the defeat of 1870, we retained the psychology and the means of a strong people. Principal artisans of the victory in 1918, we had led the others toward it. That our army should outstrip every other army in the world, our fleet be one of the best, our air force of the first order, our generals the most able—that, for us, was only natural.

Hence the collapse of 1940 and the capitulation that followed seemed to many monstrous and irremediable. The image of themselves the French had always had, the world's opinion of them, the testimony of history itself, had suddenly been abolished, annihilated. There was no opportunity for France to recover her dignity in her own eyes and in others' unless she took up arms again. But nothing was to help her re-create her unity and recover her prestige as much as this astonishing fact: that she could find in her scarcely mustered Empire, in her persecuted nation, enough conviction and military valor to reconstitute an army—and an army that would fight extremely well. After Sedan and Dunkirk, the capitulation of Rethondes and Turin, Vichy's acceptance of military defeat and the subjection of the state, it was to be an amazing

SOURCE: *The War Memoirs of Charles De Gaulle* (New York: Simon and Schuster, 1959), Vol. II, pp. 276–277, 292–293.

reversal that would bring our forces to take an important and brilliant share in the victory, though the enemy was occupying the whole of our territory, when two million Frenchmen were prisoners in their hands, when the "legal" government persisted in punishing the combatants.

There were enough men in Africa who could be mobilized to reach the strength of a campaign army. The restrictions, however, were many; for if it was possible to draw on the native populations of Algeria, Morocco, Tunisia, Equatorial Africa, and Madagascar for as many soldiers as we wished, the number of active military men and of reserves prepared to serve as officers and specialists was, on the contrary, very low. Generally, only those of French origin supplied these categories, so indispensable to the formation of large-scale modern units. Yet the population of French origin totaled no more than 1,200,000 persons in these territories. Of course, by calling up all classifications as far back as those of 1918, we would have a total of 116,000 men, a figure all the higher in consideration of the fact that the administration, economic life and law and order absorbed an important proportion of qualified elements and that many of those mobilized had been in German captivity since 1940.

●   ●   ●

Lastly, amid the confusion that would follow the German retreat and Vichy's collapse, what regime would emerge from the chaos if our army happened to be in Austria or Hungary and could not amalgamate itself with the interior forces? For England and the United States, the choice of strategy engaged their foreign policy. But for France, this choice engaged her entire destiny.

It happened that the American schemes carried the day soon enough in regard to the landing in the north of France. In December 1943, our Anglo-American allies, in response to keen urgings from the Russians, decided to execute before the spring's end that imposing strategy which they called "Operation Overlord." We could only approve this choice. But the landing in the south of France, although planned in theory and baptized "Operation Anvil" in advance, remained in the discussion stage. Mr. Churchill did not abandon his notion of focusing on Italy and the Balkans the entire Allied war effort in southern Europe: he obtained for General Maitland Wilson the high command in the Mediterranean, Alexander already being at the head of the armies in Italy; he made every effort to keep the largest possible number of American and French divisions and landing craft at their disposal; unless there were some reaction on our part, the Prime Minister's insistence would lead to the application of the British plan in the southern theater.

But how intervene? Given the game's stakes and the means we could put into the field during this phase of the conflict, it was to be expected that the French be associated with the principal decisions of the coalition; that the head of the French government participate in the conferences in which the President of the United States and the British Prime Minister decided on the strategy for the conduct of the war; that the French command—in the person of General Giraud, for example—be one of the elements of the "combined general staff" where the plans for military action were worked out. We would thereby have been in a position to make our point of view bear weight and to influence the conclusions reached. Then the Allied strategy would become as much our own as it was that of the two states who had adopted it. The fact that, in execution, an American general commanded the northern theater and a British general the southern would certainly have inspired in us a certain nostalgia for the past, but no anxiety as to the present and the future. Yet the Anglo-American powers never consented to deal with us as genuine allies. They never consulted us, as from government to government, on any of their intentions. By policy or expediency, they sought to make use of the French forces for goals they themselves had determined on, as if these forces belonged to them, and in justification citing the fact that they had contributed to their armament and supply.

Such was not my philosophy. I considered that France brought to the Allies, in a variety of forms, cooperation worth much more than the matériel they furnished her. Since she was excluded from their discussions, I felt myself justified, whenever it was necessary, to act in her own behalf and independently of the others. Such actions were not taken without disagreeable incidents, but they succeeded in forcing our allies to compromise with us and to come to the ultimate conclusion that what was to the advantage of France was to the advantage of all.

THE DEFENSE OF FRANCE MUST BE FRENCH

In 1959 the Army is committed to the war in Algeria. Relations between many of the officers and General De Gaulle will remain extremely tense until the final granting of Algerian independence in July 1962. The speech reproduced below, delivered before the

SOURCE: "Speeches and Press Conferences," (New York, French Embassy, Press and Information Service, 1959).

officers at the École de Guerre in Paris, on November 3, 1959, is one of the first steps in De Gaulle's efforts to educate and tame the Army.

The defense of France must be French. That is a necessity which has not always been too well understood in recent years. I know this. It is absolutely essential that it become recognized once more. With a country like France, if war should come, then that war must be her war. Its effort must be her effort. If it were otherwise, our country would be acting counter to everything it has been since its origins—to its role, to its self-respect, to its very soul. Naturally, should the occasion arise, French defense would be joined with that of other countries. That is in the nature of things. But it is indispensable that our defense belong to us, that France defend herself by herself, for herself, and in her own way.

If it should be otherwise, if France's defense were long allowed to remain outside the national framework or to become an integral part of, or mingled with, something else, then it would not be possible for us to maintain a State. In any period of history, the government's *raison d'être* is to defend the independence and the integrity of the territory. It arises from this necessity. Especially in France, all our regimes have been based on their ability to do so.

If you consider our history—whether in the case of the Merovingians, the Carolingians, the Capetians, the First or Second Empires, the First, Second, Third, Fourth, or Fifth Republics—you will see that considerations or necessities of defense were always at the origin of the State and of the regimes that came into being, one after another. Conversely, every invasion, every national disaster has without fail brought about the fall of whatever regime was in power. If, therefore, a government lost control of its essential responsibility, it would thereby lose its justification. Once peace was restored, it would soon be recognized that it did not fulfill its purpose.

As for the military command, which must have the incomparable responsibility of commanding on the battlefields—that is, of answering for the fate of the country—if the military command ceased to bear this honor and this burden, if it were no longer anything more than an element in a hierarchy which would not be ours, then its authority, its dignity, its prestige before the nation and, consequently, before the armed forces would soon be done for.

That is why the concept of a war or even of a battle in which France would no longer be herself and would no longer be acting in her own behalf, with a part to play all her own, and in accordance with what she wants—such a concept cannot be accepted. The system which has been called "integration" and which was inaugurated and even, to a certain extent, put into practice after the great trials we had passed through, at a time when it might have been thought that the free world was facing an imminent and boundless threat and when we had not yet recovered our national personality—this system of integration has had its day.

It goes without saying that our defense, the mobilization of our means, the way in which the conduct of war is conceived—all this must be combined for us with what exists in other countries. Our strategy must be joined with the strategy of others. On the battlefields, here is every probability that we would find ourselves side by side with our allies. But let each one have a share that is all his own.

This is a fundamental point which I ask you to reflect upon. The concept of a defense of France and of the Community which would be a French defense—that is a concept which ought to underlie the philosophy of your centers and schools.

Obviously the consequence of this is that we must know how, during the next few years, to provide ourselves with a force capable of acting in our behalf, with what is commonly called a "striking force," capable of being deployed at any time and any place. It goes without saying that the basis of this force will be atomic weapons, which—whether we manufacture them or whether we buy them—must belong to us; and since—should the circumstances arise—France could be destroyed from any point in the world, our force must be ready to act anywhere on earth.

You realize, as do I, the scope of this obligation, and all it will mean for us. From the national standpoint, we must have the courage to face up to it fully; the entire nation must be brought into this. We must have the courage to accept this obligation and to fulfill it. In the field of defense, this will be our great task during the years to come. To start with, the possible use of this force, its organization and the way in which it is to be organized and equipped—that also should be a main topic of your studies and your work, in keeping with what I have said about defense in general.

A third point which I want to present for your consideration, since I find myself among you, pertains to strictly military action. Military action—action on the battlefields—is the end result of defense. But it is an end result upon which, in turn, everything depends.

This military action, this "operation"—strategic or tactical—we are getting ready for it. You are getting ready for it through the principles you are learning. You are studying many hypotheses successively, through which you are endeavoring to determine a doctrine which can, if need should arise, inspire the action of war and a method which will enable it to be carried out.

That is excellent, for we must, in fact, practise a form of mental gymnastics which develops the ability to make decisions. In addition, we must, of course, acquire as complete and practical a knowledge as possible of the methods which can be used, of the terrain on which we will have to act, and of the enemy with whom we will have to deal.

This is what you are doing, thanks to your exercises.

But, as you well know, we must not cherish the illusion—thanks to a group of precepts established back in peacetime which are, in short, *a priori*—the illusion that we will grapple without fail, with the contingencies of war. Action in war is always contingent—that is, it always appears in an unexpected way which is infinitely variable, and always unprecedented. That is why the leader's action—while its foundation is laid through reflection, work, and study—depends, in the last resort, on his personality for what will or will not be done;—what the outcome will or will not be depends not on matters of a didactic nature, but on intelligence and character.

Those who want to prepare themselves to be leaders in war have the first duty, therefore, of striving to be men—men worthy and capable of responding—under conditions never dreamed of—to the catastrophic events which will break about their heads and in which they will be responsible, each at his own echelon.

I shall finish by telling you how much the military—and everything related to it—continues, more than ever, to be essential to the nation and the State.

It is possible to imagine, not without fear, what a conflict in the near future would be like. It is no less true that this conflict is entirely possible. We are a species and our species has its law. Undoubtedly, the means which are today at the disposal of men to destroy themselves are so far-reaching in their effects that the fearful day has thus far been avoided. But, for how long?—who knows? At any rate, a country must be capable of facing every hypothesis that might affect its destiny, including that of war. Of all the things which a nation is and, above all, which our nation is, there is nothing which is more essential than its defense.

That is why there is no military talent or genius which has not

served a vast policy. There is no great glory for a statesman which
not gained added luster from the glory of national defense.

THE IMPERATIVE OF NUCLEAR FORCE

Again on November 23, 1961, De Gaulle addresses the French
officer corps at Strasbourg, commemorating the anniversary of
its liberation. The themes of national defense and the duty of
the army to provide for it are forcefully stated.

Now, having lived through many centuries and great tragedies, she
knows that her army must be hers alone and that, without this, no
army can hold together.

Despite changing fortunes, despite the various tendencies in the ranks,
despite yesterday's oppositions between the military factions, despite
the wishes, sometimes the regrets, and even the sorrows of individuals
—the law of greatness and of service triumphed once again in the
glorious victory of Strasbourg. The lesson is an eternal one. More than
ever, it is applicable today.

For, in the midst of a world where everything is in question, we find
France once again threatened in body and soul. We find her in almost
immediate proximity to a totalitarian block that seeks to dominate and
brandishes terrible weapons. We find her to be so essential that if she
stands firm and upright, the free world can remain hopeful and united,
but if she should chance to falter, it would involve Europe and, soon
after, the freedom of the world. At no time has France had so great
a right and duty to be herself, nor has she ever had so great a need
of her soldiers. It is true that the sirens of decadence are calling to
her from all sides to give up being France, even grow angry that she
holds to it and urge her to fall in with the goals and rely on the
protection of others.

In so doing, she would be cutting down not on her men and her
money, nor, should the event occur, her ruins and her sacrifices, but
rather on her responsibilities, in other words, on her independence. It
goes without saying that such views could not be those of our country,
which has found itself once again and which is continuously growing
in resources and in influence. Most certainly the Atlantic Alliance is
absolutely necessary. Certainly it would be very desirable that the great
powers of the West permanently concert the policy that they are pursu-

SOURCE: "Speeches and Press Conferences," No. 169 (New York:
French Embassy, Press and Information Service, 1961), pp. 2–3.

ing in all parts of the globe. Certainly it is essential that they prepare together the actions of their forces and, should the occasion arise, combine their war efforts. But within this concert, this preparation and this combining of efforts, France must retain her will, her countenance and her army. This makes it necessary for our military force to be organized and equipped so that it may act in accordance with the conditions of our times. This means that it must have atomic weapons unless, of course, they cease to exist everywhere. For, however terrifying these means of destruction may be, and precisely because they are so terrifying, a great state that does not possess them while others do is not the master of its destiny.

To provide ourselves with strategic and tactical nuclear projectiles and the means for launching them, as long as these exist elsewhere, is our first aim in the field of defense. We are on the way to achieving this.

Furthermore, as the relative distance between continents is constantly diminishing, there are no longer any dangers or conflicts, wherever they may be, that do not concern every world power and, thereby, France.

What is more, in new ways adapted to our century, France is, as always, present and active overseas. The result is that her security, the assistance that she owes her allies, the aid that she is committed to furnish to her associates, may be called into question in any part of the world. A land, sea, and air striking force capable of acting anytime anywhere is therefore absolutely indispensable.

We are beginning to bring this about.

Finally, while making ourselves able to carry far the action of our weapons, we must at the same time be ready to undertake our own immediate defense on land, sea, and air. This is the third factor that constitutes our power. We must have the necessary forces with active and solid units, filled out by mobilization, and ready to use the resources of the land and of the population to combat the invader.

YES—WE SHALL CONDUCT OUR TESTS

In 1960 France began with the testing of some of her atomic devices in the Sahara. Both at the United Nations and in a number of previous public pronouncements the government had

SOURCE: *Major Addresses, Statements, and Press Conferences of General Charles De Gaulle, May 19, 1958–January 31, 1964* (New York: French Embassy, Press and Information Service), pp. 121–122.

refused to accept a halt in nuclear experiments. On April 11, 1961, De Gaulle answered his critics.

During World War II, the Americans, with the aid of a certain number of European scientists and technicians, began to build atomic bombs, then used them at the end of the war. After which a frightening nuclear arms race was unleashed between the Anglo-Saxons and the Soviets, a race which is going on worse than ever. It is true that the two sides have temporarily suspended their tests. But they no longer have any need for these tests, since those which they have already carried out have enabled them to stockpile means which, in both camps, make it possible to destroy the entire world. Now, the race is essentially concerned with the means of launching bombs, which are increasing—so to speak unlimitedly—the destructive capacity of these devices. What is frightening in this race is that it corresponds to the fundamental situation of our world, that is to say, to the rivalry between the two camps, and that it consequently takes on a sort of fatal character.

In any case, no State has ever raised its voice in a positive manner to cast the blame on one or the other of the parties which have manufactured and continue to manufacture these frightening weapons. To my knowledge, no State in the world has broken off relations with London, with Moscow, with Washington, because of this. To my knowledge the United Nations has not called on the United States, the Soviet Union, or Great Britain to destroy their atomic arsenals and their launching facilities. Then, since these two parties do not renounce their nuclear arsenals—quite the contrary—France, for reasons which concern her own defense and that of several others, has felt compelled to equip herself, in turn, with a force of this sort. It is true that the weapons she is building and which she can build will be only a very small fraction of what the others have built. It is true that the tests she is conducting are very small in number in relation to all the tests which the others have carried out. But all this is disregarded, it is against France and France alone that the outcry of indignation which you hear is directed.

Since the French tests took place in the Sahara, attempts are made to stir up terror among populations situated vast distances away—for the tests took place in a completely desert region—by invoking the danger of radioactivity.

However, no one has ever discovered, on any one, any effect whatsoever with regard to health because of the three French atomic tests which have already taken place. Moreover, why would the three French atomic tests be much more dangerous than the 120 tests—at least that many—carried out by the two parties which I mentioned a moment ago.

Since the Sahara is in Africa, attempts are being made to persuade the African States that their rights are at stake. The Americans have conducted nuclear tests in the Nevada desert and, to my knowledge, there were no ardent protests on the part of the other 47 States. The Russians have carried out their tests in Turkestan, in Siberia; to my knowledge, the 28 Asian States did not raise any protests of any great consequence. The Americans and the British have conducted tests in the Pacific; to my knowledge, the 27 countries—I have counted them— bordering on the Pacific have not considered this an encroachment.

Of course, it is understandable that the powers which possess atomic weapons, that is the United States, the Soviet Union, and Great Britain, do not wish France to acquire them. Of course, it is understandable that these three powers are finding, among the States which have more or less close ties with them, a response favorable to their arguments and unfavorable to the French plan. Of course, France owes it to herself and to all others to observe the strictest prudence in the tests which she still has to conduct, and that is what she will do, as she has already done in the preceding ones. But, so long as others have the means to destroy her, it is necessary for her to have the means to defend herself.

WHY WE ARE NOT INTERESTED IN DISARMAMENT

A year later, on May 15, 1962, De Gaulle explained why the Geneva disarmament talks did not interest France at the time. In the interval, France had successfully exploded four atomic devices in the Sahara and was preparing for nuclear tests in the Pacific.

Since we are not taking part in the negotiations of the United States with Moscow, we are not taking part in the Geneva conference either. Should you be curious, without saying so, about the reasons for our not taking part in it, I shall mention them rapidly.

It would be necessary, I believe, to have a great deal of imagination or else a great many illusions in order to believe that such a con-

SOURCE: *Major Addresses, Statements, and Press Conferences of General Charles De Gaulle, May 19, 1958–January 31, 1964* (New York: French Embassy, Press and Information Service), pp. 181–182.

ference could make the two great atomic powers that I just spoke of do away with their arms, and France is too modest to believe that her presence at such a conference would change things very much. It is not, of course, that we also do not deplore the proliferation of bombs and nuclear devices in the two camps. We have proposed in the past, on several occasions, a measure which was to our mind the only practical one and which consisted in banning, while there was still time, and perhaps there still is time, the vehicles—rockets, airplanes, submarines, etc.—for the delivery of nuclear warheads. Once again, we do not think that there is any chance for this measure to be adopted in Geneva, since it has never been adopted anywhere else. We therefore do not see any reason to increase the size of the honorable assembly that is being held there, which intends to present irreconcilable plans and can do nothing but moan a little, like the chorus of old men and women in ancient tragedy: "Insoluble difficulty! How to find a way out?"

Under these circumstances, we are not at Geneva. It is true that one might have thought that the United States and Great Britain, who seemed to have had such an idea at one time, would agree at least to refrain from making any new tests. Had they agreed on this subject, they could have expected that every other State in the world—and that includes France—would then halt its own tests. These two powers would, of course, have retained and continued to develop their terrifying weapons, but they would be giving the public, not their disarmament, of course, but an appearance of satisfaction. And then, they would be maintaining their monopoly. There was nothing there to induce France to join the seventeen countries at Geneva.

Naturally, we are quite prepared to applaud the Anglo-Saxons and the Soviets, if they decide not to carry out any more tests.

But once again, that is not the problem. The problem is disarmament: that is to say, the reciprocal controlled destruction of weapons, beginning with vehicles. In this respect, we have our problem too. So long as this disarmament is not being carried out—and there is nothing to indicate that steps are being taken in that direction—we have, with regard to ourselves, the obligation and the necessity of constituting, in our turn, our own atomic deterrent force. Consequently, we shall continue our tests in any case until the goal is reached, unless, I repeat, the others rid themselves of their means of destruction. From this point of view as well, we do not see why we should be at Geneva. Of course, if there should one day be a meeting of States that truly want to organize disarmament—and such a meeting should, in our mind, be composed of the four atomic powers—France would participate in it wholeheartedly. Until such time, she does not see the need for taking part in proceedings whose inevitable outcome is termed disillusion.

THE TEST BAN TREATY DOES NOT CHANGE THE SITUATION

And again, on July 29, 1963, De Gaulle will reiterate France's decision to continue her tests and will dismiss the Moscow Treaty between the United States and the Soviet Union to ban atmospheric testing.

The fact that the Soviets and the Anglo-Saxons decided directly to halt their nuclear tests in space, the air and the sea, is in itself satisfactory, and we share the joy that President Kennedy so eloquently expressed the day before yesterday on the subject of this event. It must be said that this is not the first time that nuclear tests would be interrupted. There have already been on several occasions long periods when neither of the two sides carried out any important tests. But this time the fact that both sides are reciprocally committed to abstention makes this much more probable. Moreover, after each side's having carried out tests, numbering several hundred, the last of them quite recently, it is hard to see what purpose new tests could now serve. Yet the area of underground tests is not included in the agreement and each partner retains the possibility of denouncing the agreement within three months if he sees fit.

However, without failing to realize that this Moscow agreement has indeed—quite the contrary—anything that can offend anyone, and in any case not us, it must be noted that it in no way alters the terrible threat that the nuclear weapons of the two rivals bring to bear on the world, and above all on the people who do not possess them.

It is a fact that both of them hold the means to annihilate the world and it is a fact that there is no quesion of their being ready to give them up.

In these conditions, the world situation in relation to this threat not being changed in any way whatsoever, it is quite natural for a country such as France, who is beginning to have the means of freeing herself to a certain degree from this permanent terror, continue along this course. All the more so since nothing prevents the two rivals, their tests having been halted, from continuing to manufacture missiles in

SOURCE: *Major Addresses, Statements, and Press Conferences of General Charles De Gaulle, May 19, 1958–January 31, 1964* (New York: French Embassy, Press and Information Service), pp. 237–238.

increasing quantities and power and to equip themselves with increasingly advanced launch vehicles, rockets, airplanes, submarines and satellites. The savings they could perhaps make from halting tests will enable them to strengthen even further their means of destruction. That is why the Moscow agreement, I say this frankly, has only limited practical importance. Unless, of course, it were the starting point for something else, which would extend to other very different areas, and for that reason the agreement, while having France's approval, nevertheless awakens her vigilance.

Then you ask me what France is going to do after the Moscow agreement?

I will tell you once again that if one day the Americans and the Soviets reach the point of disarmament, that is the controlled destruction and banning of their nuclear means, it is wholeheartedly that we ourselves would give up securing them. Nothing, unfortunately, indicates that we are about to reach that point. And the sad Geneva Conference, as was to be foreseen, will have interminably sat for nothing.

However, I can say that in any case and at all events, France was only awaiting the end of this useless performance—I am speaking of the Geneva Conference—to propose to the three other atomic powers certain initial effective disarmament measures, concerning particularly space, air, and naval launch vehicles for nuclear missles. What took place in Moscow only confirms France in this intention, and she intends before the end of the year to invite the States concerned to study with her this essential problem, while perhaps it has not yet become insoluable in its turn. But we repeat also that a mere agreement on tests between Soviets and Anglo-Saxons, already invested with immeasurable power, and who do not cease to strengthen it and thereby to confirm day by day their respective hegemonies, a mere agreement will not prevent France also from equipping herself with the same kind of means, failing which, since others have these means, France's own security and her own independence would never again belong to her.

ALLIANCE AND INDEPENDENCE

To avoid the proliferation of atomic weapons and to provide for an integrative type of nuclear defense for NATO, the United States had been pressing for some time for the so-called

SOURCE: *Major Addresses, Statements, and Press Conferences of General Charles De Gaulle, May 19, 1958–January 31, 1964* (New York: French Embassy, Press and Information Service), pp. 216–219.

Multilateral Force (MLF). It took so many forms and reflected so many equivocations on the part of the American spokesmen that it is impossible here to do justice to it. In essence it involved the establishment of an organization in which various members of NATO would operate jointly nuclear weapons either from the ground or from mobile launching sites—mostly surface vessels. However, both the bombs and the ultimate decision for their launching would be subject to American control. In a meeting between Prime Minister Macmillan and President Kennedy at Nassau in December, 1962, the British decided to abandon the construction of delivery instruments and agreed to place their own weapons in the hands of NATO force with launching devices, notably submarines, provided by the United States. Britain could withdraw and use her nuclear weapons only when her supreme national interests demanded it. France was invited to participate on the same terms and De Gaulle refused. On January 14, 1963, in the same press conference at which he declared that England should not be part of the Common Market, he rejected all such integrative schemes.

I have already had occasion several time to indicate publicly France's policy from the standpoint of her defense and also on the means with which, consequently, she deemed it necessary to equip herself. This time again I am going to try to clarify the subject. In any case I repeat, after having said it often, that France intends to have her national defense. It is obvious that one country, especially one such as ours, cannot in the present day and age and could not conduct a major modern war all by itself. To have allies goes without saying for us in the historic period we are in. But also for a great people to have the free disposition of itself and the means to struggle to preserve it is an absolute imperative, for alliances have no absolute virtues, whatever may be the sentiments on which they are based. And if one spontaneously loses, even for a while, the free disposition of oneself, there is a strong risk of never regaining it. And then, the conditions in which we presently find ourselves also make it imperative for us to act in this manner.

We are in the atomic age and we are a country that can be destroyed at any moment unless the aggressor is deterred from the undertaking by the certainty that he too will suffer frightful destruction. This justifies both alliance and independence. The Americans, our allies and our friends, have for a long time, alone, possessed a nuclear arsenal. So long as they alone had such an arsenal and so long as they showed their will to use it immediately if Europe were attacked—for at that time Europe alone could be attacked—the Americans acted in such a way that for France the question of an invasion hardly arose, since an attack was beyond all probability. It was then a matter for the Atlantic Alliance, that is to say, for the American command, of having in Europe and America a tactical and strategic air force capable of using atomic weapons—for at that time only airplanes could do that—and thus capable of protecting Europe. It was also a matter of lining up in Europe itself conventional land, naval, and air forces which could ensure the deployment and use of atomic weapons. It can be said that, during that period, the deterrent worked and that there existed a practically insuperable obstacle to an invasion of Europe. It is impossible to overestimate the extent of the service, most fortunately passive, that the Americans at that time, in that way, rendered to the freedom of the world.

Since then the Soviets have also acquired a nuclear arsenal, and that arsenal is powerful enough to endanger the very life of America. Naturally, I am not making an evaluation—if indeed it is possible to find a relation between the degree of one death and the degree of another—but the new and gigantic fact is there. From then on, the Americans found and are finding themselves confronted with the possibility of direct destruction. Thus the immediate defense, and one can say privileged defense of Europe, and the military participation of the Europeans, which were once basic factors of their strategy, moved by the force of circumstances into second place. We have just witnessed this during the Cuban affair.

The Americans, finding themselves exposed to a direct attack from the Caribbean, acted in such a way as to rid themselves of that menace and, if it had been necessary, to crush it without its having occurred either to them or to anyone else that the game would necessarily be played in Europe and without recourse to the direct assistance of the Europeans. Moreover, the means which they immediately decided to employ in order to counter a direct attack, whether it came from Cuba only or was combined with another originating elsewhere, these means were automatically set aside for something other than the defense of Europe, even if Europe had been attacked in its turn.

And then, above and beyond everything, the deterrent is now a fact for the Russians as for the Americans, which means that in the case of a general atomic war, there would inevitably be frightful and perhaps fatal destruction in both countries. In these conditions, no one in the world—particularly no one in America—can say if, where, when, how and to what extent the American nuclear weapons would be employed to defend Europe. Moreover, this does not in the least prevent the American nuclear weapons, which are the most powerful of all, from remaining the essential guarantee of world peace. This fact, and the determination with which President Kennedy used it, came into full light out of the Cuban affair. But it remains that the American nuclear power does not necessarily and immediately meet all the eventualities concerning Europe and France.

Thus principles and realities combine to lead France to equip herself with an atomic force of her own. This does not all exclude, of course, the combination of the action of this force with the action of the similar forces of its allies. But, for us, in this specific case, integration is something that is unimaginable. Indeed, as you know, we have begun with our own and only means to invent, test, and construct atomic bombs and the vehicles for launching them.

It is completely understandable that this French undertaking does not appear to be highly satisfactory to certain American circles. In politics and in strategy, as in the economy, monopoly quite naturally appears to the person who holds it to be the best possible system. Then we hear a multiple choir of Americans—unofficial persons, experts and journalists—violently and strongly attacking our autonomous armament. "The atomic force with which France intends to equip herself is and will remain," they say, "insignificant in relation to those of the United States and Russia. To build it up is thus to waste a lot of effort and money for nothing. And then, within the Alliance, the United States has an overwhelming superiority, therefore no one should run counter to its strategy through any divergent action."

It is quite true that the number of nuclear weapons with which we can equip ourselves will not equal, far from it, the mass of those of the two giants of today. But since when has it proved that a people should remain deprived of the most effective weapon for the reason that its chief possible adversary and its chief friend have means far superior to its own?

France, when formerly it was its turn to be world colossus, often experienced the worth of either the resistance of a less powerful but well-equipped adversary, or the support of an ally lining up inferior but well-tempered and well-employed weapons.

Moreover, the atomic force has a feature of its own, in that it has an efficacity that is certain and to an extent that is frightening even if it does not approach the conceivable maximum. In 1945 two bombs, then elementary, led Japan, who was not able to answer back, to capitulate. I do not want to evoke here the possibilities in which Europe could suffer nuclear actions that would be localized, but whose political and psychological consequences would be immense, unless there is a certainty that retaliation to that extent would be immediately unleashed. I only want to say that the French atomic force, from the very beginning of its establishment, will have the sombre and terrible capability of destroying in a few seconds millions and millions of men. This fact cannot fail to have at least some bearing on the intents of any possible aggressor.

Then, in the Bahamas, America and Britain concluded an agreement and we were asked to subscribe to it ourselves. Of course, I am only speaking of this proposal and agreement because they have been published and because their content is known. It is a question of constituting a so-called multilateral atomic force, in which Britain would turn over the weapons it has and will have and in which the Americans would place a few of their own. This multilateral force is assigned to the defense of Europe and is under the American NATO command. It is nevertheless understood that the British retain the possibility of withdrawing their atomic weapons for their own use should supreme national interest seem to them to demand it.

As for the bulk of American nuclear weapons, it remains outside the multilateral force and under the direct orders of the President of the United States. Furthermore and in a way by compensation, Britain may purchase from America, if it so desires, Polaris missiles which are, as you know, launched from submarines specially built for that purpose and which carry the thermonuclear warheads adapted to them for a distance of 1100–2000 miles. To build these submarines and warheads, the British receive privileged assistance from the Americans. You know —I say this in passing—that this assistance was never offered to us and you should know, despite what some report, that we have never asked for it.

France has taken note of the Anglo-American Nassau agreement. As it was conceived, undoubetedly no one will be surprised that we cannot subscribe to it. It truly would not be useful for us to buy Polaris missiles when we have neither the submarines to launch them nor the thremonuclear warheads to arm them. Doubtless the day will come when we will have these submarines and these warheads. But that day will be long in coming. For the World War, the invasion, and their consequences have slowed us down a great deal in our atomic development. When we will one day have these submarines and these warheads, what will the Polaris missiles then be worth? At that time we will probably have missiles of our own invention. In other words, for us, in terms of technology, this affair is not the question of the moment.

But also, it does not meet with the principle about which I just spoke and which consists of disposing in our own right of our deterrent force. To turn over our weapons to a multilateral force, under a foreign command, would be to act contrary to that principle of our defense and our policy. It is true that we too can theoretically retain the ability to take back in our hands, in the supreme hypothesis, our atomic weapons incorporated in the multilateral force. But how could we do it in practice during the unheard of moments of the atomic apocalypse? And then, this multilateral force necessarily entails a web of liaisons, transmissions, and interferences within itself, and on the outside a ring of obligations such that, if an integral part were suddenly snatched from it, there would be a strong risk of paralyzing it just at the moment, perhaps, when it should act.

In sum, we will adhere to the decision we have made: to construct and, if necessary, to employ our atomic force ourselves. And that without refusing, of course, cooperation, be it technological or strategic, if this cooperation is, on the other hand, desired by our allies.

OUR INDEPENDENT NUCLEAR POLICY—A SUMMING UP

On July 23, 1964, De Gaulle lectures serenely on the French nuclear effort and claims that it is a positive contribution to the establishment of a new balance of forces in the world—not simply a medium of French defense.

Nineteen years ago, suddenly, an atomic bomb caused 100,000 deaths in Hiroshima. Then, in Nagasaki, another caused as many. Suddenly Japan—a great people, courageous in the highest sense of the word, still possessing powerful military means, whose territorial nature and national character lent themselves perfectly well to the defensive to the bitter end—was seen to capitulate unconditionally, to the extent of allowing itself to be entirely occupied, governed, even transformed by its enemy.

SOURCE: *Tenth Press Conference* (New York: French Embassy, Press and Information Service, July 23, 1964), pp. 7–9.

Thus there opened in the history of our world an entirely new phase, regarding the security of peoples, consequently regarding their policy and their respective relations. To possess the atomic weapon, is for a country, to be in a position to reduce relentlessly a nation which does not possess it. But it is also to deter any nation which possesses it from carrying out atomic agression against it. For that would be tantamount to inflicting death only to receive it immediately.

Since America and Russia have both equipped themselves with such an atomic arsenal, there exists between them a kind of automatic deterrent balance. But this balance really covers only them and not the other countries of the world, even when they are linked to one or the other of the two colossal powers. For the cause and the integrity of each of the others might not seem to their great ally to be worth the trouble of being crushed itself in crushing its rival. And, nevertheless, those threatened by the ambition of one of the two giants are led to accommodate themselves, in relation to the other, with strategic, and therefore political dependence in which they think they see the only chance for their security.

Certain were able to believe that the prospect of conflict was so terrible that the United States and Russia would in concert renounce that sort of arsenal. The fruitless and interminable Geneva conference arose from this illusion. But in the present state of the world, the hypothesis is unbelievable.

The fact that America and Soviet Russia possess their nuclear arsenal provides them with such security and moreover gives them, inside their respective camps, such a reason for exercising hegemony that they will not get rid of theirs, no more than any other State in their place would get rid of its arsenal, whatever its ideology, its nature, and its propaganda. The result is that the countries which do not have an atomic arsenal believe that they have to accept a strategic and consequently a political dependency in relation to that one of the two giants which is not threatening them.

In these conditions France, while deploring the fact that the two giants in question do not disarm—except, of course, in the form of a momentary agreement which aimed only at a certain slowing down in the rate of production, but which continues to allow them to maintain and increase their gigantic power of destruction—France, I say, as soon as she was able to be herself, judged it necessary to begin the desired effort in order to become an atomic power in her turn. In this respect, it is true, she is suffering from the consequences of a long delay caused first by the war under the occupation, then by the reconstruction of everything that was demolished on her soil, and lastly by the procrastinations for her political, economic and financial recovery. Also in comparison with the United States and Russia, which have widely put to use in their time the assistance of European scientists and technicians, and with Great Britain, which profited from the American experience, France disposes of only French capacities. Lastly, it is clear that the total of our scientific, technical, and industrial means is far from reaching that of the two giants.

However, we are on the road and we are advancing according to our plan. At the same time the vast research, invention, and production activity that atomic development itself involves, introduces a most effective stimulus into our scientific, technical, and economic life. And here, at this very moment, we are reaching results. Our first atomic air unit becomes operational this year. In 1966 we will have enough Mirage IV's and refueling planes to be able to carry at one time, over a distance of thousands of miles, bombs with a total power exceeding that of 150 Hiroshima bombs. Furthermore, we are working on moving on from series A fission bombs to series H fusion bombs, the latter launched from either atomic submarines, surface vessels, or land. This very day the Premier is on his way to inspect the distant and isolated sites where, under the best testing and security conditions, the necessary tests will take place in due time. We are in a position to think that six years from now our deterrent means will reach a total instantaneous power of 2,000 Hiroshima bombs. This is what certain, obviously unthinking, opponents call France's "little bomb."

The field of deterrence is thus henceforth open to us. For to attack France would be equivalent, for whomever it might be, to undergoing frightful destruction itself. Doubtless the megatons that we could launch would not equal in number those that Americans and Russians are able to unleash. But, once reaching a certain nuclear capability, and with regard to one's own direct defense, the proportion of respective means has no absolute value. Indeed, since a man and a people can die only once, the deterrent exists provided that one has the means to wound the possible aggressor mortally, that one is very determined to do it and that the aggressor is convinced of it. That is why France's modern arsenal not only constitutes for her the incomparable guarantee of her security, but also introduces into a dangerous world a new and powerful element of wisdom and circumspection.

However, our advent to the rank of an atomic power is not failing to arouse diverse opposition here. To condemn this new force, the classic marriage of eternal demagogy and eternal routine is taking place; a marriage which once caused the failure of our Army's transformation in the face of Bismarck's ambitions and which was thus greatly responsible for our defeat in 1870; a marriage which, before 1914, deprived us of heavy artillery, for the lack of which, during the World War, our human losses far exceeded those of the enemy until we were finally able, after three years of exhausting combat, to equip ourselves with the necessary cannon; a marriage which, on the eve of World War II, led the public powers and military command to refuse to build the mechanized armored force, while Germany gave itself Panzer divisions, the effects of which are known; a marriage which today loudly stigmatizes the so-called excessive cost of atomic weapons, while not only does this cost not annually exceed one hundredth of our national income, or one quarter of our military expenditures, or half what the State pays to its pensioners and retired people, or the total of the social benefits paid to farmers, but permits us to reduce by half our Army personnel and the length of military service.

However, this time the opposition does not come only from an oversimple refusal of reform. It is in reality inspired by adherents to two political prejudices, doubtless opposed, but both aimed at France's effacement under the hegemony of one or another foreign State. There are those, on the one hand, who would like to establish a totalitarian dictatorship in our country and who therefore desire to see us deprived of the means with which to defend ourselves against the East. There are, on the other hand, the partisans of the American protectorate who are alarmed at the prospect of a France mistress of herself with regard to her allies. But I believe, less than ever, that these objections, coming from two very different horizons, but both originating with the intention that our country be subordinated, are persuading the French nation. We will thus continue our atomic effort over the short, medium, and long term, convinced to be thereby helping the nation's scientific, technical, and industrial development, to be reviving the body and soul of our army as modern times command, and to be giving France the means for her security and her independence, consequently those for her action in behalf of equilibrium and peace in the world.

PART III

FRENCH INDEPENDENCE

In Part III some of De Gaulle's major pronouncements on contemporary world problems are reproduced. De Gaulle returned to power in 1958 confronting a world that had greatly changed since he had last held office. The two superpowers were now both equipped with nuclear weapons and the "balance of terror" appeared to be the only deterrent to war; Stalin's successor was providing for the first time a relaxation of the hard Soviet foreign and domestic line; coexistence was much in evidence despite the many abortive attempts by the Soviet Union to settle the fate of Berlin by threats of force; the Sino-Soviet dispute based, as De Gaulle had often intimated, upon national rivalries which no ideological labels could any longer camouflage, opened up once more the prospects of a change in Soviet policy; under the nuclear umbrella of the two superpowers, nationalisms stirred and came into being—in Eastern Europe, in Africa, in Latin America, in Southeast Asia, and in western Europe itself. France was coming of age industrially. The Common Market had been signed in the wake of the Coal and Steel Community, and West Germany was part of it. NATO under American leadership provided a military association of most of the western nations—including a recovered Germany. American leadership and dominance were obvious and, as in World War II, an American general was in charge of all Atlantic forces with headquarters near Paris. But, while the Americans pursued their

151

interests outside of NATO at their discretion, France and Great
Britain were thwarted in what many considered to be their
legitimate interests in Egypt and elsewhere.

All these changes called for new tactics in the pursuit of
De Gaulle's original goal to secure French independence. Relations with West Germany and western Europe had to be recon-
sidered; the shifting character of Soviet policies called also for
watchful reconsideration; the tight American hold over her allies
in most parts of the world but also in Western Europe appeared
to be, in the context of changing Soviet policy, both dangerous
and unwarranted. Finally, nationalist stirrings in Eastern Europe
provided the hope that what had been done at Yalta could be
undone and the balance of Europe as De Gaulle envisaged it
after the Liberation could be, with proper accommodations to
the problem of German reunification, restored. As we have seen,
De Gaulle's first effort was to attain status and rank within the
Alliance by pressing for cooperation and consultations through a
tripartite arrangement. When this failed, De Gaulle proceeded to
carry out his threat. Gradually French participation in NATO
was whittled down, through the withdrawal of French forces
under the NATO command and the interdiction of storing on
French soil nuclear weapons over which France had no control.

But De Gaulle's major objective was to achieve a new synthesis
both in Western Europe and in the world. The heart of the matter
was Europe—and with it Germany. This had two aspects. First,
Western Europe, with West Germany to be sure, should develop
political consultative organs that ultimately, but only ultimately,
might lead to some kind of political unity. As De Gaulle argues
in the passages we reproduce, such a Western Europe should be
built upon the hard realities of the existing situation. This calls
for cooperation rather than integration of states. It called for a
"center of gravity" consisting of a core of the most powerful
states—and this led him to advocate a Franco-German alliance.
Second, De Gaulle never set aside the vision of French leadership
and the possession of atomic weapons gave to the French pre-
eminence in Europe. The stumbling block to this policy was the
United States, with its increasing influence among business
groups; its development of special relations with both Germany

and, in particular, England; with its troops and atomic weapons deployed in the heart of Europe, and on whose protection in the last analysis all the European nations had to count in case of Soviet attack. And the United States, poised in the center of Europe, did not allow the Russians a moment of relaxation that might pave the way to the liberalization of the eastern regimes and ultimately the withdrawal of the Soviet armies.

Furthermore, the Americans apparently had no intention of returning home. On the contrary, through NATO, SEATO, CENTO, etc., they appeared everywhere to be shaping policy and often blundering, according to De Gaulle, into policies that were tolerated only because of their overwhelming strength and their nuclear monopoly—a monopoly which the English went out of their way to support! Therefore, *as long as the Soviets do not threaten,* De Gaulle will take a clearly anti-American stance. The polarization of nuclear power—and with it of course the American monopoly within the free world—must be broken; NATO, as long as it underwrites American leadership, must be undermined; Americans must be kept out of the legitimate spheres of interest of other nations. If not, they shall discover that a friendly and allied nation like France will attempt to weaken their influence even in their own backyard. Finally, if the Americans do not accept the principle of consultations and joint decisions within NATO, they shall get a taste of their own medicine—France will proceed on her own, no matter how distasteful this may prove to be.

Much has been written about De Gaulle's "anti-Americanism," a subject that is treated separately in this part. It should be said, however, that De Gaulle has simply steered a course between what he considers, in terms of the interests of France, to be two evils—Soviet *or* American domination. Whenever the choice is stark and unavoidable he will support the United States. But when events do not press a clear choice upon him, his course is simply to maneuver between a potential enemy and a very irksome friend. At times American acts or pressures—as was the case with the MLF, with Southeast Asia, and the sending of marines to Santo Domingo—have appeared to him to be dangerous to France's independence or interests, and he therefore has taken issue with these policies. When, however, the Soviet Union threatened Berlin, when the summit conference failed, and when missiles were installed in Cuba, De Gaulle took the American side. He is only playing the traditional game of balance by refusing to accept a protector. In fact, the more the United States pressured for control of the Alliance, the more recalcitrant De Gaulle became, until he finally unfolded his scheme of a *European Europe* and began to contemplate the possibility of direct negotiations with the Soviet Union on the future of Germany. Ultimately, a European Europe meant the realization of an old dream he had evoked so often—the reestablishment of French leadership in Western Europe; the withdrawal of Soviet troops from East Europe; the development, perhaps, of a neutralized zone including part of Germany; and the withdrawal of American troops. Western Europe then would become a genuine Third Force between the two superpowers but one which, given her resources and the newly acquired French nuclear armaments, could become an equal in its own right, asserting once more its former world-wide interests.

Many have seen in this dream the presence of anachronistic elements and the danger of a revival of nationalism. This may well be so. But it should be pointed out that in De Gaulle's scheme of things "nationalism" is not a terminal point. In western Europe he sees great possibilities of union; in the liberalization of the Eastern European regimes he sees also enormous possibilities of humanizing and liberalizing the totalitarian thrust of the Soviet Union; in the withdrawal of American forces he sees perhaps a development that carries the promise of stability and peace—a solution more conducive to peace, in his mind, than the confrontation of the Soviet Union and the United States in the heart of Europe. Whatever the case, this is De Gaulle's global view. The central issue, of course, is Europe—because for De Gaulle Europe continues to be the center of a power and civilization capable of generating a way of life that may appeal to the uncommitted nations by avoiding both the shortcomings of the economic liberalism practiced in the United States and the harshness of Soviet totalitarianism.

7. THE EUROPEAN VOCATION

❧

When De Gaulle returned to power in 1958 he accepted the European Common Market and implemented its provisions. Like the previous leaders of the Fourth Republic, De Gaulle drove a hard bargain and often appeared to gain advantages disproportionate to his bargaining power. While seeming to accept in principle the idea of political unity, he insisted that the time was not ripe for "integration." Indeed, he scoffed at the idea time after time. Instead, he argued for political consultations in the form of periodic meetings of Heads of States; the Franco-German alliance provided for such meetings for the purpose of coordinating common policies—including foreign affairs and defense.

In his speech at Strasbourg in 1945, he seemed to consider the intellectual and ideological affinities of Europe. But all his later pronouncements reflect a realization that Europe is and will remain a "Europe of States" and that the best that can be done is to establish cooperation among those states. Such cooperation is, he argues, a political phenomenon even when only economic issues are to be decided. Gradually it will create the instrumentalities of closer cooperation that may lead to political union. At this stage integration is a fiction. It is inconceivable that Germans or French or Belgians will be loyal to and obey a disemboweled entity called "United Europe"; we should not lull ourselves with tales from *A Thousand and One Nights*. But De Gaulle himself had spoken of the anachronistic character of small units in an age of empires, and at the time of the Liberation he spoke of "great wholes" and larger associations among smaller states. He seems to have accepted that economic unity means political participation and cooperation that inevitably bind the individual states. The hard lines of national sovereignties

155

have been blurred in the Economic Market that De Gaulle has supported.

Why then his intransigence? I think there are two related reasons. First, doubts about Germany: in an integrated Europe Germany might not only play an important role on a level of equality, but also attempt to dominate the whole in a manner inconsistent with French interests. Second, and more important, "integration" may create a political entity that will be, at least in the beginning, so lacking in authority and organization as to be dominated by the United States. Thus, in De Gaulle's mind a united Europe with integrated political organs (which ultimately would mean supranational organs for defense and foreign policy) would be less European than a Europe consisting of nation-states cooperating on the basis of common interests and affinities.

There is, however, one capital consideration that may cause De Gaulle to seriously reconsider France's continuing participation in the Common Market. This is not so much the agricultural policies over which the progress of the Common Market seems to be stalemated now, but the political and military position of West Germany and of the United States. De Gaulle has offered, in his own terms, the Germans a privileged position in Western Europe. If the Bonn Republic prefers to maintain its own special position with the United States, as England did, then De Gaulle will not hesitate to negotiate directly with the Soviet Union or at least to threaten the Germans of so doing. This scheme was clearly unveiled in his press conference of September 9, 1965, in which he spoke of a larger Europe that was to include Eastern European states, attacked strongly any tendency toward the development of supranational arrangements in the Common Market and, finally, spoke in favor of radically revising and perhaps withdrawing from NATO.

THE PROSPECTS OF UNITY

Where can I say it better than here in Strasbourg what is now the great task ahead for this part of France? Yesterday, the Rhine, your river, our river, was a barrier, a frontier, a war front. Today, since the

SOURCE: *Discours et Messages, 1940–1946* (Paris: Berger-Levrault, 1946), pp. 561–563.

enemy has collapsed thanks to our victory, since the furious temptations that led Germany toward evil have disappeared, the Rhine may again play the role assigned to it by history and geography. It may become a link for the west. Let us look at it: from Switzerland through Alsace and Moselle, through Baden and the areas of Main and Ruhr and the Low Countries where it reaches the sea close to the coast of England, the ships can and must now freely circulate up and down the river from one end to the other. The same is true for ideas that influence the mind and the soul. The same is true for civilization. . . . Yes, the link of western Europe is two feet away. It is the Rhine that flows through Strasbourg. Thus, it is your city—a great port, a great intellectual center, which is now called upon to spread the energy and ideas of France through the medium it has used for so long. To do so you can count on the help of the whole of France. I promise this in the name of the Republic. I have the feeling that in Strasbourg everybody has understood; I have the feeling that people realize the greatness of this eternal effort of France—which is primarily yours.

THE BASIS OF COOPERATION

On September 5, 1960, De Gaulle urged the members of the "Six" to realize that cooperation among independent states was the best and most feasible type of cooperation—thus rejecting all arguments in favor of integration or federation.

Along with the Premier and the Minister of Foreign Affairs and, moreover, in line with the policy clearly defined and followed by the Government, we have in fact recently inaugurated a series of consultations with the Heads of State or of Government of the countries of Western Europe, more specifically those of what is called the Europe of the Six. Moreover, this has not prevented us from seeing, and we hope indeed that it will not keep us from seeing the British Prime Minister again on an occasion which will necessarily be a happy occasion.

To build Europe, that is to say, to unite it, is evidently something essential. It is trite to ask why this great center of civilization, of strength, of reason, of prosperity is being smothered by its own ashes. All that is necessary, in such a domain, is to proceed, not by following our dreams, but according to realities.

SOURCE: *Major Addresses, Statements, and Press Conferences of General Charles De Gaulle, May 19, 1958–January 31, 1964* (New York: French Embassy, Press and Information Service), pp. 92–93.

Now, what are the realities of Europe? What are the pillars on which it can be built? The States are, in truth, certainly very different from one another, each of which has its own spirit, its own history, its own language, its own misfortunes, glories, and ambitions; but these States are the only entities that have the right to order and the authority to act. To imagine that something can be built that would be effective for action and that would be approved by the peoples outside and above the States—this is a dream.

Of course it is true that, while waiting to come to grips with Europe's problem and tackle it as a whole, it has been possible to institute certain organs that are more or less extranational. These organs have their technical value, but they do not have, they cannot have authority and, consequently, political effectiveness. As long as nothing serious happens, they function without much difficulty, but as soon as a tragic situation appears, a major problem to be solved, it can then be seen that one "High Authority" or another has no authority over the various national categories and that only the States have it. This is what was proved not long ago with regard to the coal crisis, and it is what may be seen with regard to the Common Market when there are problems of agricultural products and economic aid to be furnished to the African States or of the relations between the Common Market and the free trade area.

Once again, it is quite natural that the States of Europe have at their disposal specialized organs for the problems that they have in common, in order to help formulate and, if need be, follow up their decisions; but the right to take these decisions is theirs alone. To ensure regular cooperation between the States of Western Europe is what France con-siders as desirable, possible, and practical in the political, economic, and cultural domains and in that of defense.

This requires organized, regular consultation between responsible Governments, and then the work of specialized organs in each of the common domains which are subordinate to the Governments. This requires periodic deliberations by an assembly formed of delegates from the national parliaments, and in my opinion, this will have to require, as soon as possible, a formal European referendum so as to give this launching of Europe the character of popular support and initiative that is indispensable.

As it happens the States of Europe have at present between them, in common, great means of action and also very great problems. As it happens, their former enmities are being reduced to minor proportions. In short, as it happens, the opportunity is at hand. Certainly, if this course is taken, if one can hope that we shall embark on it, ties will be increased and habits will take shape. Then, as time does its work, little by little, it is possible that new steps will be taken toward European unity.

Let me repeat, this is what France is proposing. It is all this and nothing else.

THE FALLACIES OF INTEGRATION

Two years later—on May 15, 1962—he returns to the same theme in order to reject in far more caustic terms the arguments in favor of the development of supranational organs.

In a world such as ours, where everything is permeated by the threat of a world conflict, the idea of a united Western Europe with sufficient strength, sufficient means, and sufficient cohesion to exist by itself—an idea such as this occurs quite naturally and all the more so as the enmities that had for centuries torn Europe apart, particularly the differences between Germany and France, have now come in an end. Suddenly, we perceive first of all, what may be termed the complementary character—from the geographic, strategic, economic, cultural, and other points of view—of the peoples of this part of the old continent, Western Europe; then, at the same time, the global capacity that they represent in terms of power, production, creativity, and trade, in relation to the general activity of the world; and, finally, the opportunities that their union would present to the two billion people that inhabit the underdeveloped countries. Such is the factual data that has led six States of the Continent to attempt to establish special bonds beween them.

Already during World War II, I shall take the liberty of recalling, I declared that this evolution was one of France's chief goals. Along this line, something positive has already been accomplished. It is the European Economic Community, which was created in principle by the Treaty of Rome and implemented, first of all, thanks to our economic and financial recovery of 1958–1959—for if we had not made this recovery, there could have been no enduring Community; implemented, secondly, thanks to the fact that last January we obtained the inclusion of agriculture in the Common Market and, correlatively, the agreement of the participants to move on to the second stage, in other

SOURCE: *Major Addresses, Statements, and Press Conferences of General Charles De Gaulle, May 19, 1958–January 31, 1964* (New York: French Embassy, Press and Information Service), pp. 173–177.

words, to real implementation. We thus have an economic organization of a kind that will lead to the gradual removal of trade barriers between the Six—a fact which is not failing to stimulate their efforts—while their respective production will gradually be adjusted and regulated, in such a way that the Common Market can, in orderly fashion, either absorb this production itself or else trade it with other countries. This is something; this is a great deal; but it is not everything.

In the French view, this economic construction is not enough. Western Europe—whether it be a matter of its action vis-à-vis other peoples, of its own defense, of its contribution to the development of regions that are in need of it, or of its duty to European balance and international détente—Western Europe must form itself politically. Moreover, if it did not succeed in doing so, the Economic Community itself could not in the long run become stronger or even continue to exist. In other words, Europe must have institutions that will lead it to form a political union, just as it is already a union in the economic sphere.

Thus France took the initiative of proposing such an organization and, as you know, last year in April the six Heads of State or of Government met in Paris to discuss France's project. They did so again in Bonn in July. Then a political commission was formed in Paris—the Fouchet Commission—which was given the task of drawing up the final text for a treaty of union. In the meantime, many bilateral and multilateral contacts were made on this subject. Finally it was agreed that there would be a summit meeting of the Six in Rome in order to conclude matters, should this be possible. You know the reasons why we have not yet succeeded.

What is it that France is proposing to her five partners? I shall repeat it once again: to organize ourselves politically, let us begin at the beginning. Let us organize our cooperation, let our Heads of State or of Government meet periodically to examine our problems together and to make decisions with regard to these problems which will be the decisions of Europe. Let us set up a political commission, a defense commission and a cultural commission, just as we have already formed an economic commission in Brussels which studies common questions and prepares the decision of the six Governments. Naturally the political commission and the others will proceed, in this regard, in conditions that are appropriate to their particular domains. Moreover, the Ministers in charge of these various fields will meet whenever necessary to implement in concert the decisions that will be taken by the Council. Finally, we have a European parliamentary assembly that meets in Strasbourg and is composed of delegations from our six national Parliaments. Let us enable this assembly to discuss common political questions as it already discusses economic questions. After we have tried it, we shall see, in three years' time, what we can do to strengthen our ties; but at least we shall have begun to acquire the habit of living and acting together. This is what France has proposed. She believes that this is the most practical thing that can be done.

• • •

I would like incidentally, since the opportunity has arisen, to point out to you, gentlemen of the press—and you are perhaps going to be very surprised by this—that I have never personally, in any of my statements, spoken of a "Europe of nations," although it is always being claimed that I have done so. It is not, of course, that I am repudiating my own; quite the contrary, I am more attached to France than ever, and I do not believe that Europe can have any living reality if it does not include France and her Frenchmen, Germany and its Germans, Italy and its Italians, and so forth. Dante, Goethe, Chateaubriand belong to all Europe to the very extent that they were respectively and eminently Italian, German, and French. They would not have served Europe very well if they had been stateless, or if they had thought and written in some kind of integrated Esperanto or Volapük.

But it is true that the nation is a human and sentimental element, whereas Europe can be built on the basis of active, authoritative, and responsible elements. What elements? The States, of course; for, in this respect, it is only the States that are valid, legitimate, and capable of achievement. I have already said, and I repeat, that at the present time there cannot be any other Europe than a Europe of States, apart, of course, from myths, stories, and parades. What is happening with regard to the Economic Community proves this every day, for it is the States, and only the States, that created this Economic Community, that furnished it with funds, that provided it with staff members; and it is the States that give it reality and efficiency, all the more so as it is impossible to take any far-reaching economic measure without committing a political action.

It is a political action, when tariffs are dealt with in common, when coal-mining areas are converted, when wages and social welfare funds are made the same in the six States, when each State allows workers from the five other States to settle on its territory, when decrees are consequently taken, and when Parliament is asked to vote necessary laws, funds, and sanctions. It is a political action when agriculture is included in the Common Market, and it is the six States, and they alone, that succeeded in doing so last January by means of their political bodies. It is a political action when the association of Greece or of the African States or of the Malagasy Republic is being dealt with.

It is a political action when one negotiates with Great Britain on the request that it has made to enter the Common Market. It is again a political action when the applications of other States for participation or association are considered. It is still a political action when one comes to consider the requests that the United States announces that it will make with regard to its economic relations with the Community.

In fact, the economic development of Europe cannot be assured without its political union and, in this regard, I want to point out the arbitrary nature of a certain idea that was voiced during the recent discussions in Paris and that claimed to keep economic matters out of the meetings of the heads of State or of Government, whereas, for each of them in their respective countries, economy is the constant and primary issue.

I should like to speak more particularly about the objection to integration. The objection is presented to us with the words, "Let us merge the six States into a supranational entity; this way, things will be quite simple and practical." But such an entity cannot be found without there being in Europe today a federator with sufficient power, authority, and skill. That is why one falls back on a type of hybird, in which the six States would undertake to comply with what will be decided upon by a certain majority. At the same time, although there are already six national Parliaments, plus the European Parliament, plus the Consultative Assembly of the Council of Europe—which did, it is true, predate the conception of the Six and which, I am told, is dying on the shore where it was abandoned—we must, it seems, elect yet another parliament, a so-called European one—which would lay down the law for the six States.

These are ideas that may, perhaps, beguile certain minds, but I certainly do not see how they could be carried out in practice, even if there were six signatures on the dotted line. Is there a France, a Germany, an Italy, a Holland, a Belgium, a Luxembourg, that would be ready—in a matter that is important for them from the national or the international point of view—to do something that they would consider bad because this would be dictated to them by others? Would the French people, the German people, the Italian people, the Dutch people, the Belgian people, or the Luxembourg people dream of submitting to laws voted by foreign deputies if these laws were to run contrary to their own deep-seated will? This is not so; there is no way, at the present time, for a foreign majority to be able to constrain recalcitrant nations. It is true that, in this "integrated" Europe, as they say, there would perhaps be no policy at all. This would simplify things a great deal. Indeed, once there would be no France and no Europe, once there would be no policy—since no one policy could be imposed on each of the six States—one would refrain from making any policies at all. But then, perhaps, this world would follow the lead of some outsider who did have a policy. There would perhaps be a federator, but the federator would not be European. And it would not be an integrated Europe, it would be something quite different, much broader and much more extensive with, I repeat, a federator. Perhaps it is this which, sometimes and to a certain degree, is at the basis of some remarks of such or such an advocate of European integration. In that case, it would be best to say so.

You see, when one's mind dwells on matters of great import, it is pleasant to dream of the marvelous lamp that Aladdin had only to rub in order to soar above the real. But there is no magic formula that will make it possible to build something as difficult as a united Europe. Thus, let us place reality at the basis of the edifice and, when we shall have completed the work, this will be the time for us to lull ourselves to sleep with the tales of *A Thousand and One Nights*.

A EUROPEAN EUROPE

Europe does not need either a "federator" or a "protector," De Gaulle says in 1964—thus rejecting all efforts on the part of the United States to promote European unity within NATO. Europe must become European, he warns the German leaders who, deeply concerned by De Gaulle's pronouncements, become particularly sensitive to the need of closer ties with the United States.

In discussing Europe and in trying to distinguish what it should be, it is always necessary to ascertain what the world is.

At the end of the last World War, the distribution of forces in the world was as simple, as brutal as possible. It appeared suddenly at Yalta. Only America and Russia had remained powers, and all the more considerable powers in that all the rest found themselves dislocated, the vanquished engulfed in their unconditional defeat and the European victors destroyed to their foundations.

For the countries of the free world, threatened by the Soviets' ambition, American leadership could then seem inevitable. The New

SOURCE: *Tenth Press Conference* (New York: French Embassy, Press and Information Service, July 23, 1964), pp. 3–7.

World was, of all of them, the great victor of the war. Under the command of the United States, owner of atomic bombs, the Atlantic Alliance ensured their security. Thanks to the Marshall Plan their economies were being revived. Wherever the colonial powers were effecting under more or less violent conditions, the transfer of their sovereignty to self-governing regimes, there pressure was felt, openly or not, from Washington. At the same time, America was seen to assume the conduct of political and strategic affairs in all the regions where the free world found itself in contact with the direct or indirect action of the Soviets. It did this either unilaterally or through the channels of regional international bodies which in practice were at its disposal: in Europe, NATO; in Western Asia, CENTO; in Southeast Asia, SEATO; in America, the OAS; or, thanks to its supremacy in the North Pacific, or, finally, through military or diplomatic intervention, in Korea, in the Congo, or during the Suez crisis through the offices of the United Nations Organization which it dominated by its preponderance.

It is clear that things have changed. The Western States of our old continent have rebuilt their economies. They are rebuilding their military forces. One of them—France—is becoming a nuclear power. Above all they have become aware of their natural ties. In short, Western Europe appears likely to constitute a major entity full of merit and resources, capable of living its own life, indeed not in opposition to the New World, but right alongside it.

On the other hand, the monolithic nature of the totalitarian world is in the process of dislocation. China, separated from Moscow, enters on the world scene by its mass, its needs, and its resources, avid for progress and consideration. The Soviet Empire, the last and the largest colonial power of this time, is seeing first the Chinese contest the domination it exercises over vast regions of Asia, and second is seeing the European satellites which it had subjugated by force moving further and further away. At the same time the Communist regime, despite the enormous effort it has been making in Russia for half a century and despite the results it has achieved in certain massive undertakings, is meeting with failure with respect to the standard of living, the satisfaction and the dignity of men in comparison with the system that applies in Western Europe which combines "dirigisme" with freedom. Lastly, great aspirations and great difficulties are deeply agitating the developing countries.

The result of all these new factors, complicated, and interrelated, is that the division of the world into two camps led by Washington and Moscow respectively corresponds less and less to the real situation.

With respect to the gradually splitting totalitarian world, or the problems posed by China, or the conduct to be adopted toward many countries of Asia, Africa, and Latin America, or the remodeling of the United Nations Organization that necessarily ensues, or the adjustment of world exchanges of all kinds, etc., it appears that Europe, provided that it wishes it, is henceforth called upon to play a role which is its own.

Undoubtedly it should maintain an alliance with America in which, in the North Atlantic, both are interested so long as the Soviet threat remains. But the reasons which, for Europe, made this alliance a form of subordination are fading away day by day. Europe must assume its share of the responsibilities. Everything indicates, moreover, that this event would be in accordance with the interest of the United States, whatever may be its merit, its power, and its good intentions. For the multiplicity and complexity of the tasks henceforth go beyond, and perhaps dangerously, its means and its capacity. That is why the United States declares that it wishes to see the old continent unite and organize itself while many among the Gallic, Germanic, and Latin people cry out "Let us build Europe!"

But which Europe? That is the question. Indeed, the established conveniences, the accepted renunciations, the deep-rooted reservations do not fade away easily. We French feel that it is a question of Europe's being made in order for it to be European. A European Europe means that it exists by itself for itself, in other words in the midst of the world it has its own policy. But that is precisely what is rejected consciously or unconsciously by some who claim, however, to want it to be established. In reality, the fact that Europe, not having a policy, would be subject to the policy that came to it from the other side of the Atlantic appears to them, even today, normal and satisfactory.

We have seen many people—quite often, what is more, worthy and sincere—advocate for Europe not an independent policy, which in reality they do not visualize, but an organization unsuited to have one, linked in this field, as in that of defense and the economy, to an Atlantic system, in other words American, and consequently subordinate to what the United States calls its leadership. This organization, entitled federal, would have had as its bases on the one hand a council of experts withdrawn from the affiliation to the States, and which would have been dubbed "executive"; and on the other hand a Parliament without national qualifications and which would have been called "legislative." Doubtless each of these two elements would have supplied that for which it would have been fitted, that is to say, studies for the council and debates for the Parliament. But, without a doubt, neither of the two would have made what indeed no one wanted them to make, that is, a policy . . .

A policy is an action, that is to say a body of decisions taken, of things done, of risks assumed, all this with the support of a people. The governments of nations alone can be capable of and responsible for making policy. It is of course not forbidden to imagine that a day will come when all the peoples of our continent will become one and that then there could be a Government of Europe, but it would be ridiculous to act as if that day had come.

That is why France—refusing to let Europe get bogged down, becoming bogged down herself in a guileful undertaking that would have stripped States, misled peoples, and prevented the independence of our continent—took the initiative of proposing to her five partners of the Rome Treaty a beginning for the organization of their cooperation. Thus we would begin to live in common, pending the time when habit and evolution would gradually draw the ties closer together. We know that the German Government adhered in principle to this project. We know that a meeting of the six States in Paris, then another one in Bonn, seemed at first on the road to success, but that Rome refused to call the decisive meeting, its objections, joined with those of The Hague and Brussels, being powerful enough to halt everything. Finally, we know that the opponents invoked two arguments, moreover contradictory. The first argument: the French plan, which maintains the sovereignty of the States, does not conform to our conception of a Europe having as its Executive a commission of experts, and as its Legislative a Parliament cut off from national realities. The second argument: although Britain does not agree to lose its sovereignty, we will not enter into any European political organization to which it would not belong.

The French plan for European organization not being adopted by Italy and by the Benelux countries; moreover, integration not being able to lead to anything other than an American protectorate; finally, Great Britain having shown throughout the interminable Brussels negotiations that it was not in a position to accept the common economic rules and, by the Nassau agreement, that its defense force, particularly in the nuclear domain, would not be European for lack of being autonomous in relation to the United States—it seemed to the Government of the Federal Republic of Germany and to the Government of the French Republic that their bilateral cooperation could have some value. It was then that, on the proposal of the German Government, the Franco-

German Treaty of January 22, 1963, was concluded, which I had the honor of signing right here with Chancellor Adenauer.

However, it must be noted that, if the Franco-German Treaty made possible limited results in some areas, also if it led the two Governments and their services to establish contacts which, for our part, and altogether, we judge can be useful and which are, in any case, very pleasant, up to now a common line of conduct has not emerged. As-suredly there is not, and there could not be any opposition, strictly speaking, between Bonn and Paris. But, whether it is a matter of the effective solidarity of France and Germany concerning their defense, or even of the stand to take and the action to pursue toward the East, above all the Moscow satellites, or correlatively of the question of boundaries and nationalities in Central and Eastern Europe, or of the recognition of China and of the diplomatic and economic mission which can be opened to Europe in relation to that great people, or of peace in Asia and particularly Indochina and Indonesia, or of the aid to give to the developing countries in Africa, Asia, and Latin America, or of the organization of the agricultural common market and consequently the future of the Community of the Six—one could not say that Germany and France have yet agreed to make together a policy and one could not dispute that this results from the fact that Bonn has not believed, up to now, that this policy should be European and independent. If this state of affairs were to last, there would be the risk, in the long run, of doubts among the French people, of misgivings among the German people and, among their four partners of the Rome Treaty, an increased tendency to leave things as they are, while waiting, perhaps, to be split up.

But, throughout the world, the force of things is doing its work. In wanting and in proposing the organization of a Europe having its own policy, France is sure of serving the balance, the peace, and progress of the world. Moreover, she is now strong enough and sure enough of herself to be able to be patient, except for major external changes which would jeopardize everything and therefore lead her to change her direction. Besides, at the last meeting just held between the Governments in Bonn and Paris, Chancellor Erhard gave an indication of a forthcoming German initiative. In waiting for the sky to clear, France is pursuing, by her own means, that which a European and independent policy can and should be. It is a fact that people everywhere are pleased with it and that for herself it is not an unsatisfactory situation.

8. THE ATLANTIC COMMUNITY

❖

The North Atlantic Treaty Organization agreement was signed in 1949 and has since been the basis of the defense of western Europe and North America. It binds the signatories to come to the aid of any member that is attacked, and establishes institutions that provide for continuing deliberations on matters of military policy and preparedness. Individual states place their national forces at the disposal of the organization so that they can be used by the Commander in Chief, whose headquarters are at Fontainebleau, south of Paris. Nuclear weapons (under American control) are available and conventional naval and ground units (including American forces) are deployed in Western Europe and the Mediterranean. The eastern Mediterranean is covered, thanks to the participation of Greece and Turkey. Western Germany became a member in 1954—with the right to rearm but not to manufacture nuclear weapons. In the light of American predominance in nuclear weapons the American government has made every effort to encourage the allies to develop conventional forces so that these could be used to contain any Soviet aggressive thrust, thus providing a pause before nuclear arms could come into play.

De Gaulle was absent from the political scene when NATO was signed, and remained out of all deliberations and plans until he returned to power. Time after time he stated that the Atlantic Alliance was a necessity, but at the same time he made it clear that he envisaged its organization, operation, and purpose in different terms. In the famous Memorandum of September 23, 1958, to which we have already referred, he argued for a genuine tripartite direction of NATO to assume responsibility for the Atlantic Community, including its global interests and commit-

168

ments. This directorate, composed of France, England, and the United States, was to be the controlling group within NATO—to deliberate on military policy, pool military resources, provide for a division of labor in theaters of command, and act in unison on the basis of common strategic decisions and agreements. This would apply to the use of all types of weapons, with the proviso that each member would be in the last analysis free to use these weapons for the defense of its own territory. Such a formulation struck hard at the American position that nuclear weapons, even when located on European sites, could be used only with the permission of the Americans and, secondly, that NATO was not an alliance with global responsibilities, but was limited to a certain area. The United States claimed to be free to act alone in other parts of the world.

De Gaulle realized that the situation expressed in classic terms the existing balance of power in favor of the United States, but was unwilling to allow it to become a permanent pattern. First there was the question of changing conditions—when the NATO treaty was signed the European nations were impoverished, unarmed, and on the brink of internal disorder. In 1958 this was no longer true. Second, when the NATO treaty was signed the United States alone held the power of nuclear destruction; after 1958 the use of American weapons upon Soviet territory could provoke retaliation which would in turn destroy North America. Third, the location of American controlled nuclear weapons on European soil could tempt the Russians to destroy them, thus making Europe a holocaust while sparing the territories of the two major adversaries. The atomic guarantee of the United States was thus weakened and the European countries—especially France—were left without their own means of riposte if their territories were attacked. These three basic considerations account for De Gaulle's first gradual and then outspoken opposition to the existing NATO arrangements. Underlying these considerations was the belief that the Soviet danger was not what it had been in 1949 and that therefore it was possible to assume an increasing liberty and independence vis-à-vis the United States.

When in 1960 the first French atomic bomb was exploded, and when further tests gave grounds for belief that some French atomic weapons were to some degree operational, the compelling need for American protection was lost and with it the argument in favor of American control of NATO forces. France now had her own deterrent with which she could not only protect herself but also give some pledge of protection to her European allies. The whole logic of NATO had therefore changed so completely that De Gaulle seemed determined to drastically overhaul the alliance or to withdraw from it. This was virtually explicitly stated in his press conference of September 9, 1965.

THE NEED FOR DIVISION OF LABOR

When it became clear that the United States was unwilling to seriously entertain the possibility of a NATO directorate consisting of France, England, and the United States, as suggested in his memorandum of September 23, 1958, De Gaulle decided to withdraw the Mediterranean Fleet from the NATO Command. On March 25, 1959, he gave his reasons.

This is neither the time nor the place to set forth France's position on how world security and the Atlantic Alliance should be organized. Today I merely state that the zone of possible NATO action does not extend south of the Mediterranean. The Middle East, North Africa, Black Africa, the Red Sea, etc., are not a part of it. Who can deny that France may possibly find herself obliged to act in these different areas? She would therefore have to act independently of NATO. But how could she do so if her fleet were not available? Without her fleet, how could she carry on any type of action in the regions that I have just referred to?

I observe, furthermore, that the two other great world powers of the Atlantic Alliance—the United States and Great Britain—have taken steps to prevent the greater part of their naval forces from being integrated into NATO. I add that Americans and British have kept in their hands alone the principal element of their strength, their atomic bombers.

The fact that France has resumed the power to dispose of her own fleet certainly would not prevent her from using it, should the occasion arise, in a common battle in the Mediterranean. Thus there is nothing in this change that might weaken the Alliance. Quite the contrary.

SOURCE: *Major Addresses, Statements, and Press Conferences of General Charles De Gaulle, May 19, 1958–January 31, 1964* (New York: French Embassy, Press and Information Service), p. 49.

Indeed, I believe that the Alliance will be all the more vital and strong as the great powers unite on the basis of a cooperation in which each carries its own load, rather than on the basis of an integration in which peoples and governments find themselves more or less deprived of their roles and responsibilities in the domain of their own defense.

DEFENSE: A NATIONAL PROBLEM

On September 5, 1960, De Gaulle expounded his favorite theme —defense is a national problem and integrative schemes therefore impair national defense.

It is more than ten years since the Atlantic Alliance was organized in its present form. At that time, as I remember, the burning question, the immediate question, was merely the security of Europe. So we made an alliance limited to Europe, and one with a very narrow field of action. And furthermore, at that same time it appeared that the United States alone had the means for defense and that the States of Western Europe, of Continental Europe at least, found themselves in a political, economic, and social position, of which the best that can be said was that it was uncertain. Moreover, these States postponed the revival of their personality in the international sphere until a much later date, if they did not renounce it altogether. So the Alliance was set up on the basis of integration, that is to say, of a system whereby the defense of each of the countries of Continental Europe, of Western Europe—not counting England—does not have a national character; a system in which, in fact, everything is under the command of the Americans and in which the Americans decide on the use of the principal weapons, in other words, the atomic weapons.

But during the past ten years, much has changed. First of all, it became evident that the possibilities of conflict, and consequently of military operations, were spreading far beyond Europe, were spreading all over the world. It became evident that the Middle East and Africa, in particular, were danger spots quite as much as Europe, and that there existed, between the principal members of the Atlantic Alliance, political differences concerning them which, if the occasion arose, might turn into disagreements on strategy. Then, too, the countries of Continental Europe, France in particular—we may be allowed to say

SOURCE: *Major Addresses, Statements, and Press Conferences of General Charles De Gaulle, May 19, 1958–January 31, 1964* (New York: French Embassy, Press and Information Service), pp. 95–97.

so—regained their balance and began to prosper once more, and consequently as this occurred they regained awareness of themselves, especially where their defense was concerned. Finally one of them—you know which one—began to build an atomic arsenal of its own. Now under these circumstances, France considers that what was done ten years ago within this limited field and on the single, exclusive basis of integration must be brought up to date. I shall naturally speak only of the points in which France is directly interested. As for the other countries, if one day there is a general confrontation, they will speak for themselves.

With regard to France, there are at least two points on which the treaty must be revised. Moreover, you know that when the Treaty of the North Atlantic Organization was drawn up, its text specified that it could be revised at the end of ten years, and the ten years have elapsed.

What are the two essential points for France? The first, as I have indicated, is the limitation of the Alliance to the single area of Europe. We feel that, at least among the world powers of the West, there must be something organized—where the Alliance is concerned—as to their political conduct and, should the occasion arise, their strategic conduct outside Europe, especially in the Middle East, and in Africa, where these three powers are constantly involved. Furthermore, if there is no agreement among the principal members of the Atlantic Alliance on matters other than Europe, how can the Alliance be indefinitely maintained in Europe? This must be remedied.

The second point on which France thinks there should be a change is that of integration in the defense of Europe. It seems to us that the defense of a country, while being of course combined with that of other countries, must have a national character. How indeed in the long run could a Government, a Parliament, a people give their money and their services with all their heart in time of peace, and make their sacrifices in time of war, for a system in which they are not responsible for their own defense? That is why from this point of view as well, a revival of the Alliance seems indispensable to us. Moreover, as you know, we have already taken a few steps in this direction. That is why, for example, France keeps her fleet directly under her own orders. For exactly what is a fleet? It is a means of distant action. And how could it be imagined that France would leave this means of distant action to the discretion of an exclusively European organization which has nothing to do with Africa, while she herself, through her interests and her responsibilities, is continually involved in Africa?

Furthermore, France feels that if atomic weapons are to be stockpiled on her territory, these weapons should be in her own hands. Given the nature of these weapons and the possible consequences of their use, France obviously can not leave her own destiny and even her own life to the discretion of others.

This is what France understands by the reform of the Atlantic Organization, while repeating that there is certainly no question, of course, of separating from each other, for never has the Atlantic Alliance met such a great need.

CHANGING CONDITIONS AND NATO

On April 11, 1961, De Gaulle returns to a comprehensive discussion of changing world conditions, about which he expects to talk with President Kennedy during the latter's trip to Paris.

I cannot anticipate what President Kennedy and I will say to each other. In any case, on the question of the Atlantic Alliance, I can repeat and clarify what I have already said.

No one is more convinced than I that it is necessary for the free peoples to be allied in case of a conflict between East and West. Of course, this applies particularly to those who are on one or the other side of the Atlantic. What I question, therefore, is not the Atlantic Alliance, but the present organization of the Atlantic Alliance.

Everyone feels that a change is necessary, and with regard to this change I can say that, in my view, it must take into account three essential points.

First, the right and the duty of the European continental powers to have their own national defense. It is intolerable for a great State to leave its destiny up to the decisions and action of another State, however friendly it may be. In addition, it happens that, in integration —for it is integration that I mean—the integrated country loses interest in its national defense, since it is not responsible for it. The whole structure of the Alliance then loses its resilience and its strength. And what would it be like in timee of war?

Another point: it is necessary to clarify thoroughly the question of the use of nuclear weapons by the two Western powers which possess them, and also the question of the use of their other arms. For the European States of the continent, which are by far the most exposed, must

SOURCE: *Major Addresses, Statements, and Press Conferences of General Charles De Gaulle, May 19, 1958–January 31, 1964* (French Embassy, Press and Information Service), pp. 123–124.

know exactly with which weapons and under which conditions their overseas allies would join them in battle.

Finally, the third point: since the Atlantic Alliance was created, the threats of war are no longer limited to Europe. They extend over the entire world, Africa and Asia in particular. Under these conditions the Atlantic Alliance, in order to endure, must be extended to all these new fields. If it did not do so, it would lose the basic, the close solidarity between its members, which is indispensable to it. If it does so, then it must revise its organization which does not encompass these extra-European questions.

We shall soon have, I repeat, the great honor and the great pleasure of seeing President Kennedy. I suppose that this is one of the subjects which we will discuss as good friends and good allies.

THE NEED TO OVERHAUL

These changing conditions call for drastic reform of NATO. As far as France is concerned, the immediate course of action is to put her Army under direct national command.

The Atlantic Alliance exists. So long as the Soviets threaten the world, this alliance must be maintained. France is an integral part of it. If the free world were attacked, on the old or the new continent, France would take part in the common defense of the coasts of her allies and with all the means that she has.

Having made this statement—which is indisputable—there is within the Atlantic Alliance a certain military organization, NATO, which was built thirteen years ago, in conditions which are greatly changed today. Since that time, a certain number of new elements have appeared on the scene and one has only to mention them in order to make everyone understand that, with regard to the defense of France, the problem is no longer what it was in the past. At the beginning, America, and to a certain extent Great Britain, were the only countries in the world with nuclear weapons. Then Western Europe found it most expedient to turn over to the United States the responsibility for its protection, granted the fact that the American bombs would suffice to prevent any aggressive action that might be launched against Europe. In exchange, Western Europe—or at least continental Western Europe—turned over

SOURCE: *Major Addresses, Statements, and Press Conferences of General Charles De Gaulle, May 19, 1958–January 31, 1964* (New York: French Embassy, Press and Information Service), pp. 179–181.

to the United States the command of its forces, and, thereby, its defense policy and strategy. This is what was termed integration. On this basis, America transported a part of its atomic weapons to Europe and organized an expeditionary corps there. At the same time, it kept for itself enormous capabilities for using them should the occasion arise, wherever it may arise, according to the circumstances.

England, for its part, set aside certain land and air units for the defense of Europe, and it reserved the rest for itself.

In the case of France, it was agreed at that time that everything which she possessed in Europe belonged to NATO. Only, since the major part of her military resources were committed overseas, her direct contribution was fairly limited. But, since then, new elements of an extraordinary dimension have been introduced into the picture, and France must take them into consideration. First, Soviet Russia also now has an enormous nuclear arsenal which is increasing every day, as moreover, is that of the United States. Henceforth, America and Soviet Russia will be capable of striking each other directly and, doubtless, of reciprocally destroying each other. It is not certain that they will take this risk. No one can tell today when, how, or why one or the other of these great atomic powers would employ its nuclear arsenal. It is enough to say this in order to understand that, as regards the defense of France, the battle of Europe and even a world war as they were imagined when NATO was born, everything is now in question. On the other hand, a French atomic deterrent force is coming into existence and is going to grow continuously. It is a relatively modest force, it is true, but one which is changing and will completely change the conditions of our own defense, those of our intervention in faraway lands and those of the contribution that we would be able to make to the safeguard of our allies. Furthermore, the gradual return of our military forces from Algeria is enabling us to acquire a modernized army; an army which is not, I daresay, destined to play a separate or isolated role, but one which must and can play a role that would be France's own. Finally, it is absolutely necessary, morally and politically, for us to make our army a more integral part of the nation. Therefore, it is necessary for us to restation it, for the most part, on our soil; for us to give it once again a direct responsibility in the external security of the country; in short, for our defense to become once again a national defense. It is indispensable, I repeat, both morally and politically.

Without further developing the new elements of the problem, it will be understood that they lead us to make far-reaching changes in what we have done in this respect up to now.

9. GERMANY—THE
PERENNIAL PROBLEM

⚜

In the ruins of Germany in 1944 De Gaulle already saw the beginnings of a new situation that might end the secular rivalry with France and possibly lead to a new European equilibrium. But at the time a policy of reconciliation was unrealistic and impossible. De Gaulle therefore turned to the Soviet Union. In 1958, however, the defeated and truncated enemy was back on its feet, with an economy more powerful and a population larger than that of France. Thus West Germany became in his eyes the basis of a European system—but also a pawn to be manipulated by France in her designs to assume the leadership of Europe. In one of his first press conferences, De Gaulle firmly supported the status quo for Germany and Berlin, because "Germany does not threaten us today." He was willing to consider "neutralization" only if the Soviet troops also withdrew to the Urals. He also advocated slow and gradual communications and exchanges between the two parts of Germany until a viable solution could be found. He stood squarely behind the Atlantic Alliance "which is unimaginable without the participation of France" in pledging France's readiness to defend and fight with her allies for the preservation of the status quo in Berlin. When in 1962 the United States and England undertook conversations with the Soviet Union on the status of Berlin, De Gaulle appeared to be more adamant than any of his allies. He could not "object" of course to the American efforts, but he felt that the time for a change of the status of Berlin or Germany was inopportune and he declared that the unity of Europe depended upon the solidarity between Germany and France. In 1963 this solidarity was solemnly reasserted, and while England was unceremoniously declared to be a non-European power, a treaty be-

176

tween West Germany and France was signed, providing for common cooperation on a variety of crucial issues. Its text is reproduced below (pp. 186–191).

In De Gaulle's words, Germany continued to be the "burning issue of the world." It certainly appeared to be so for the Soviet Union and the United States. Both had vied for the control of Germany, finally leaving it divided and failing to reach a definitive peace settlement. Both seemed willing to reconsider a settlement when De Gaulle assumed the role of the staunchest supporter of the status quo. The offer of French cooperation was of course most welcome to Germany, but when De Gaulle phrased it in an exclusive manner, it became apparent to many German statesmen that American protection was worth even more. When De Gaulle appeared to intimate that the Franco-German rapprochement was to be made at the expense of NATO, serious misgivings developed both in Germany and the United States. The result, naturally, was a sharper conflict between France and the United States and a serious reassessment on the part of West German and American leaders of relations between the two countries—a relationship which at the economic and military levels has since grown more intimate. De Gaulle's effort appeared therefore doomed when he produced his last trump. In the same manner that he had excluded England from the Common Market, primarily because of the intimate military relations between Britain and the United States, he criticized German dependence upon the United States and German endorsement of the MLF arrangements. Furthermore, he declared on February 4, 1965, that the solution of the German problem after all was a European problem to be solved by Germany's neighbors, in particular France and the Soviet Union. In other words, from a defender of the German status quo when modifications were considered by the United States and the Soviet Union, he became a revisionist when the same matter was to be arranged between France and the Soviet Union. This amounted indirectly to a threat to West Germany if it continued its cooperation with the United States.

This classic maneuver, in which professions of support alternate with threats, is bound in the last analysis to undermine

what De Gaulle professes to be his objective—European unity
based on a close Franco-German rapprochement. The former
enemy and present ally, with the power it represents, continues
to be a thorny problem in Gaullist diplomacy.

THE DEFENDER OF THE STATUS QUO UNLESS . . .

The first clear statement of the new Gaullist policy vis-à-vis
West Germany came in De Gaulle's first press conference, on
March 25, 1959, in which he appears to be the staunchest de-
fender of the status quo for Berlin.

The crisis opened by Soviet Russia on the subject of Berlin plunges
the world into grave anxiety.

Three closely related questions are put by Moscow:

—The possibility of measures which would raise an obstacle to the
movement of American, British, and French military units between West
Berlin and the Western zone.

—The destiny of the German people, which would be profoundly
affected by the formal separation of Germany into two states and by
the fact that the former capital of the Reich would become incorporated
in territories under totalitarian dictatorship or subjected to conditions
which would lend to this servitude.

—Finally, neutralization of a zone in Europe of which Germany would
be an essential part.

Let us add that the Soviet Government, in pressing the West to open
negotiations on the fate of Berlin and on a peace treaty with the two
Germanies, made it known that it envisaged transferring its rights and
responsibilities regarding the city to the Pankow [East German] authorities. In this case, the goings and comings of American, British, and
French forces would have to be made in agreement with Pankow, a
situation which Washington, London, and Paris would find themselves
forced to recognize.

Should the Western powers see the way barred to them and should
they want to open it by force, they would come up against Soviet
troops stationed in East Germany who, we have been told, are "not
there to play marbles."

SOURCE: *Major Addresses, Statements, and Press Conferences of
General Charles De Gaulle, May 19, 1958–January 31, 1963* (New
York: French Embassy, Press and Information Service), pp. 41–44.

This being so, it might be thought that France wishes to profit from the crisis and, joining the move to split the German people, ensure for herself, at the expense of that country, advantages parallel to those which the Soviet Union seems to wish to seize for itself. That is a policy that others have been able to practice toward an unfortunate neighbor.

It is not our policy. If the present Germany seemed dangerous to us, then no doubt the memory of trials suffered by its actions and the desire to prevent their recurrence would motivate our demands. But Germany, as it is, in no way threatens us. We even think that with its capabilities, its energy, its resources, it constitutes an essential element in the life and progress of Europe and the whole world.

Even more, as is normal for two old adversaries who have given up fighting and destroying each other, France and Germany have resolved to cooperate. On this point, the policy of Chancellor Adenauer coincides with ours. Quite recently, Mr. Segni assured me that it was also that of Italy.

We shall thus support nothing which would be such as to lead the German people to despair or to compromise its peaceful future or to wreck the hope which, after so many shocks and tears, has arisen on both sides of the Rhine.

One might think, on the other hand, that France might consider keeping out of the quarrel. Being without means of action, that is to say of destruction, equal to those in the hands of the Americans and the Russians, and thus, without the power to try and impose her policy, she might endeavor to keep outside the conflict and, should it come to that, out of the war. This would amount to France, in an attempt to keep her life, giving up her reasons for living. But also this would be to destroy the Atlantic Alliance, an alliance which is unimaginable without the participation of France.

Thus nothing except atomic war could prevent Soviet domination from spreading over all Europe and all Africa, before it went on to cover the rest of the world. After which, the human race, or as much of it as would have survived, would everywhere be given up to the oppression of dictatorship and to the frightful upheavals brought about by dictatorial trends and leaders.

We prefer to maintain the Alliance until the day when the future of peace is assured.

We hold it necessary in the first place that America, Britain, and France should not agree to allow anyone to put obstacles in the way of the comings and goings of their troops to and from Berlin. As a result of the victory, as well as of arrangements concluded in the past with Soviet Russia, the three powers have the right of passage. If anybody opposes this, they and all others who might come to support them would commit an act of hostility toward the Western powers and would thus be responsible for the clashes which could follow.

As regards the fate of the city itself, we note that those of its inhabitants who have the opportunity to express their views are unanimous in wishing it to stay Western. For this reason and for others, we would not allow West Berlin to be given up to the Pankow regime.

Furthermore, we are not prepared to recognize this regime as a sovereign and independent state because it could not have been born and could not exist except by virtue of the Soviet occupation and because of an implacable dictatorship.

From the point of view of the foreign relations of the French Republic, we cannot put on the same level, on the one hand, this arbitrary construction and on the other, the German Federal Republic, where citizens say, read, and hear what they like, come and go as they please and, in complete freedom, elect their representatives and their government.

The reunification of the two parts into a single Germany which would be entirely free seems to us the normal destiny of the German people, provided they do not reopen the question of their present frontiers to the west, the east, the north, and the south, and that they move toward integrating themselves one day in a contractual organization of all Europe for cooperation, liberty, and peace.

But, pending the time when this ideal can be achieved, we believe that the two separated sections of the German people should be able to multiply the ties and relations between themselves in all practical fields. Transport, communications, economic activity, literature, science, the arts, the goings and comings of people, etc., would be the subject of arrangements which would bring together the Germans within and for the benefit of that which I would call "Germanness" and which after all is common to them, in spite of differences in regimes and conditions.

As regards turning Germany into a neutralized territory, this "extrication" or "disengagement" in itself has no meaning for us which is of any value. For if disarmament did not cover a zone which is as near to the Urals as it is to the Atlantic, how would France be protected? What then, in case of conflict, would prevent an aggressor from crossing by a leap or a flight the undefended German no man's land?

What narrow strip would remain between the Meuse and the ocean, in which to deploy and use the means of the West? Certainly, we are supporters of the control and limitation of all weapons of war. But, in order for these measures, apparently humanitarian, not to risk leading to our disappearance, they must cover an area deep enough and large enough for France to be covered and not, on the contrary, exposed.

On these different subjects and on others, I do not see, for my part, any objection of principle to the opening of negotiations, whatever precedents there may or may not have been. M. Couve de Murville would thus attend a conference of foreign ministers, should one be held.

If it were to develop that that conference, after thorough examination of the problems, succeeded in sifting out the elements of an agreement on important points, then, with Premier Michel Debré at my side, I could myself take part in a meeting of those charged with the supreme responsibilities of the great powers.

But it is clear that, in order to achieve something worthwhile, it is necessary to prepare the topics for discussion in such a forum, and discussions must be carried out in a peaceful atmosphere. In this matter, I am in complete agreement with what President Eisenhower said recently.

On this serious occasion, France feels qualified to speak clearly and calmly. First of all, because she has no feeling of competition or animosity toward the Russian people. Quite the contrary, she has a real and traditional friendship. In the next place, for the reason that in the matter of Germany, which is the stake in the crisis, she has been able to master her grievances and, taking into account the changes which have occurred there, to consider this country not as an enemy, but as a partner.

Lastly, because France herself does not yet have atomic bombs, and, unlike the three others, is not subject to the obsession of launching her bombs before those of the adversary have been able to accomplish their mission. In short, France looks at the present crisis in her own way, with clarity and even with impartiality.

That is why, speaking in her name, I am sure of speaking the thoughts of more than two billion human beings who think as she does. Because of, and in comparison with, the risks run by our species and the immense human tasks that we could and should accomplish in common, any summons which might be addressed to the West with a view to forcing a decision by intimidation would be hateful and absurd. When, in both camps, everything is arranged so that means of destruction, capable of annihilating continents, could be unleashed in the space of a few seconds—at a time like that, creating a state of tension, such that any error, any incident might unleash the cataclysm, would be tantamount to presenting the very existence of humanity with an unpardonable challenge.

When two thirds of the inhabitants of the earth lead a miserable existence, while certain peoples have at their disposal what is necessary to ensure the progress of all—what is the use of the dangerous wrangling over West Berlin, the [East] German Democratic Republic and German disengagement?

For, in our time, the only quarrel worthwhile is that of mankind. It is mankind that must be saved, made to live and enabled to advance.

A CLEAR EYE AND A FIRM HEART

This stand was reiterated in the most unequivocal terms on September 5, 1961.

One may, indeed, wonder why the Soviets have suddenly used the pretext of Berlin in order to demand that the city's status be changed, by will or by force; one may also wonder why this Berlin situation, which has seemed tolerable to them for the past sixteen years and which they themselves organized and set up with the United States and Great Britain at the Potsdam meeting at which France, moreover, was not present—one can also wonder why, suddenly, this situation seems intolerable to them. One may wonder why they are suddenly mixing their demands with frightening threats. One may wonder if there is someone who truly believes that the Federal German Republic, such as it is, is a danger to the present Russia. And one may finally wonder if there is a Soviet citizen who believes this when the Kremlin states that it is in a position to crush totally, immediately, under bombs equivalent to 100 million tons of TNT, whoever would raise his hand against the Communist world.

Actually, there is in this uproar of imprecations and demands organized by the Soviets something so arbitrary and so artificial that one is led to attribute it either to the premeditated unleashing of frantic ambitions, or to the desire of drawing attention away from great difficulties: this second hypothesis seems all the more plausible to me since, despite the coercions, isolation, and acts of force in which the Communist system encloses the countries which are under its yoke,

SOURCE: *Major Addresses, Statements, and Press Conferences of General Charles De Gaulle, May 19, 1958–January 31, 1964* (New York: French Embassy, Press and Information Service), pp. 140–142.

and despite certain collective successes which it has achieved by drawing upon the substance of its subjects, actually its gaps, its shortages, its internal failures, and above that its character of inhuman oppression, are felt more and more by the elites and the masses, whom it is more and more difficult to deceive and to subjugate.

And then, also, the satellites that the Soviet regime holds under its sway are feeling to an increasing degree in their national sentiment the element of cruelty in the annexation which they have suffered. It may then be understood that, under these circumstances, the Soviets consider that the Berlin question may be a suitable opportunity to deceive themselves and to deceive others. And, in fact, where Berlin is located, it is relatively easy for them to make demonstrations on the spot, and the measures of restraint which they are taking involve limited risks for them. And, in addition, they may think that the United States, England, and France, will allow themselves to be somewhat discouraged and somewhat resigned, and therefore that the retreat of these three powers will deal a serious blow to the Atlantic Alliance; that, above all, throughout the world, it will look as if the totalitarian regime, the totalitarian camp in the face of an uncertain and divided West, is clearly the stronger.

But, in fact, this is not true. Admittedly the Soviets possess terrible nuclear weapons, but the Western powers also have some formidable ones. If world conflict were to break out, the use of forces of destruction would undoubtedly result, in particular, in the complete disruption of Russia and the countries which are a prey to Communism. What is the good of ruling over dead men? And then, in addition, the rule itself would also come to an end because in this disaster the framework would be broken, the framework of a regime which only keeps going by means of an authoritarian mechanism, a rigidly planned and relentlessly imposed police rule. This, moreover, the Soviet leaders are aware of despite all their boasting.

Then the Western powers have no reason not to consider the Soviet demonstrations with a clear eye and a firm heart. It is true, I repeat, that on the spot, in Berlin, the act of force which would be undertaken could bring some advantage to the Soviets, as it would obviously be difficult for the Western powers to act from such a distance on the soil and in the sky of the former German capital. But the Western powers could well fight back on the seas and in the skies traveled by Soviet ships and planes, which would also be far from their bases. There would then be an exchange of wrongdoings which undoubtedly would not end to the benefit of the Soviets. In short, if the Soviets want to reduce the positions and cut the communications of the Allies in Berlin, by force, the Allies must maintain by force their positions and their communications. Clearly one thing leads to another, as they say, and if all this tends to multiply the hostile acts committed by the Soviets, to which we shall be obliged to reply, we may end up with a general war. But then, this would be what the Soviets deliberately wanted, and in that case any retreat has the effect of overexciting the aggressor, of pushing him to redouble his pressure and, finally, to facilitate and hasten his assaults. To sum up, the Western powers have no better means of serving world peace at present than to remain resolute and firm.

Does this mean that the two camps must oppose each other forever? This is by no means what France believes, because it would really be extremely foolish and extremely costly. If world conflict is to break out, then modern technical progress will have led to death. If that is not the case, we must try to make peace. Let the Soviets stop issuing threats. Let them help ease the situation instead of hindering it. Let them encourage a peaceful international atmosphere instead of creating a suffocating one. Then it will be possible for the three Western powers to study all the world problems with them and, in particular, that of Germany.

In that case, France could be counted upon to put forth solutions. Indeed France—who, for her part, is not prepared to give way before the threats of the totalitarian empire—nonetheless retains a deep and sincere friendship for the countries which live in this empire. Furthermore, France believes that the future of modern civilization can lie only in the understanding, then the cooperation and, finally, the osmosis between the countries that created civilization and continue to create it, and which have spread it throughout the world and continue to spread it and, above all, the osmosis of all the European peoples. That is how I can answer you.

BETTER COOPERATION

Early in 1963 De Gaulle presented his thesis that European unity and the revival of western Europe as a world power should be based upon Franco-German cooperation.

SOURCE: *Major Addresses, Statements, and Press Conferences of General Charles De Gaulle, May 19, 1958–January 31, 1964* (New York: French Embassy, Press and Information Service), pp. 219–221.

Among the new elements that are in the process of shaping the world at present, I believe that there is none more striking and more fruitful than the Franco-German fact. Two great peoples, which have for so long and so terribly opposed and fought each other, are now turning toward each other with the same impulse of sympathy and understanding. It is not only a question of a reconciliation demanded by circumstances. What is happening in reality is a kind of mutual discovery of two neighbors, each noticing the extent to which the other is valid, worthy, and attractive.

It is from this then that springs the desire for a rapprochement manifest everywhere in the two countries which conforms with reality and which commands politics, because for the first time in many generations, the Germans and Gauls realize their solidarity. This solidarity exists obviously from the standpoint of their security, since the same threat of foreign domination confronts them and because their territories constitute a single strategic area. It exists from the economic standpoint because for each of them, mutual trade is an essential and preponderant element. It exists from the standpoint of their cultural influence and development, for in thought, philosophy, science, the arts and technology they are complementary.

And now the voice of the peoples makes it heard that these currents deeply reflect something decisive and, without a doubt, something historic. Already, when President Luebke, in our capital, and later when Chancellor Adenauer, officially in Paris and in the Provinces, visited France there arose from our people such homage and such testimony that there could be no doubt about the completely new course—to say the least—that feelings in our country had taken. When I myself, last September, had the honor of bearing the greetings of the French people to Germany, when I was received in Bonn, Cologne, Düsseldorf, Duisburg, Hamburg, Munich, Stuttgart, and other cities, all those who were able to see and hear were overwhelmed by the elemental and extraordinary outburst of enthusiasm displayed then in favor of the friendship of Germany and France, of the union of Europe as they both wish it and of their common action in the world. I for my part —I must admit—I was touched by it to the very depths of my soul and strengthened in my conviction that the new policy of Franco-German relations is based on an incomparable popular basis.

Now, all along this policy has been—we must pay him this tribute— that of Chancellor Adenauer. This great statesman has never ceased to think and proclaim that Franco-German cooperation was an absolute necessity for the life and modern development of the two countries;

that it was also the condition and the very basis of the construction of Europe; and finally that it was at present the most basic factor in the security of our continent and perhaps, in the future, a factor of balance and peace among the nations that people our continent from East to West. Since we think in exactly the same way, the Governments in Bonn and Paris did not have much difficulty in reaching an agreement to establish closer relations in the political, economic, cultural, and defense sectors.

The Franco-German meeting that will shortly be held here will permit us, we most sincerely hope, to organize our cooperation better than it is organized already. It goes without saying that there is nothing there that either resembles or tends toward the building up between Germany and France of some kind of exclusive community. The two countries have decided and are committed to being an integral part of Europe, such as it is built on the basis of the Rome Treaty. Moreover, it is absolutely impossible to see how the more effective rapprochement between the French and German peoples would in any way whatsoever harm the fraternity of Italy and France, a fraternity that is two thousand years old and which is today more alive than ever, or harm the close links that the centuries have forged between us and Belgium, the Netherlands, and Luxembourg.

But it is true that by tightening their cooperation, Germany and France are setting an example which may be useful to the cooperation of everyone.

THE TREATY

This cooperation within a few days became embodied in a treaty, the text of which is reproduced below.

THE COMMON DECLARATION AND THE TREATY BETWEEN THE FRENCH REPUBLIC AND THE FEDERAL REPUBLIC OF GERMANY OF JANUARY 22, 1963

COMMON DECLARATION

General Charles De Gaulle, President of the French Republic, and Dr. Konrad Adenauer, Chancellor of the Federal Republic of Germany,

At the close of the conference which was held in Paris on January 21 and 22, 1963 and which was attended, on the French side, by the Premier, the Minister of Foreign Affairs, the Minister of the Armed

SOURCE: French Embassy, Press and Information Service, 1963.

Forces, and the Minister of National Education and, on the German side, by the Minister of Foreign Affairs, the Minister of Defense, and the Minister of Family and Youth Affairs,

Convinced that the reconciliation of the German people and the French people, bringing an end to the age-old rivalries, constitutes a historic event which profoundly transforms the relations of the two peoples,

Conscious of the solidarity which unites the two peoples both with respect to their security and with respect to their economic and cultural development,

Observing particularly that young people have become aware of this solidarity and find themselves called upon to play the determinant role in the consolidation of Franco-German friendship,

Recognizing that a strengthening of the cooperation between the two countries constitutes a vital stage along the road to a united Europe, which is the goal of the two peoples,

Have agreed to the organization and to the principles of the cooperation between the two States as they are stated in the Treaty signed this day.

THE TREATY

Following the Common Declaration of the President of the French Republic and the Chancellor of the Federal Republic of Germany, dated January 22, 1963, on the organization and the principles of the cooperation between the two States, the following provisions have been agreed upon:

I—Organization

1. The Heads of State and of Government will give whenever required the necessary directives and will follow regularly the implementation of the program set hereinunder. They will meet for this purpose whenever this is necessary and, in principle, at least twice a year.

2. The Ministers of Foreign Affairs will see to the implementation of the program as a whole. They will meet at least once every three months. Without prejudice to the contacts normally established through the channels of the embassies, high officials of the two Ministries of Foreign Affairs, responsible respectively for political, economic and cultural affairs, will meet each month in Paris and Bonn alternately to survey current problems and to prepare the Ministers' meeting. In addition, the diplomatic missions and the consulates of the two countries, and also the permanent missions to the international organiza-

tions, will make all the necessary contacts on problems of common interest.

3. Regular meetings will take place between the responsible authorities of the two countries in the fields of defense, education and youth. These meetings will not in any way affect the functioning of the already existing bodies—Franco-German Cultural Commission, Permanent General Staff Group—whose activities will on the contrary be extended. Both the Ministers of Foreign Affairs will be represented at these meetings in order to ensure the overall coordination of the cooperation.

(a) The Ministers of the Armed Forces or of Defense will meet at least once every three months. Similarly, the French Minister of National Education will meet, at the same intervals, with the person who will be designated by Germany to follow up the program of cooperation on the cultural level.

(b) The Chiefs of Staff of the two countries will meet at least once every two months; in the event of their being unable to meet, they will be replaced by their responsible representatives.

(c) The French High Commissioner for Youth and Sports will meet, at least once every two months, with the Federal Minister for Family and Youth Affairs or his representative.

4. In each of the countries, an interministerial commission will be charged with following problems of cooperation. It will be presided over by a high Foreign Ministry official and it will include representatives of all the administrations concerned. Its role will be to coordinate the action of the Ministries concerned and to report periodically to its Government on the state of Franco-German cooperation. It will also have the task of presenting all useful suggestions with a view to implementing the program of cooperation and to its ultimate extension to new domains.

II—Program
A—Foreign Affairs

1. The two Governments will consult each other, prior to any decision, on all important questions of foreign policy, and in the first place on questions of common interest, with a view to arriving, insofar as possible, at a similar position.

This consultation will cover, among other subjects, the following:

—Problems relative to the European Communities and to European political cooperation;

—East-West relations, both on the political and economic levels;

—Subjects dealt with in the North Atlantic Treaty Organization and the various international organizations in which the two Governments are interested, notably the Council of Europe, Western European Union, the Organization for Economic Cooperation and Development, the United Nations and its specialized agencies.

2. The cooperation already established in the area of information will be continued and developed between the services concerned in Paris and Bonn and between the [diplomatic] missions in other countries.

3. With regard to aid to the emergent countries, both Governments will systematically compare their programs with a view to maintaining close cooperation. They will study the possibility of engaging in joint undertakings. Since several Ministerial departments are responsible for these matters in both France and Germany, it will be the duty of the two Ministries of Foreign Affairs to determine together the practical bases for this cooperation.

4. The two Governments will study together the means for strengthening their cooperation in other important sectors of economic policy, such as agricultural and forest policy; energy policy; communications and transportation problems and industrial development, within the framework of the Common Market; as well as export credits policy.

B—Defense

1. The following objectives will be pursued in this domain:

(a) On the level of strategy and tactics, the competent authorities of both countries will endeavor to harmonize their doctrines with a view to arriving at mutual concepts. Franco-German Institutes for operational research will be created.

(b) Exchanges of personnel between the armed forces will be increased. These particularly concern professors and students from the general staff schools. They may include temporary detachments of entire units. In order to facilitate these exchanges, an effort will be made on both sides to give the trainees practical language instruction.

(c) With regard to armaments, both Governments will endeavor to organize a joint program from the time of drafting appropriate armaments projects and formulating financing plans.

To this end, joint committees will study the research being conducted on these projects in both countries and will carry out a comparative study. They will submit proposals to the Ministers, who will examine them during their quarterly meetings and will give the necessary directives for implementation.

2. The Governments will make a study of the conditions in which Franco-German cooperation could be established in the area of civil defense.

C—Education and Youth

With regard to education and youth, the proposals contained in the French and German memoranda of September 19 and November 8, 1962 will be studied, in accordance with the procedures indicated hereinabove.

1. In the field of education, the effort will chiefly concern the following points:

(a) Language instruction:

The two Governments recognize the essential importance that the knowledge in each of the two countries of the other's language holds for Franco-German cooperation. They will endeavor, to this end, to take concrete measures with a view to increasing the number of German students learning the French language and that of French students learning the German language.

The Federal Government will examine, with the governments of the Laender competent in this matter, how it is possible to introduce regulations making it possible to achieve this objective.

In all the establishments for higher education, practical courses in French will be organized in Germany and practical courses in German will be organized in France, which will be open to all students.

(b) The problem of equivalences:

The competent authorities of both countries will be asked to accelerate the adoption of provisions concerning the equivalence of academic periods, examinations and university degrees and diplomas.

(c) Cooperation in scientific research:

Research bodies and scientific institutes will increase their contacts, beginning with more extensive reciprocal information. Concerted research programs will be established in the areas in which it will appear possible.

2. All opportunities will be offered to the young people of both countries in order to draw closer the ties that unite them and to strengthen their mutual cooperation. Collective exchanges, particularly, will be increased.

A body whose purpose will be to develop these possibilities and to promote exchanges will be created by the two countries with an autonomous administrative council at its head. This body will have at its disposal a joint Franco-German fund for the exchange between the two countries of pupils, students, young artists, and workers.

III—Final Provisions

1. The necessary directives will be given in each country for the immediate enactment of the above. The Ministers of Foreign Affairs will examine the progress made at each of their meetings.

2. The two Governments will keep the Governments of the member States of the European Communities informed on the development of Franco-German cooperation.

3. With the exception of the provisions concerning defense, the present Treaty will also be applied to the Land of Berlin, barring a contrary declaration made by the Government of the Federal Republic of Germany to the Government of the French Republic in the three months following the entry into force of the present Treaty.

4. The two Governments may make any improvements which might appear desirable for the implementation of the present Treaty.

5. The present Treaty will enter into force as soon as each of the two Governments will have made known to the other that, on the domestic level, the necessary conditions for its implementation have been fulfilled.

THE GERMAN PROBLEM IS A EUROPEAN PROBLEM

At the very moment of success, however, the resignation of Chancellor Adenauer and the apparent manner in which De Gaulle envisaged European unity by excluding the United States accounted for a serious reconsideration on the part of the new German Chancellor and his cabinet. Germany, while attracted by the Franco-German rapprochement was unwilling to implement it at the expense of NATO and its relations with the United States. The treaty, with its provisions for cooperation and consultation was, after all, not implemented. In this statement, delivered two years after the conclusion of the treaty, De Gaulle reminds the Germans of their European vocation and emphasizes that the German problem is a European one.

During the conversations which I had the honor and satisfaction of having at Rambouillet two weeks ago with Chancellor Erhard, and which enabled us to establish confident and friendly contact between us, the problem of Germany was, of course, considered. I will not tell you what was explicity advanced by both sides on that very serious subject. But I can give you some indications of France's over-all views, insofar as they have not already been formulated.

The German problem is, indeed, *the* European problem. European, you can guess, since the time of the Roman Empire, that is, when historic

SOURCE: De Gaulle's Eleventh Press Conference, February 4, 1965 (New York: French Embassy, Press and Information Service).

Europe ceased to confine itself to the Mediterranean basin and moved toward the Rhine. European, because of the location of the Germans in the center of our continent, between Gauls, Latins, and Slavs. European, because a long and difficult history filled it with ferment and burdened it with sequels which left cruel rancor and manifold prejudices among all the neighbors of that country constantly in the making. European, because the German people are a great people, through both economic activity, as in the realm of philosophy, science and art, or in the area of military capacity, and because Europe sees in them a vital part of itself. European, lastly, because Germany has always felt an anguish, and at times a fury, created by its own uncertainty about its boundaries, its unity, its political system, its international role, so that the more its destiny remains undetermined, the more disturbing it always appears to the whole continent.

Is it necessary to say that the events which have occurred during the first half of this century have made this problem more disturbing and burning than ever? Already, because of the German Empire, the first World War had caused a gigantic shock in the west, east, north, and south of Europe. But then the Third Reich's immense effort to dominate; its armies' invasion on one side as far as the Channel, the Atlantic, the Pyrenees, the Adriatic, and the two shores of the Mediterranean, on the other as far as the Arctic, the approaches to Moscow, the heart of the Caucasus, the Black Sea, the Aegean; the action of its submarines on all the oceans of the globe; its tyranny established over twelve European States, its hegemony over four others; the violent death of forty million men, military and civilian, as a result of its acts, particularly the systematic extermination of ten million prisoners——all that inflicted terrible wounds on the body and soul of the peoples.

Doubtless, the final crushing of the Third Reich put an end to the ordeal. Doubtless, the subordination imposed on the vanquished—demolished and decimated—the accomplished facts in the territories which were once East Prussia, Posnania, and Silesia, the end of the Austrian Anschluss and of the "protectorate" over Czechoslovakia, the country's organic partition through the creation of zones and the Berlin statute, had first made the direct fears which Germany had for so long inspired recede. Doubtless, the reasonable and skillful policy adopted by Chancellor Adenauer's Government reassured many minds in the West. But the tragedy nonetheless left very deep scars. In short, it was with circumspection, indeed, even with some uneasiness, that public opinion in Western Europe sometimes viewed the economic expansion, military rebirth, and political recovery of the Federal Republic, while the Sovietized regimes in eastern Europe made use of the peoples' instinctive distrust of the Germans to justify the cold war against the free world, inveigled, so to speak, by the "German revengers."

The problem has thus arisen once again in history. For France, everything can be reduced to three closely linked questions: to see that Germany henceforth becomes a definite element of progress and peace; on this condition, to help with its reunification; to make a start and select the framework which would make this possible.

It is true that, up to now, the issue has not always been considered in this light. Following the last World War, with the memory of the ordeals suffered and risks run by the peoples of the Old Continent, many sides envisaged preventing the return of such misfortunes by eliminating what had been the cause, that is, the German might. Hence the projects aimed at forbidding the reconstitution of a central government, at placing the Ruhr under international control and at keeping Germany disarmed. You know that France was at first inclined, and for good reason, toward this concept. But the fact that the confrontation of the free world and the Soviet world became the major affair, and that Germany was one of its stakes, modified our outlook. Moreover, because in the depths of their misfortune our neighbors across the Rhine no longer seemed threatening, many were feeling, and despite everything, the basic attraction to them which their qualities deserved. Lastly and above all, the union of Europe—which became the indispensable condition for its independence and development—demanded reconciliation and cooperation between Germany and France.

However, the rivalry between East and West which was taking place on Germany's soil could only aggravate its political and territorial division. It is true that the Soviets, having in their zone imposed a regime modeled on their own, were trying to make it appear that, sooner or later, Germany could be reunited under a system of the same kind. But the Atlantic Alliance, the Federal Republic's economic and social success, the repugnance which communism created in the entire German population, made this pretention futile. For the Soviets to have had a chance of unifying Germany under a system like their own, they would have had to triumph in a world conflict.

Now, despite the tension they were maintaining in Berlin, they were careful not to start such a conflict. On the other hand, the United States, whose policy was at that time led by John Foster Dulles, could think that by strongly reinforcing NATO, the West would make Moscow withdraw and thus restore Germany's unity. But that was only a dream, unless someone made war—something which Washington and its allies were in no way disposed to do. Moreover, a large part of world opinion, while recognizing the precarious nature of what had become of the old Reich, and while disapproving of the brutal ruse of the wall and barbed wire, accommodated itself to a situation which, for whatever it was worth, was not preventing coexistence. Twenty years have thus elapsed without determining Germany's new destiny.

Such indetermination, in such a region of the world and at such a time, obviously cannot go on forever. Oh, doubtless one can imagine things continuing as they are for a long time without provoking tomorrow, any more that they aroused yesterday, a general conflagration, since the reciprocal nuclear deterrence is succeeding in preventing the worst. But it is clear that real peace and, even more, fruitful relations between East and West, will not be established so long as the German anomalies, the concern they cause and the suffering they entail continue. It is no less clear that, unless there is fighting so that one or the other imposes its solution, and without failing to recognize the reasons for constantly keeping the problem before the conscience of nations, this matter will not be settled by the direct confrontation of ideologies and forces of the two camps today rivaling each other in the world. What must be done will not be done, one day, except by the understanding and combined action of the peoples who have always been, who are and who will remain principally concerned by the fate of the German neighbor—in short, the European peoples. For those peoples to envisage first examining together, then settling in common, and lastly guaranteeing conjointly the solution to a question which is essentially that of their continent—this is the only way that can make reappear, this is the only link that can maintain, a Europe in the state of equilibrium, peace, and cooperation from one end to the other of the territory which nature has given it.

Certainly, the success of such a vast and difficult undertaking implies many conditions. Russia must evolve in such a way that it sees its future, not through totalitarian constraint imposed on its own land and on others, but through progress accomplished in common by free men and peoples. The nations which it has satellized must be able to play their role in a renewed Europe. It must be recognized, first of all by Germany, that any settlement of which it would be the subject would necessarily imply a settlement of its frontiers and of its armament in agreement with all its neighbors, those on the East and those on the West. The six nations which, let us hope, are in the process of establishing the economic community of Western Europe, must succeed in organizing themselves in the political domain as well as in that of defense, in order to make a new equilibrium possible on our continent. Europe, the mother of modern civilization, must establish herself, from the Atlantic to the Urals, in harmony and cooperation, with a view to the development of her vast resources and so as to play, in conjunction with America, her daughter, the role which falls to her in the progress of two billion men who desperately need it. What a role Germany could play in this world ambition of the rejuvenated old continent!

Doubtless, these conditions appear very complex and these delays seem quite long. But, after all, the solution to a problem as vast as that of Germany can only have large dimensions and consequences.

France, for her part, believes that this problem cannot be resolved except by Europe herself, because it is on the scale of the whole of Europe. This, ultimately, is the basic objective on this continent of the policy of France.

❧

De Gaulle's famous "no" to England's request to enter the Common Market was the culmination of many frictions and misunderstandings. It was also a calculated move on his part designed to promote French leadership in Europe. Not for a single moment had De Gaulle lost sight of the fact that Anglo-American relations had a special and privileged character. In a stormy meeting with Churchill during the war Churchill is reported to have declared that British interests were inextricably associated with American ones and that any time a question of choice was involved England would follow American leadership. The Prime Minister, De Gaulle concluded in his *Memoirs*, "made for himself a rule to do nothing except in agreement with Roosevelt."[1] In the last year of the war he offered to the British Prime Minister a special type of alliance that would have enabled France and England together to assume responsibility for Europe and form a solid bloc that might arbitrate between the two superpowers —only to be rebuffed. From then on the expression "the Anglosaxons" assumed a special connotation: the British and the Americans acting in unison to safeguard their particular interests at the expense of all others—particularly of France and Europe.

A number of other reasons influenced De Gaulle. The British had received atomic secrets and had developed a nuclear force

[1]*The War Memoirs of Charles De Gaulle* (New York: Simon and Schuster, 1959), Vol. I, p. 232.

only to gradually renounce it and return it, so to speak, to American command. Such a know-how, however, could have been used by the French, and a Franco-British nuclear cooperation might have provided the best guarantee for Europe. In December, 1962—three weeks before the fate of the British application to enter the Common Market was to be decided, Macmillan and Kennedy met at Bermuda and reached an agreement that virtually surrendered the British nuclear deterrent. Thus the British seemed to have wittingly renounced the only strong trump they had in negotiating their entry into the Common Market, and had again shown that they were ready to follow American leadership. During the various efforts to create an economic union of Europe with the Coal and Steel Community and then, more particularly, with the Common Market, the British who were invited to participate seemed first to hesitate and then to demur. When, much to their surprise, the Common Market became a reality, they attempted to counter it by organizing their own special trade area— the Free Trade Area with special ties for its members and, indirectly, some of the members of the British Commonwealth.

It is in this context that De Gaulle's "No" must be understood. To be sure, there are strong arguments on the other side and a different kind of attitude on his part might well have paved the way to England's entry, especially as it was ardently desired by the other members of the Common Market. For De Gaulle, the reasons for refusing England's entry were political and military. England's entry into the Common Market seemed like that of a Trojan horse: England was likely to promote within the Common Market political, economic, and military interests that would in fact be predominantly American. From a political point of view, De Gaulle shrewdly argued, England's entry might well be incompatible with the development of a political union in Europe, since the British were against the supranational development that was so much desired by the same European countries that favored British membership. Despite their many differences, these six countries were closer together; England might dilute the Community, unless she were willing to pull down the sails that were constantly hoisted in the direction

198   FRENCH INDEPENDENCE

of the United States. This, De Gaulle claimed, England was not
ready to do.

"NO" TO ENGLAND

When we talk about economic matters, and even more when we are
dealing with them, it is essential for what is said and what is done to
conform to reality, for otherwise we end up in deadlocks and sometimes even ruin.

Concerning this very important question of the European Economic
Community and also that of the possible membership of Great Britain,
it is the facts which must be considered first. Sentiments, as favorable
as they might be and as they are, cannot be put forward in opposition
to the real factors of the problem. What are these factors?

The Treaty of Rome was concluded between six continental States,
States which are, in short, economically of the same nature. Whether
in terms of their industrial or agricultural production, of their foreign
trade, of their commercial customs and clients, or of their living and
working conditions, there are many more similarities than differences
between them. Moreover, they are adjacent, they interpenetrate, they
are extensions of each other through their communications. The very
fact of grouping them and linking them together in such a way that
what they produce, buy, sell, and consume by preference within their own
grouping thus conforms to reality.

It must be added, moreover, that from the standpoint of their economic development, their social progress and their technological capability they are, in short, in stride with each other and they are moving
forward at more or less the same pace. Furthermore, it happens that
there exists between them no kind of political grievance, no border
disputes, no rivalry for domination or power. To the contrary, there is
a feeling of solidarity between them, firstly owing to the awareness
they have of together possessing an important part of the origins of
our civilization, and also with regard to their security, because they
are continental countries and they are confronted by the same single
threat from one end of their territorial grouping to the other. Finally,
they have a feeling of solidarity because not one of them is linked on
the outside by any special political or military agreement.

SOURCE: *Major Addresses, Statements, and Press Conferences of
General Charles De Gaulle, May 19, 1958–January 31, 1964* (New
York: French Embassy, Press and Information Service), pp. 211–216.

Thus it has been psychologically and materially possible to organize an economic community of the Six. Moreover, this was not without difficulty. When the Treaty of Rome was signed in 1957, it was after long discussions, and once concluded, so that something could be accomplished, it was necessary for us French to straighten ourselves out in the economic, financial, and monetary domain. And this was done in 1959.

From that time on, the Community was workable in principle, but it was then necessary to implement the Treaty. Now this Treaty, which was quite specific and complete on the subject of industry, was not at all specific and complete on the subject of agriculture. And yet, it was essential for our country that this be settled.

For it is indeed quite obvious that agriculture is an essential element of our national activity as a whole. We cannot conceive of a Common Market in which French agriculture would not find outlets commensurate with its production, and we agree, moreover, that, among the Six, we are the country for which this necessity is the most imperative.

That is why last January, when consideration was being given to implementing the second stage of the Treaty, in other words, to a practical beginning of application, we were led to set the entry of agriculture into the Common Market as a formal condition.

This was finally accepted by our partners, but very complex and difficult arrangements were needed. And some of these arrangements are still being worked out. I will note in passing that, in this vast undertaking, all the decisions taken were taken by the Governments, for nowhere else is there any authority or responsibility. But I should say that, in order to prepare and clarify matters, the Brussels Commission worked in a highly objective and pertinent fashion.

Then Great Britain applied for membership in the Common Market. It did so after refusing earlier to participate in the community that was being built, and after then having created a free trade area with six other States, and finally—I can say this, the negotiations conducted for so long on this subject can be recalled—after having put some pressure on the Six in order to prevent the application of the Common Market from really getting started. Britain thus in its turn requested membership, but on its own conditions.

This undoubtedly raises for each of the six States and for England problems of a very great dimension.

England is, in effect, insular, maritime, linked through its trade, markets, and food supply to very diverse and often very distant countries. Its activities are essentially industrial and commercial, and only slightly agricultural. It has, throughout its work, very marked and original customs and traditions. In short, the nature, structure, and economic context of England differ profoundly from those of the other States of the Continent.

What is to be done so that Britain, such as it lives, such as it produces and such as it trades, be incorporated into the Common Market such as it has been conceived and such as it functions?

For example, the means by which the people of Great Britain nourish themselves is in fact by importing foodstuffs purchased at low prices in the two Americas or in the former dominions, while still granting large subsidies to British farmers. This means is obviously incompatible with the system the Six have quite naturally set up for themselves.

The system of the Six consists of making a pool of the agricultural products of the entire Community, of strictly determining their prices of forbidding subsidizing, of organizing their consumption between all the members and of making it obligatory for each of these members to pay to the Community any savings they might make by having foodstuffs brought in from outside instead of consuming those offered by the Common Market.

Once again, what is to be done to make Britain, such as it is, enter that system?

One was sometimes led to believe that our British friends, in applying for membership in the Common Market, agreed to change their own ways even to the point of applying all the conditions accepted and practiced by the Six, but, the question is to know if Great Britain can at present place itself, with the Continent and like it, within a tariff that is truly common, give up all preference with regard to the Commonwealth, cease to claim that its agriculture be privileged and, even more, consider as null and void the commitments it has made with the countries that are part of its free trade area. That question is the one at issue.

One cannot say that is has now been resolved. Will it be so one day? Obviously Britain alone can answer that.

The question is raised all he more since, following Briain, oher States which are, I repeat, linked to it in the Free Trade Area, for the same reasons as Great Britain, would or will want to enter the Common Market.

It must be agreed that the entry first of Great Britain and then that of those other States will completely change the series of adjustments, agreements, compensations, and regulations already established between the Six, because all these States, like Britain, have very important traits of their own. We would then have to envisage the construction of another Common Market. But the 11-member, then 13-member, and then perhaps 18-member Common Market that would be built would, without any doubt, hardly resemble the one the Six have built.

Moreover, this Community, growing in that way, would be confronted with all the problems of its economic relations with a crowd of other States, and first of all with the United States.

It is foreseeable that the cohesion of all its members, who would be very numerous and very diverse, would not hold for long and that in the end there would appear a colossal Atlantic Community under American dependence and leadership which would soon completely swallow up the European Community.

This is an assumption that can be perfectly justified in the eyes of some, but it is not at all what France wanted to do and what France is doing, which is a strictly European construction.

Then, it is possible that Britain would one day come round to transforming itself enough to belong to the European Community without restriction and without reservation, and placing it ahead of anything else, and in that case the Six would open the door to it and France would place no obstacle in its path, although obviously the mere membership of Britain in the Community would completely change its nature and its volume.

It is also possible that England is not yet prepared to do this, and that indeed appears to be the outcome of the long, long Brussels talks. But if this is the case, there is nothing there that can be dramatic.

First of all, whatever decision Britain finally makes in this regard, there is no reason, as far as we are concerned, for the relations we have with it to be changed in any way. The consideration and the respect due that great State and that great people will not be altered in the least.

What Britain has done over the centuries and throughout the world is recognized as gigantic, even though there have often been conflicts with France. The glorious participation of Great Britain in the victory that crowned the first World War, we French will always admire. As for the role played by Britain at the most dramatic and decisive moment of the second World War, no one has the right to forget it.

Truly, the fate of the free world, and first of all our own and even that of the United States and of Russia, has depended to a large extent on the resolution, the solidity, and the courage of the British people such as Churchill gave them the will to be. This very day no one can dispute the fitness and the valor of the British.

Therefore, I repeat, if the Brussels negotiations were not to succeed at this time, nothing would prevent the conclusion of an agreement of association between the Common Market and Great Britain in such a way as to safeguard trade; neither would anything prevent the maintenance of the close relations between Britain and France and the continuation and development of their cooperation in all fields, especially those of science, technology and industry as, indeed, the two countries have just proven by deciding on the joint construction of the supersonic Concorde aircraft.

Lastly, it is possible that Great Britain's own evolution and the evolution of the world would lead the British to the Continent, whatever may be the delays before complete realization. For my part, this is what I am inclined to believe, and that is why, in my opinion, it will be in any case a great honor for the British Prime Minister, for my friend Harold Macmillan, and for his Government, to have perceived this so early, to have had enough political courage to proclaim it and to have had their country take the first steps along the path that, one day perhaps, will bring it to make fast to the Continent.

❖

I have tried to assemble here some of De Gaulle's most representative statements concerning the United States. It is not an easy matter. From the very moment that he assumed the leadership of the Free French, De Gaulle encountered a certain amount of distrust on the part of American officials—a distrust that he often exaggerated. The greater his reliance upon the United States, the greater his resentment when the aid he demanded was not forthcoming. And the greater his admiration for American power, the more severe his despondency that he himself did not possess the same resources and make better use of them. As he realized that the United States would inevitably win the war and be in a position to shape the future peace, his frustration increased, for he felt that France would be excluded. Finally, he saw in the United States a future partner and friend, true, but a friend that would dwarf France and shape the destiny of Europe wherein lay France's primary interests. In American anticolonialism he saw nothing but a pretext to open up new areas of influence and power for the United States. The American colossus would shatter the existing balance or would replace it with one from which France would be eliminated.

De Gaulle's doubts regarding the United States waxed every time he conferred with American statesmen. They assumed increasing virulence when the United States refused to consider him as the only legitimate spokesman for France, ignored him in important military and diplomatic steps taken during the war and stringently doled out economic and military aid. Failure to invite him to Yalta and Potsdam was squarely attributed to the United States. Churchill, Stalin, and even Mussolini receive words of praise or sympathy from De Gaulle—but not Roosevelt. Indeed, according to him, Roosevelt and the United States wantonly shattered the equilibrium of Europe and totally misunderstood the motives and ambitions of the Soviet Union. The peace he wrote wrecked Europe and upset the balance of world power. Both in his conversations with Roosevelt and Hopkins, and later with Truman, De Gaulle reverted to the theme of European reconstruction and accused the United States of ignoring it for the sake of an illusory rapprochement with the Soviet Union, or for the sake of arrangements that were based upon the cooperation of what was then the Big Four—China, Russia, England, and the United States.

But De Gaulle is a realist. The destruction of Europe and the disregard of France did not permit him to delude himself and to ignore the fact that his own future and that of France depended in the last analysis upon the United States. In his conversaiton with Hopkins (pp. 210–213) he tried once more to state his case, only to be later rebuffed. From then on all he could do was to cooperate grudgingly until France was liberated. He retired from power at the very time when French weakness and American supremacy became even more pronounced than they were during World War II. But the sentiments he harbored came to the fore after 1958 in a world where American power, if still needed, appeared no longer as indispensable to France. From then on he simply tried to assert his independence, to correct the errors of the past and, hopefully, to recreate an equilibrium of forces that would restrict American initiative and power while promoting that of France and Europe. This meant the weakening of NATO, the rejection of any integrative schemes of defense such as the MLF, the building of French nuclear power and the attempt to assert supremacy in Europe. While he insists that the Atlantic Alliance is vital, he construes it simply as an alliance among equals; while he agrees that ultimately defense is in great part an American burden, he refuses to accept an American monopoly. Alliances may change, and since defense is a national prerogative the interests of France must be promoted through bilateral agreements and treaties with other powers. Above all, he refuses to accept the permanent interests of the United States in Europe—even for purposes of defense. When conditions demand, it is natural for Europe and her "daughter" to march hand in hand. If conditions change, there is no reason why the daughter should not be disavowed in favor of the prodigal cousin beyond Eastern Europe, provided that she abandons her dissolute and dangerous ways and returns to the European family.

ELEMENTARY FEELINGS

De Gaulle, like so many French intellectuals and political leaders, attributes to the United States—an upstart in the old game of diplomacy—a lack of understanding and know-how. To this primarily De Gaulle will attribute his many misunderstandings with Roosevelt who had "the ambition to make law and dictate rights throughout the World."

The United States brings to great affairs elementary feelings and a complicated policy. This was the case in 1941 with their attitude toward France. While in the depths of American opinion the enterprise of General De Gaulle aroused passionate response, the whole fringe of officialdom persisted in treating it with coldness or indifference. As for the officials, they kept their relations with Vichy unchanged, claiming thus to be wresting France from German influence, preventing the fleet from being handed over, maintaining contact with Weygand, Noguès, and Boisson, whom Roosevelt expected one day to open to him the gates of Africa. But, with an astonishing self-contradiction, the policy of the United States, while keeping diplomatic relations with Pétain, held aloof from Free France on the pretext that it was impossible to prejudge what government the French nation would give itself when it was liberated. At bottom, what the American policymakers took for granted was the effacement of France. They therefore came to terms with Vichy. If, nonetheless, at certain points of the world they contemplated collaborating with this or that French authority as the struggle might dictate, they intended that this should be only by episodic and local arrangements.

These conditions made agreement with Washington difficult for us. Besides, the personal equation of the President affected the problem

SOURCE: *The War Memoirs of Charles De Gaulle* (New York: Simon and Schuster, 1959), Vol. I, pp. 209–210.

with a factor that was the opposite of favourable. Although Franklin Roosevelt and I had not yet been able to meet, various signs made me aware of his reserve toward me. I wanted, nonetheless, to do everything possible to prevent the United States, then about to enter the war, and France, for whom I was ready to answer that she had never left it, from following divergent paths.

As for the form of the relations to be established—a subject which the politicians, diplomats, and publicists were to discuss to their hearts' content—I must say that to me at that time it was almost a matter of indifference. I attached much more importance to the reality and content of the relations than to the successive formulas which the jurists of Washington would drape about the "recognition." At the same time, in face of America's enormous resources and the ambition of Roosevelt to make law and dictate rights throughout the world, I felt that independence was well and truly at stake. In short, while I wanted to try to reach an understanding with Washington, we had to do so on practical foundations and yet standing on our own feet.

FRANKLIN DELANO ROOSEVELT

De Gaulle was very sensitive to Roosevelt's disparaging remarks. The two men never got along together; indeed, it seems that they developed a genuine dislike for each other. Roosevelt referred to De Gaulle as a prima donna, and refused to acknowledge him as the spokesman for France. De Gaulle's comments about the American leader reveal his equally hostile feelings.

Franklin Roosevelt was governed by the loftiest ambitions. His intelligence, his knowledge, and his audacity gave him the ability, the powerful state of which he was the leader afforded him the means, and the war offered him the occasion to realize them. If the great nation he directed had long been inclined to isolate itself from distant enterprises and to mistrust a Europe ceaselessly lacerated by wars and revolutions, a kind of messianic impulse now swelled the American spirit and oriented it toward vast undertakings. The United States, delighting in her resources, feeling that she no longer had within herself sufficient scope for her energies, wishing to help those who were in misery or bondage the world over, yielded in her turn to that taste

SOURCE: *The War Memoirs of Charles De Gaulle* (New York: Simon and Schuster, 1959), Vol. II, pp. 81, 88–89, 268–271.

for intervention in which the instinct for domination cloaked itself. It was precisely this tendency that President Roosevelt espoused. He had therefore done everything to enable his country to take part in the world conflict. He was now fulfilling his destiny, impelled as he was by the secret admonition of death.

But from the moment America entered the war, Roosevelt meant the peace to be an American peace, convinced that he must be the one to dictate its structure, that the states which had been overrun should be subject to his judgment, and that France in particular should recognize him as its savior and its arbiter. Therefore the fact that France was reviving in the heat of battle, not in terms of a fragmentary and hence convenient resistance but as a sovereign and independent nation, thwarted his intentions. Politically he felt no inclination toward me—all the less since he found himself ceaselessly criticized by public opinion in his own country. It was America that conferred his power; during the course of the war Roosevelt twice had to submit to elections, and during the intervals the press, the radio, and every sort of special interest harassed the President. Diligent at charming others, but hampered deep within himself by the painful infirmity against which he struggled on valiantly, Roosevelt was sensitive to partisan reproaches and gibes. Yet it was precisely his policy in regard to General De Gaulle that aroused the fiercest controversies in America. It must be added that like any star performer he was touchy as to the roles that fell to other actors. In short, beneath his patrician mask of courtesy, Roosevelt regarded me without benevolence.

* * *

As a matter of fact, President Roosevelt, under cover of proclamations to the contrary, intended that French affairs should fall within his own sphere of influence, that the leading strings of our divisions should end up in his hands, and that the public powers eventually emerging from this disorder should derive from his arbitration. That is why he had bet on both De Gaulle and Pétain at the start, then launched Giraud onto the track when a rupture with the Marshall was inevitable, then lowered the barrier in front of Darlan as soon as Giraud's failure was apparent, and finally put Giraud back on the track after the Admiral's assassination. Now the President found it convenient to keep Fighting France and the system at Algiers separate until the moment when he himself would impose on both parties the solution of his choice, which, furthermore, would certainly not be the formation of a true French government.

* * *

During five days in the [American] capital, I observed with admiration the flood of confidence that sustained the American elite and discovered how becoming optimism is to those who can afford it.

President Roosevelt, of course, did not doubt for a moment that he could. During our meetings, he avoided any reference to immediate issues, but permitted me to glimpse the political objectives he wished to achieve through victory. His conception seemed to me an imposing one although disquieting for Europe and for France. It was true that the isolationism of the United States was, according to the President, a great error now ended. But passing from one extreme to the other, it was a permanent system of intervention that he intended to institute by international law. In his mind, a four-power directory—America, Soviet Russia, China, and Great Britain—would settle the world's problems. A parliament of the allied nations would give a democratic appearance to the authority of the "big four." But, short of handing over the quasi-totality of the earth's surface to the other three, such an organization, according to him, would have to involve the installation of American forces on bases distributed throughout the world and of which a number would be located in French territory.

Roosevelt thus intended to lure the Soviets into a group that would contain their ambitions and in which America could unite its dependents. Among the "four," he knew, in fact, that Chiang Kai-shek's China needed his cooperation and that the British, in danger of losing their dominions, would yield to his policy. As for the horde of small and middle-size states, he would be in a position to act upon them by the aid he could provide. Lastly, the right of peoples to decide for themselves, the support offered by Washington, the existence of American bases would give rise to new sovereignties in Africa, Asia, and Australasia, which would increase the number of states under obligation to the United States. In such a prospect, the questions relative to Europe, notably the fate of Germany, the destiny of the states along the Vistula and the Danube, as well as of the Balkans, and Italy's destiny, seemed to him quite subordinate. In order to find a satisfactory solution for them, he would certainly not go to the lengths of sacrificing the monumental conception that he dreamed of turning into a reality.

I listened to Roosevelt describe his plans to me. As was only human, his will to power cloaked itself in idealism. The President, moreover, did not explain matters as a professor setting down principles, nor as a politician who flatters passions and interests. It was by light touches that he sketched in his notions, and so skillfully that it was difficult to contradict this artist, this seducer, in any categorical way. I answered him, nevertheless, that in my opinion his plan risked endangering the Western world. By considering Western Europe as a secondary matter, was he not going to weaken the very cause he meant to serve— that of civilization? In order to obtain Soviet approval, would he not have to yield them, to the detriment of Poland and the Baltic, Danubian and Balkan states, certain advantages that threatened the general equilibrium? How could he be assured that China, emerging from the ordeals in which its nationalism was being forged, would remain what she was now? If it was true, as I was the first to think and say, that the colonial powers must renounce the direct administration of the peoples they ruled and practice with them a regime of association, it was also true that this enfranchisement could not be effected against those powers themselves, at the risk of unleashing, among the unorganized masses, a xenophobia and an anarchy dangerous for the entire world.

"It is the West," I told President Roosevelt, "that must be restored. If it regains its balance, the rest of the world, whether it wishes to or not, will take it for an example. If it declines, barbarism will ultimately sweep everything away. Now, Western Europe, despite its dissensions and its distress, is essential to the West. Nothing can replace the value, the power, the shining examples of these ancient peoples. This is true of France above all, which of all the great nations of Europe is the only one which was, is, and always will be your ally. I know that you are preparing to aid France materially, and that aid will be invaluable to her. But it is in the political realm that she must recover her vigor, her self-reliance and, consequently, her role. How can she do this if she is excluded from the organization of the great world powers and their decisions, if she loses her African and Asian territories—in short, if the settlement of the war definitively imposes upon her the psychology of the vanquished?"

Roosevelt's powerful mind was open to these considerations. Furthermore, he felt a genuine affection for France, or at least for the notion of it he had once been able to conceive. But it was precisely because of this inclination of his that he was at heart disappointed and irritated by yesterday's disaster among us and by the mediocre reactions the latter had aroused among so many Frenchmen, particularly those whom he knew personally. He told me so quite plainly. As for the future, he was anything but convinced of the rebirth and renewal of our regime. With bitterness he described what his feelings were when before the war he watched the spectacle of our political impotence unfold before his eyes. "Even I, the President of the United States," he told me, "would sometimes find myself incapable of remembering the name of the current head of the French government. For the moment, you are there, and you see with what kind attentions my country welcomes you. But will you still be there at the tragedy's end?"

It would have been easy but pointless to remind Roosevelt how much America's voluntary isolation had counted in our discouragement after the First World War, and again in our collapse at the beginning of the Second. It would have been equally futile to point out to him to what degree his own attitude toward General De Gaulle and Fighting France, having aided a great part of our elite to play a waiting game, encouraged in advance the French nation's return to that political inconsistency he had so justly condemned. The American President's remarks ultimately proved to me that, in foreign affairs, logic and sentiment do not weigh heavily in comparison with the realities of power; that what matters is what one takes and what one can hold on to; that to regain her place, France must count only on herself. I told him this. He smiled and concluded: "We shall do what we can. But it is true that to serve France no one can replace the French people."

Our conversations ended.

THE CONVERSATION WITH HOPKINS—FRANCO-AMERICAN RELATIONS IN 1944

In his conversation with Harry Hopkins De Gaulle attempted once more to bridge the gap that had separated him from Roosevelt, and to reconsider the existing state of relations with the United States as they had developed during the war.

I asked Hopkins what, in American eyes, was the cause of the unfortunate state of relations between the two nations. "The cause," he replied, "is above all the stupefying disappointment we suffered when we saw France collapse and surrender in the disaster of 1940. Our traditional conception of her value and her energy was overthrown in an instant. Add to this the fact that those French military or political leaders in whom we successively placed our trust because they seemed to symbolize that France we had believed in did not show thmselves —and this is the least that can be said—worthy of our hopes. Do not seek elsewhere for the true source of the attitude we have adopted toward your country. Judging that France was no longer what she had been, we could not trust her to play one of the leading roles.

SOURCE: *The War Memoirs of Charles De Gaulle* (New York: Simon and Schuster, 1960), Vol. III, pp. 92–95.

"It is true that you yourself, General De Gaulle, appeared on the scene; that a French resistance movement formed around you; that French forces have returned to combat; that today all France acclaims you and recognizes your government. Since at first we had no motive for believing in this prodigy, since you then became the living proof of our mistake, since you yourself, finally, have not dealt sparingly with us, we have not favored you up to the present. But we acknowledge what you have accomplished and are delighted to see France reappear among the Allies. Yet how could we forget what we have lived through on her account? Furthermore, knowing the political inconsistency that riddles your country, what reasons have we to suppose General De Gaulle will be in a position to lead her for long? Are we not then justified in using circumspection as to the share we expect of France to bear of the burden of tomorrow's peace?"

Listening to Harry Hopkins, I felt I was hearing again what President Roosevelt had said to me about France in Washington, six months before. But at that time the liberation had not yet taken place. I and my government were still established in Algeria; there was still some excuse for American doubts as to the mind of Metropolitan France. But at present, everything was decided. It was known that our people wanted to take part in the victory. It was apparent what our reviving army was worth. It was recognized that I had been installed in Paris at the head of a government surrounded and supported by national fervor. Yet was the United States any more convinced that France was capable of becoming a great power once again? Did it truly wish to help her? These were the questions which, from the French point of view, dominated the present and future of our relations with the United States.

I declared as much to the President's special envoy. "You have told me why, on your part, our relations are flawed. I am going to show you what, on our side, contributes to the same result. Let us pass over the episodic and secondary frictions provoked by the abnormal conditions under which our alliance is operating. For us, this is the essential matter: In the mortal dangers we French have survived since the beginning of the century, the United States does not give us the impression that it regards its own destiny as linked with that of France, that it wishes France to be great and strong, that it is doing all it can to help her to remain or become so once again. Perhaps, in fact, we are not worth the trouble. In that case, you are right. But perhaps we shall rise again. Then you will have been wrong. In either case, your behavior tends to alienate us."

I reminded him that the disaster of 1940 was the result of the excessive ordeals the French had endured. Yet during World War I the United States intervened only after three years of combat in which we had exhausted ourselves repulsing German aggression. America, moreover, had entered the conflict solely because of the damage to her commerce by German submarines and after attempting to effect a peace by compromise, according to the terms of which France would not even have recovered Alsace and Lorraine. Once the Reich was conquered, America had refused France the security pledges formally promised her, had exercised a stubborn pressure upon her to renounce the guarantees and the reparations due to her, and lastly had furnished Germany all the aid necessary for a return to power. "The result," I said, "was Hitler."

I recalled the immobility the United States had observed when the Third Reich attempted to dominate Europe; the neutrality she had clung to while France suffered the disaster of 1940; the rejection Franklin Roosevelt had offered Paul Reynaud's appeal, when a mere promise of aid, even secret and long-term, would have been enough to persuade our government to continue the war; the support granted for so long by Washington to those French leaders who had subscribed to capitulation and the rebuffs continually offered to those who had continued the combat. "It is true," I added, "that you were obliged to enter the conflict when the Japanese, as Germany's allies, attacked Pearl Harbor. The colossal war effort you have since mustered is about to render victory a certainty. Rest assured that France is thoroughly aware of the fact. She will never forget that without you her liberation would not have been possible. Still, while she is slowly recovering, it cannot escape her notice that America is counting on her only as a subordinate, as is proved by the fact that Washington is furnishing only a limited supply of arms for the French Army, as well as by what you yourself have just told me."

"You have explained the past," remarked Mr. Harry Hopkins, "in an incisive but accurate manner. Now America and France face the future. Once again, how shall we act so that henceforth they may act in agreement and in full mutual confidence?"

"If this is really America's intention," I replied, "I cannot understand how she can undertake to settle Europe's future in France's absence. Especially since after pretending to ignore her in the imminent 'Big Three' discussions, she must ask Paris to consent to whatever has been decided."

Messrs. Hopkins and Caffery agreed. They declared that their government now attached the highest importance to France's participation in the London "European Commission," on equal footing with America, Russia, and Great Britain. They even added that so far as the Rhine was concerned, the United States was more disposed than our two other great allies to settle the question in accord with our wishes. As for this last point, the question of the Rhine would not be settled by America any more than by Russia or Great Britain. The solution, if there was one, could eventually be found only by France or by Germany. Both had long sought for it, one contending against the other. Tomorrow, they would perhaps discover it in association.

To conclude the meeting, I said to the two ambassadors: "You have come in behalf of the President of the United States to discuss the profound problems of Franco-American relations. I think that we have done so. The French have the impression that you no longer consider the greatness of France necessary to the world and to yourself. This is responsible for the coolness you feel in our country and even in this office. If you want relations between our countries to be established on a different footing, it is up to you to do what must be done. Until you reach a decision, I send President Roosevelt the salute of my friendship on the eve of the conference that will bring him to Europe."

TRUMAN SIMPLIFIES EVERYTHING

Roosevelt's death and the accession of Truman to the presidency did not much alter the situation. De Gaulle again comments on the simplicity with which Truman's mind worked, but attributes to him a greater sense of realism than he was willing to grant his predecessor.

The collapse of Germany, soon followed by that of Japan, placed the United States in a kind of political void. Hitherto, the war had dictated its plans, its efforts, its alliances. All had had no other object beyond victory. Now the universe was changing, and at an ultrarapid tempo. Yet America, the only one of the great powers completely intact, remained invested during the peace with the same responsibility she had finally had to assume in the conflict, for she was to enter a national and ideological rivalry with a state that was her equal in size and power. Confronting the Soviet Union, the United States wondered which course to take, which foreign causes to espouse or reject, which peoples to aid or ignore. In short, isolationism had become impossible. But when one is powerful and undamaged, one must accept the encumbrances of a great policy.

It was natural for President Truman to lose no time consulting France. The latter, despite the ordeals she had just survived, was the only

SOURCE: *The War Memoirs of Charles De Gaulle* (New York: Simon and Schuster, 1960), Vol. III, pp. 236–237, 238–241.

nation on the European continent on which Western policy could count. She remained, moreover, a major African reality. Her sovereignty attended as far as the territories of America and Oceania. She had not left the Middle East. Nothing could keep her from returning to the Far East. Her prestige and her influence were gaining all over the world. Whether America tried to organize the peace by the collaboration of nations, attempted to institute balance of powers, or was merely obliged to prepare her own defense, how do so without France?

• • •

This, certainly, was President Truman's sense of the situation. For seven hours on August 22, 23, and 25, I conferred with him, attended by James Byrnes and Georges Bidault and Ambassadors Jefferson Caffery and Henri Bonnet. Mr. Truman, for all his simplicity of manner, proved to be an extremely positive man. His speech suggested an attitude remote from the vast idealism which his illustrious predecessor had developed in the same office. The new President had abandoned the plan of a world harmony and admitted that the rivalry between the free world and the Soviet bloc now dominated every other international consideration. It was therefore essential to avoid dissension and revolutionary upheaval, so that states not yet Communist would not be led to become so.

As for the complex problems of the Old World, they in no way intimidated Harry Truman, who regarded them from a position which simplified everything: For a nation to be happy, it need only institute a democracy like that of the New World; to put an end to the antagonisms which opposed neighboring countries, for instance France and Germany, all that was necessary was to establish a federation of rivals, as the states of North America had done among themselves. There existed one infallible formula to influence the underdeveloped countries to favor the West, independence; the proof, America herself, who once free of her former possessors had become a pillar of civilization. Finally, confronted with its present danger, the free world could do nothing better, and nothing else, than adopt the "leadership" of Washington.

President Truman, as a matter of fact, was convinced that the mission of serving as guide fell to the American people, exempt as they were from exterior shackles and internal contradictions that encumbered all other states. Moreover, to what power, to what wealth could America's be compared? I must admit that by the end of the summer of 1945, one was struck, at first contact with the United States, by the impression of an overpowering activity and an intense optimism that swept all before them. Among the former belligerents, this nation was the only one still intact. Its economy, based on apparently unlimited resources, quickly emerged from the wartime regime to produce enormous quantities of consumer goods. The avidity of the buyers and, abroad, the needs of a ravaged world guaranteed an outlet to the greatest enterprises, and full employment to the workers. Thus the United States was assured of being the most prosperous nation for some time. Then, too, it was the strongest! A few days before my visit to Washington, the atom bombs had reduced Japan to capitulation.

The President, therefore, did not expect that Russia could risk an actual war for a long time to come. This was why, he explained to me, the American forces were entirely withdrawing from Europe, with the exception of occupation forces in Germany and in Austria. But he considered that in many areas an extreme of devastation, poverty and disorder could result in the succession of Communism and afford the Soviets so many victories without the need for battle. The peace problem, according to Truman, was therefore of a largely economic order. The nations of western Europe, whether they had won or lost the war, had to resume the normal course of their existence as soon as possible. In Asia and Africa, the underdeveloped peoples should receive the means of raising their standard of living. This was what mattered, not frontiers, grievances and guarantees!

It was with these convictions that President Truman examined with me the problems raised by the victory. He listened to me explain how we French envisaged the fate of the German territories and made no direct objection to any of our proposals—termination of the centralized Reich, autonomy of the left bank of the Rhine, international government of the Ruhr. But he remained reserved on these points. On the other hand, he was categorical as to the necessity of materially aiding Germany. While eager—like myself—to assist the Westphalian basin to resume its coal production on a large scale and at once, he did not favor the notion of handing over certain quantities of its output to France, Belgium, and Holland in compensation for the devastation of which they had been the victims. At best, he suggested that these nations buy—in dollars—a share of the fuel. Similarly, the President opposed the withdrawal from Germany of raw materials, machinery, and manufactured objects. Even the recovery of the machinery which the Germans had taken from France disturbed Harry Truman. On the other hand, he was quite favorable to the reattachment of the Saar to France, since her coal and steel production would certainly be increased thereby.

I explained to the President why France conceived of the world in a less abstract manner than the United States. "You Americans," I said, "have taken part in two world wars with an effectiveness and a courage which one must certainly salute. Nevertheless, invasion, devastation, and revolution are for you unknown ordeals. But in France, an old man has seen our nation thrice invaded during his own lifetime, the last time completely. The resulting amount of human loss, destruction, and expense is actually incalculable. Each of these crises, particularly the last, has provoked in our people divisions whose profundity cannot even be estimated. Our inner unity and our international status will long be compromised. My government and I must therefore take the necessary measures to prevent the German threat from ever reappearing. Our intention, of course, is not to drive the German people to despair. On the contrary, we desire that people to live, to flourish and even to draw closer to us. But we must have guarantees. I have specified which ones. If, later on, it appears that our neighbors have changed their ways, we could modify these initial precautions. But at present, the armature Germany is to be given must be pacific and it must be forged while the Lord's fire has rendered the iron malleable."

I observed to Mr. Truman that here lay the hope of one day re-establishing European equilibrium. "This equilibrium has been shattered," I said, "because with the consent of America and Great Britain, the states of Central Europe and the Balkans are forced to serve as satellites to the Soviet Union. If these states have in common with their 'protector' the same national dread of seeing an ambitious Germany reappear, the bonds which link them by force to the Soviet policy will be all the stronger. If they realize, on the contrary, that the German menace no longer exists, their national interest will be contrary to the Soviet camp. Thus, between them and their suzerain, inevitable discords will turn the Kremlin from belligerent enterprises, particularly since Russia herself will be profoundly less inclined to such adventures. Even Germany will be able to take advantage of the new structure which must be established, for a truly federal regime would be her unique opportunity to induce the Soviets to permit the Prussian and Saxon territories to rejoin the common body. The road France proposes to the former Reich is the only one which can lead to European reorganization and regrouping."

TWENTY YEARS AFTER: FRANCE IS INDEPENDENT

Almost twenty years after his conversation with Hopkins, De Gaulle returns to the problem of the deterioration of Franco-American relations. Now, however, the shadow of war is lifted,

SOURCE: Eighth Press Conference, July 29, 1963 *Major Addresses, Statements, and Press Conferences of General Charles De Gaulle, May 19, 1958–January 31, 1964* (New York: French Embassy, Press and Information Service), pp. 231–236.

and the United States, despite her power, is beset by problems that belie the earlier optimism of her leaders; France is united and prosperous and has developed her own limited nuclear capabilities. De Gaulle's lofty expressions and detached manner cannot hide his satisfaction in declaring French independence vis-à-vis the United States and in rejecting American schemes for the unification of Europe and the integration of nuclear weapons under American leadership.

There has been much agitation, particularly in the American press, in the last few months. I can tell you after my personal experience of nearly 25 years of public reactions in the United States, I am hardly surprised by the ups and downs of what it is customary there to call opinion. But, all the same, I must confess that recently the tone and the song, as regards France, have seemed rather excessive to me.

It is true that to judge this one has to take into account a certain tension which exists there and which is naturally caused by pressing domestic and foreign concerns, as well as by an electoral situation which is continually recurring. Needless to say I myself many times noted how this pounding was as useless as it was exaggerated.

Some of you will remember that it was the case, for instance, in the heroic times when I was led to occupy the islands of Saint Pierre and Miquelon, or at the time of the formation of the liberation government in North Africa, or when I happened to disapprove of Yalta and to decline to go to Algiers for a meeting with Roosevelt who was returning from that deplorable conference or, after victory, when it was a question of maintaining our troops in Stuttgart until France was recognized an occupation zone in Germany. This was the case later with regard to the project of a European Defense Community, which consisted in depriving our country not, of course, of its military expenses but indeed of its army, and which, from my retirement, I categorically opposed. And it is also the case today on very important issues, such as the organization of Europe, the creation of a French atomic force, the Franco-German treaty, etc.

But I believe it useful to stress right away that this agitation by the press, political circles and more or less semiofficial bodies, which rages on the other side of the Atlantic and which naturally finds a ready echo in the various sorts of unconditional opponents, all this agitation, I say, cannot alter in France what is fundamental as regards America. For us, the fundamental factors of Franco-American relations are friendship and alliance.

This friendship has existed for close on 200 years as an outstanding psychological reality in keeping with the nature of the two countries, special and reciprocal bonds maintained by the fact that among all the world powers France is the only one, with the exception, I should say, of Russia, with which the United States never exchanged a single cannon shot, while it is the only power without exception which fought at its side in three wars—the War of Independence and the First and Second World Wars—under conditions forever unforgettable.

For such a moral capital to be jeopardized would require infinitely serious and infinitely long dissension. There can be, there are, political divergencies between Paris and Washington. There is journalistic ill will. But it is not these divergencies, and it is not this journalistic ill will of the moment which can lead France to believe that the United States seeks to wrong her. Conversely, for the United States to imagine that France seeks to harm it would be a ridiculous absurdity.

As regards the Franco-American alliance, if, since the days of Washington and Franklin, of Lafayette, of de Grasse, of Rochambeau, it was forged only during the First World War, in 1917 and 1918, and during the Second after December 1941, it is a fact that it now exists and that everything makes it vital for the two countries to maintain it. Indeed, so long as the free world is faced with the Soviet bloc, which is capable of suddenly submerging this or that territory, and which is moved by a dominating and detestable ideology, it will be essential that the peoples on both sides of the ocean, if they wish to defend themselves, be linked together to do so.

The Atlantic Alliance is an elemental necessity, and it is obvious that in this respect the United States and France have a capital responsibility, the United States because it disposes of a nuclear armament without which the fate of the world would be rapidly settled and France because, whatever the present inferiority of its means, it is politically, geographically, morally, militarily essential to the coalition.

Thus if, once again, there are divergencies between Washington and Paris on the functioning of the organization of the Alliance, the Alliance itself—that is, the fact that in the event of a general war, France, with the means it has, would be at the side of the United States, and this I believe is mutual—is not in question except in the wanderings of those who make it their profession to alarm the good people by depicting each scratch as an incurable wound. Thus neither the Franco-American friendship nor the alliance could be questioned, nor are they. But it is true that in the presence of the problems now facing the two countries, their policies are not always in agreement. Moreover, there is nothing that is essential or fundamentally disturbing or even surprising. But we both must adapt ourselves to this new situation.

To my mind, these present differences are purely and simply the result of the intrinsic changes which took place in the last few years and which are continuing with regard to the absolute and relative situation of the United States and France. France had been materially and morally destroyed by the collapse of 1940 and by the capitulation of the Vichy people. Doubtless, the recovery achieved by the Resistance, at the sides of the Allies, gave her back, as though by a miracle, her integrity, her sovereignty and her dignity. But France came out of the ordeal greatly weakened in every respect.

In addition, the inconsistency of the regime which she fell back upon prevented her from achieving her growth within and her rank without. Moreover, failing to adopt and to apply the decisions necessary with a view to decolonization, France's national development and international action were hampered by distant and fruitless struggles.

That is why, with regard to the United States—rich, active, and powerful—she found herself in a position of dependence. France constantly needed its assistance in order to avoid monetary collapse. It was from America that she received the weapons for her soldiers. France's security was dependent entirely on its protection. With regard to the international undertakings in which its leaders at that time were taking part, it was often with a view to dissolving France in them, as if self-renunciation were henceforth its sole possibility and even its only ambition, while these undertakings in the guise of integration were automatically taking American authority as a postulate. This was the case with regard to the project for a so-called supranational Europe, in which France as such would have disappeared, except to pay and to orate; a Europe governed in appearance by anonymous, technocratic, and stateless committees; in other words, a Europe without political reality, without economic drive, without a capacity for defense, and therefore doomed, in the face of the Soviet bloc, to being nothing more than a dependent of that great Western power, which itself had a policy, an economy, and a defense—the United States of America.

But it happens that, since then, France's position has considerably changed. Her new institutions put her in a position to wish and to act. Her internal development brings her prosperity and gives her access to the means of power. She has restored her currency, her finances, her balance of trade, to such an extent that, from this standpoint, she no longer needs anyone, but to the contrary she finds herself receiving requests from many sides, and so, far from borrowing from others,

220   FRENCH INDEPENDENCE

particularly from the Americans, she is paying back her debts to them and even on occasion is granting them certain facilities. She has transformed into cooperation between States the system of colonization which she once applied to her African territories and, for the first time in a quarter of a century, she is living in complete peace. France is modernizing her armed forces, is equipping them herself with materiel and is undertaking to endow herself with her own atomic force. She has cleared away the clouds which were surrounding and paralyzing the construction of Europe and is undertaking this great task on the basis of realities, beginning with the setting up of the economic community by giving, together with Germany, an example of the beginnings of political cooperation and by indicating that she wishes to be France within a Europe which must be European. Once again the national and international condition of our country resembles less and less what it used to be. How could the terms and conditions of her relations with the United States fail to be altered thereby? All the more so since the United States, on its side, as regards its own problems, is undergoing great changes which modify the character of hegemonic solidarity which, since the last World War, has marked its relations with France.

From the political standpoint it is true that the Soviet bloc holds to its totalitarian and threatening ideology and again recently the Berlin wall, the scandal of the Berlin wall, or the installation of nuclear arms in Cuba have shown that, because of the Soviet bloc, peace remained precarious. On the other hand, human evolution in Russia and its satellites, considerable economic and social difficulties in the life of those countries, and above all the beginnings of an opposition which is appearing between a European empire possessing immense Asiatic territories which make it the greatest colonial power of our times, and the empire of China, its neighbor for 6,000 miles, inhabited by 700 million men, an empire that is indestructible, ambitious, and deprived of everything—all this can, in effect, introduce some new elements into the concerns of the Kremlin and lead it to insert a note of sincerity in the couplets that it devotes to peaceful coexistence. And thus the United States which, since Yalta and Potsdam, has nothing, after all, to ask from the Soviets, the United States sees tempting prospects opening up before it. Hence, for instance, all the separate negotiations between the Anglo-Saxons and the Soviets which, starting with the limited agreement on nuclear testing, seem likely to be extended to other questions, notably Europeans ones, until now in the absence of the Europeans, which clearly goes against the views of France.

France, in effect, has for a long time believed that the day might come when a real détente, and even a sincere entente, will enable the relations between East and West in Europe to be completely changed and she intends, if this day comes—I have said this on other occasions—to make constructive proposals with regard to the peace, balance, and destiny of Europe. But for the time being, France will not subscribe to any arrangement that would be made above her head and which would concern Europe and particularly Germany. As for a draft nonaggression pact—which, we are told, was discussed in Moscow—between the States belonging to NATO and the leaders of the countries subjected to the Kremlin's yoke, I must say right away that France does not appreciate this assimilation between the Atlantic Alliance and Communist servitude. And then, moreover, there is no need for a pact in order for France to declare that she will never be the first to attack, its being understood that she will defend herself with whatever means she may have against whomsoever would attack either her or her allies. But today France solemnly declares through the voice of the President of the Republic that there will never be any French aggression. And consequently our eventual participation in a nonaggression pact no longer has any kind of purpose.

But it remains that what happened in Moscow shows that the course followed by the policy of the United States is not identical with ours. With regard to defense, until recently the Americans, thanks to their nuclear weapons, were in a position to assure the free world almost complete protection, but they have lost this monopoly, while continuing at great expense to strengthen their power. Owing to the fact that the Russians also now have the means to destroy the world and particularly the new continent, it is quite natural that America is seeing its own survival as the principal objective in a possible conflict and is not considering the time, degree, terms, and conditions of its nuclear intervention for the defense of other regions, particularly Europe, except in relation to this natural and primary objective. This, moreover, is one of the reasons that France is equipping herself with her own atomic weapons. The result of this is that, as far as the French Government is concerned, important modifications are necessary with regard to the terms and conditions of our participation in the Alliance, since this organization has been built on the basis of integration, which today is no longer valid for us.

Lastly, on the economic level, the time has come when the United States, whose enormous production and trade capacity is not at all impaired, sees that of the European countries, particularly of France, rising, to the point of making them quite disturbing competitors.

Furthermore, the burden represented for the United States by the financial support it grants to many States and by the military forces it maintains abroad, these burdens cannot but weigh heavily upon it, while a considerable part of its capital is being invested abroad. For these reasons the balance of payments and the dollar problem of the United States are becoming essential concerns. It is therefore perfectly understandable that its intentions are no longer those it formerly had on the subject of the organization of a European Europe and of the role that France can play in it, but it is also understandable that France, who is industrial and agricultural, cannot and does not wish to see either the nascent economy of Europe or her own dissolved in a system of a type of Atlantic community which would only be a new form of that famous integration. In sum, for France, and I believe, for the United States, the friendship that unites them and the alliance that links them are above and beyond all jeopardy, but it is true that there are differences between the two countries in the face of certain international problems. The evolution of both countries has created this state of things which, once again, is not at all surprising, however disturbing it may perhaps appear to the Americans. In any case, in the relations between the two peoples, we believe that each must accept this new situation. That being done, it will doubtless be advisable to harmonize, in each case and to the greatest extent possible, the respective policies. France for her part is cordially, very cordially disposed to this.

12. THE "SO-CALLED"
UNITED NATIONS

⚜

De Gaulle's experience with the League of Nations and his firm conviction that only nation-states, on the basis of consultations and cooperation, can provide for international order naturally colored his assessment of the United Nations. To be sure, as he wrote, "its universal object was highly estimable in itself and consonant with the genius of France" but despite what Stalin, Roosevelt, and Churchill seemed to think, De Gaulle would not allow himself to exaggerate the value of this organization. He was gratified that France was asked to be a permanent member of the Security Council and that French became one of the official languages of the organization.

His subsequent analysis of what happened to the United Nations, however, is for him also a vindication of his original doubts. The admission of so many new nations, coupled with the conflict between the United States and the Soviet Union, paralyzed decisions and actions of any kind both at the level of the Council and of the Assembly. The orderly conduct of international affairs was thrown into confusion and, as had been the case with the League, the United Nations became unable to provide even an adequate forum for deliberations that lead to resolution of conflict. De Gaulle has continued to insist that only the large powers should be permitted to decide on global questions, thus in effect urging a return to nineteenth-century diplomacy.

THE BIRTH OF THE UNITED NATIONS

Reviving an idea which had haunted the minds of many philosophers and several statesmen, had given birth to the League of Nations and then had foundered because of the defection of the United States

SOURCE: *The War Memoirs of Charles De Gaulle* (New York: Simon and Schuster, 1960), Vol. III, pp. 227–229.

and the weakness of the democracies, Roosevelt had wanted a world peace organization to emerge from the conflict. In our conversations in Washington the year before, the President had made me understand how close this monumental edifice was to his heart. In his ideology, international democracy was a sort of panacea; he felt that the nations, thus confronting each other, would examine their grievances and in each case take the measures necessary to keep matters from reaching a state of war. They would also cooperate in behalf of the progress of the human race. "Thanks to this institution," he told me, "the old American isolationism will come to an end and we will also be able to associate Russia, long isolated from us, with the rest of the Western world." Besides, although he did not mention it, Roosevelt expected that the crowd of small nations would force the hand of the "colonialist" powers and assure the United States an enormous political and economic clientele.

First at Dumbarton Oaks and later at Yalta, America, Great Britain, and Russia had reached agreements on a constitution for the United Nations. China's consent had been obtained. When the Crimean conference was over, France's approval was asked, and Paris was invited to join Washington, London, Moscow and Chung-king in issuing invitations to the San Francisco Conference. After careful consideration, we declined the offer the other four "big powers" had made to us to be a sponsoring power along with them. It was not suitable for us to recommend to fifty-one nations that they subscribe to articles drawn up without our participation.

On my part, it was with sympathy but not without circumspection that I envisaged the nascent organization. Of course its universal object was highly estimable in itself and consonant with the genius of France. It could appear salutary that cases of imminent conflict be referred to international intervention, and that the latter be employed to effect compromises. In any case, it was good that the states make contact with each other periodically, in full view of world-wide opinion. Nevertheless, despite what Roosevelt thought, what Churchill implied, what Stalin appeared to believe, I did not permit myself to exaggerate the value of the "United Nations."

Its members would be states, that is, the least impartial and the most partisan bodies in the world. Their meeting could, assuredly, formulate political motions, but not render decisions. Yet it was inevitable that such an organization would claim to be as qualified for the one endeavor as for the other. Furthermore, its more or less tumultuous deliberations, developing in the presence of innumerable transcribers, broadcasters, and cameramen, ran every risk of balking genuine diplomatic negotiation, which is almost always fruitful only when characterized by precision and discretion. Lastly, it was to be presumed that many small countries would automatically oppose the great powers, whose presence and territories extended the world over, touched many frontiers and inspired frequent envy or anxiety. America and Russia certainly had strength enough to inspire more than respect. England, relatively intact, retained its maneuverability. But France, terribly damaged by the war and assailed by all kinds of claims from Africa and Asia—what hearing would she obtain on the occasion of her difficulties?

This was why I instructed our delegation not to give way to high-sounding declarations, as many of our representatives had once done in Geneva, but instead to observe an attitude of restraint. This was done, and done well, under the successive direction of Georges Bidault, participating for the first time in an international council, and President Paul Boncour, whose experience with the League of Nations made him a master of such subjects. The discretion shown by our representatives did not, of course, keep France from taking her place in the Areopagus of the five "big powers" which conducted the affair. It achieved, in San Francisco, all that we were most eager to obtain. Thus, despite a certain amount of opposition, French was recognized as one of the three official languages of the United Nations. Further, beyond the right of veto appertaining to France as to the other great powers, the Charter's original draft was amended so as to make the "General Assembly" counter-balance the "Security Council" and, at the same time, to control the tendencies of the Assembly by requiring a two-thirds majority for its motions. It was further specified that the examination of litigations by the organization would in no way impede the drafting and signing of treaties of alliance. Lastly, the system of "trusteeships," under which malevolent intentions with regard to the French Union were apparent, would be subject to severe restrictions.

The United Nations was born. . . .

A SCENE OF DISTURBANCE

The reservations that were expressed by General De Gaulle and his representatives at the time the United Nations was founded were soon to be replaced by caustic remarks against the "so-

SOURCE: *Major Addresses, Statements, and Press Conferences of General Charles De Gaulle, May 19, 1958–January 31, 1964* (New York: French Embassy, Press and Information Service), pp. 119–120.

called" United Nations. On April 11, 1961, De Gaulle called it a scene of disturbance.

The United Nations Organization and its institutions were created in 1945 on the basis of a Charter, and with purposes which France at that time approved. I was, myself, at that time at the head of my country and in that capacity I was one of the founders of the United Nations at the request of President Roosevelt and then of President Truman, who were its promoters.

There was an executive council, the Security Council, which was a sort of Government composed of the five big powers, that is to say, the United States, the Soviet Union, Great Britain, China, and France. And then there was a kind of nonlegislative deliberative parliament, the General Assembly. The General Assembly, at that time, was supposed to debate only on subjects which were submitted to it by the Security Council. I will add that the General Assembly then included only about forty States which had been in existence for a long time, which were endowed with cohesion and unity and which were used to international relations and to the traditions, obligations, and responsibilities which these relations entail.

In the Security Council each of the members—each of the big powers—had the veto power. And then finally in the General Assembly, in accordance with what France had wanted and had obtained in San Francisco, it was necessary—and it still is—to have a two-thirds majority in order to pass a resolution.

It seems that all these procedures would enable the States to establish contact with each other, to examine world questions jointly and to promote peace while restricting demagogic activities.

As for the Charter, it was designed to prevent the Organization from interfering in the affairs of each State and it could intervene only on the explicit request of a Government.

Finally, among the intentions which had inspired its creation, there was the desire, perhaps the illusion of the Western nations—in any case of the Americans—to bring the Soviets to cooperate with the West. We know what has happened.

Today it must be said that the United Nations really does not in any way resemble what it was or ought to have been at the start. First of all, the Security Council no longer comprises—it is far from comprising—only the big powers, but also several powers elected in turn, and then there is an undetermined number of delegations attending all debates of the Security Council, depending on the subjects under discussion. As for the General Assembly, at the present time it has assumed all powers. It can deliberate on everything, without and even against the advice of the Security Council which is thus dispossessed of its essential prerogative. In addition, this General Assembly now includes the representatives of more than 100 States—soon they will number 120—most of which, at least many of which, are improvised States and believe it their duty to stress grievances or demands with regard to the older nations, rather than elements of reason and progress.

As for the Charter, it now inconveniences every one and there is no one who can enforce its application. As regards the hoped-for cooperation between East and West within the United Nations, we can see its results.

So that now the meetings of the United Nations are no more than riotous and scandalous sessions where there is no way to organize an objective debate and which are filled with invectives and insults thrown out, especially by the Communists and those who are allied with them against the Western nations.

And then as the United Nations becomes a scene of disturbance, confusion and division, it acquires the ambition to intervene in all kinds of matters. This is especially true of its officers. It is anxious to assert itself—even by force of arms—as it did in the Congo.

THE BIG FIVE

In 1965 he urges what he has always favored—diplomacy by the great powers of the world—England, the United States, France, the Soviet Union, and Communist China. Then the United Nations can play a ceremonial role. This, it should be repeated, has been consistently De Gaulle's position: Only the great powers can make policy.

QUESTION: Mr. President, in view of the gravity of the United Nations crisis, what is your opinion on this crisis and what measures do you recommend for solving it?

ANSWER: I am going to go back rather far, for the idea of the United Nations is an old one. It emerged, of course, from the war. "War gives birth to everything," said the ancient Greeks. From the first World War came the League of Nations, which France, Great Britain, the United States, and their allies decided to establish in the hope that the combined action of peace-loving nations would prevent a repetition of

SOURCE: Eleventh Press Conference, February 4, 1965 (New York: French Embassy, Press and Information Service), pp. 7–9.

the catastrophe. Subsequently, it is true, America abstained from taking part. But, so long as the factors of the world situation remained as they had been fixed by the Treaty of Versailles, the League of Nations was able to exist and function by extolling its own ideals, especially when it concerned the theoretical condemnation of war.

However, the world was to see that, men being men and nations being nations, it had set its sights too high. As imperialist Japan, Nazi Germany and Fascist Italy attacked the established order, and as the necessity appeared not only to speak, but to act against them, the League of Naions showed its impotence. Indeed, the conjunction of so many calculations, reservations, fears and diverse interests could not result in action, that is to say, in determination, commitment, and risk. The second global conflict caused the bankruptcy of the Geneva institution, while its principal members, divided into two camps, came to blows.

However, even before the guns were silenced, the idea again appeared of offering nations a framework in which they could be equally represented, discuss world problems, establish a consensus of peoples on them, repudiate the warlike intentions of the ambitious, centralize information on each country's material, social, and moral position, and set in motion collective efforts toward their development. I had the honor, with Roosevelt, Churchill, Stalin, and Chiang Kai-shek, of drawing up the draft Charter which was adopted by fifty-one nations in San Francisco.

We know that, by virtue of that constitution, the United Nations was composed firstly of a Council charged with watching over international security and able to mobilize the means desired to make it respected, and secondly of an Assembly whose debates would result in recommendations, with the right to take action belonging, nevertheless, to the Council alone. Among the eleven members of the latter were five permanent members, that is, the five victorious powers, each one having the veto power. An Economic and Social Council and a Court of Justice were added to these two great bodies. A Secretary General was to ensure the practical functioning of the Organization. In addition, the Charter provided that the United Nations should not intervene in the internal affairs of a State.

This Charter was reasonable. It resulted in the normal and continuous meeting and confrontation within the Assembly of almost all the world's nations in a kind of forum from which international public opinion could emerge and which, by virtue of the equality of all its members, conferred upon each of them, especially those which had just acquired sovereignty and independence, a highly esteemed dignity. Within the Council, moreover, five powers whose policies, economy, armed forces, and influence gave them world-wide responsibilities, were brought to meet, and if possible to collaborate, in maintaining the peace. These arrangements thus corresponded to what was both possible and prudent; they undoubtedly did not establish a world government and a world parliament, which in this century could exist only in dreams. But, given the realities, and especially the rivalry between Soviet Russia and the United States which was spreading over the whole world among an increasing number of nations, it was a wise idea that the Organization gave itself the conditions for balance and impartiality, rather than aspiring to impose the impossible.

We all know what happened. Under the pressure of events in Korea, Suez, and Hungary, and the Soviets' excessive use of the veto, the so-called "united" nations, which were so no more, permitted themselves to exceed their nature and their possibilities. Failing to recognize the competence of the Security Council, they deviated from their Charter. In 1950 the General Assembly arrogated to itself the right to decide on the use of force, which made it the scene of quarrels between the two rivals. Through the disorder thus created, the then Secretary General was led to set himself up as a superior and arbitrary authority. Continuing these abuses, the Organization involved itself directly in the internal affairs of the Congo, sent there at great cost military troops furnished by States that were too often interested—which State is not?—and political, administrative, and economic missions which, in fact, corresponded to the intentions of the great power. To be sure, this intervention has ceased thanks to the wisdom of the present Secretary General, and because of the expenditures—which France, let it be said in passing, could not for her part assume, since she has never ceased to disapprove of an unjustified undertaking and a procedure contrary to the San Francisco Treaty. But the profound transformation which the United Nations has undergone because of such legal distortions clearly compromise its unity, its prestige, and its functioning. Hence the present crisis into which it is plunged.

I will say frankly that, in my opinion, it is by returning to prudence and to the Charter that the United Nations can regain its equilibrium. In the present circumstances, it is clearly necessary for Washington, Moscow, London, Peking, and Paris to agree to return to the point of departure, as they agreed to once in order to establish the United Nations. France, for her part, is ready to contribute to such an agreement by the five, and she feels that Geneva would be the obvious place for such negotiations, or, moreover, for any others which you are thinking of. Indeed, we regard as desirable the salvation of an institution in which the world has put so much hope for furthering the solidarity and progress of all mankind.

13. FRANCE HAS
INTERESTS EVERYWHERE

❧

While Europe has been De Gaulle's primary concern, he has never relinquished the world-wide interests of France. Not only in North Africa, the Mediterranean, and Africa, but also in the Far East and Latin America, France's interests must be maintained and promoted. Indeed, as the self-proclaimed head of a powerful European political bloc, France's accession to the status of a world power must be accompanied by overt expressions of interest even when it is not congruent with the other Atlantic nations—especially the United States. There is also a tactical reason for the expression of such interest: to force both England and the United States to reconsider the joint character of the global responsibilities of the three major NATO powers. Without appropriate deliberations and consultations their interests are bound to collide. It is in this double sense that De Gaulle's trip to Latin America and his insistence on negotiations for a Vietnamese settlement must be interpreted. France has interests in that area and can not admit a unilateral American policy.

The recognition of China may be a different story. In part it was a realistic move since China with its present government is an inescapable reality; in part it opened up the prospect of European (as opposed to American or Soviet) influence in the Far East; in part it was an effort to re-establish contact with a region where France had been present economically, culturally, politically, and militarily for about seventy years. But above all it was an assertion of French independence vis-à-vis the United States that looked with great disfavor upon the recognition of China. De Gaulle was again clearly indicating that the United States would either have to make NATO a genuine consultative organization for all global problems or acknowledge that the logic of its own position applied also to its allies. If the United States could act alone, so could France!

THE SALUTE TO MEXICO

During his state visit to Mexico in March, 1964, De Gaulle evoked the common cultural and political heritage, that Mexico shared with France, and held out prospects of economic cooperation. This was a symbolic gesture, but in 1965 De Gaulle expressed his concern at the American intervention in the domestic affairs of Santo Domingo. The parallel between Algeria and Santo Domingo is only too obvious. If the United States could take a position that seemed for so long contrary to French policy in what was at least legally a French Department—Algeria, there was nothing to prevent France from doing the same to the United States by castigating American military intervention in her own backyard.

Mexicans,
    I bring to Mexico the greetings of France.
    France salutes Mexico in friendship. My country, ardent, proud and free, is attracted to your own, free, proud, and ardent. No doctrine, no quarrel, no divergent interests separate us. Quite the contrary, we have many reasons that urge us to draw closer together.
    France salutes Mexico with respect. We are aware of the impressive American origins from which your nation springs. We are aware with what courage you fought for and maintained your independence. We know what an immense effort toward the liberation of man and modern development your revolution represents.
    And you Mexicans, you know to what extent the French—during the whole course of their long and hard struggle as a people—fought for the liberty and dignity of man. You know how today they are working with their hands, their heads, and their hearts to raise up their country and to help many others.
    France salutes Mexico with confidence. The world we live in is undergoing a complete transformation. But, at the same time, it is threatened by frightful trials.

SOURCE: Mexico City speech, March 16, 1964 (New York: French Embassy, Press and Information Service).

The problems that all States are thereby facing are known as progress and peace. In order to solve them nothing is more important than the cooperation of two countries like ours, which yesterday responded to the same ideal, which today follow the same path and which, tomorrow, feel themselves destined to the same future.

This, then, is what the French people suggest to the Mexican people: "Let us walk hand in hand."

Long live Mexico!

THE CONCERN FOR VIETNAM

The same appears to be the case with Vietnam—a former French colony and in a real sense an unfortunate legacy of the unsuccessful French war to subdue Indochina that lasted from 1946 to 1954. De Gaulle's reassertion of French interests is couched in economic and political terms now that French colonialism has come to an end.

M. Alain Peyrefitte, French Minister of Information, at the close of the meeting of the Council of Ministers held on August 29, 1963, read a statement reporting the following declaration on the situation in Vietnam made by General De Gaulle during the course of the meeting:

"The French Government is following with attention and emotion the grave events occurring in Vietnam. The task accomplished in the past by France in Cochin China, Annam, and Tonkin, the ties she has maintained in the country as a whole, and the interest she takes in its development explains why she understands so well and shares sincerely in the trials of the Vietnamese people. In addition, France's knowledge of the merits of this people makes her appreciate the role they would be capable of playing in the current situation in Asia for their own progress and to further international understanding, once they could go ahead with their activities independently of the outside, in internal peace and unity and in harmony with their neighbors. Today more than ever, this is what France wishes for Vietnam as a whole. Naturally it is up to this people, and to them alone, to choose the means of achieving it, but any national effort that would be carried out in Vietnam would

SOURCE: *Major Addresses, Statements, and Press Conferences of General Charles De Gaulle, May 19, 1958–January 31, 1964* (New York: French Embassy, Press and Information Service), p. 241.

find France ready, to the extent of her own possibilities, to establish cordial cooperation with this country."

CHINA: A GREAT PEOPLE

On January 31, 1964, De Gaulle announced the recognition of Communist China. What he had formerly called the "multitude" or the "hordes" is now elevated to "China, a great people," whose industry and civilization are extolled.

China, a great people, the most numerous on the earth, a race in which the capacity for patience, labor, and industry of its individuals has, for thousands of years, arduously compensated for its collective lack of method and cohesion, and has built a very special and very profound civilization; a tremendous country, geographically compact though without unity, extending from Asia Minor and the steppes of Europe to the long shoreline of the Pacific, and from the Siberian ice to the tropical regions of India and Tonkin; a State older than history, steadily resolved upon independence, tirelessly striving for centralization, instinctively inward-looking and scornful of foreigners, but conscious and proud of an immutable duration—such is Eternal China.

Her first contact with modern nations was very abrupt and very costly. In one country, many interventions, demands, expeditions, invasions—European, American, Japanese—inflicted as many humiliations and dismemberments. These terrible national shocks, as well as the determination of her leaders to transform their country at any cost, so that she might achieve the same power and the same condition as the nations that had oppressed her, led China to revolution. Doubtless Marshall Chiang Kai-shek—to whose worth, patriotism, and nobility of spirit it is my duty to pay homage, certain that the day will come when history and the Chinese people will do as much—Marshall Chiang Kai-shek, after having led China to the Allied victory which concluded the Second World War in the Pacific, tried to channel the flood. But matters were at the point where they overrode everything, except the extreme. Once the United States, which had lent the Marshall the direct assistance of its forces on the continent, was obliged to forego doing so, he fell back to Formosa, and the Communist regime, long

SOURCE: *Major Addresses, Statements, and Press Conferences of General Charles De Gaulle, May 19, 1918–January 31, 1964* (New York: French Embassy, Press and Information Service), pp. 256–258.

prepared by Mao Tse-tung, established its dictatorship. That was fifteen years ago.

Since then, the enormous effort which was requisite in any case for the exploitation of natural resources, industrial development, agricultural production, national education, the struggle against the scourges inherent in this nation—hunger, pestilence, erosion, floods—has been put into effect throughout the territory. As is always the case in the Communist system, what could be achieved involved terrible suffering among the people, an implacable constraint for the masses, tremendous losses and waste of property, the collapse and decimation of countless human values. It appears, however, that at the cost of so many sacrifices, certain results have been achieved, due in part to the action of the totalitarian system and also, in large measure, to the ardor of a proud people, resolved in its depths to raise itself in every instance, and to the wealth of courage and ingenuity which that people is capable of lavishing, whatever the circumstances.

It is true that Soviet Russia at first lent China considerable aid: establishing credit for the purchase of tools and supplies, furnishing mining and industrial equipment and specialists, sending engineers, technicians, skilled workers to the spot, and so on. This was the period when the Kremlin, utilizing here as elsewhere its rigorous preponderance within the Communist Church to support the supremacy of Russia over the peoples whom a dictatorship similar to its own had subordinated to it, intended to keep China under its rule and thereby dominate Asia. But the illusion has been dispelled. Doubtless there still remains, between the regimes in power in Moscow and in Peking, a certain doctrinal solidarity that may be manifested in the world rivalry of ideologies. Yet under a cloak that is torn a little more every day, appears the inevitable difference in national policies. The least we can say in this regard is that in Asia, where the frontier between the two States, from the Hindu Kush to Vladivostok, is the longest that exists in the world, Russia's interest, which is to conserve and to maintain, and China's, which is to grow and to acquire, cannot be considered identical. As a result, the attitude and the action of a nation of 700 million inhabitants are effectively settled only by its own government.

Given the fact that for fifteen years almost the whole of China is gathered under a government which imposes its laws, and that externally China has shown herself to be a sovereign and independent power, France has been disposed to begin regular relations with Peking. Doubtless certain economic and cultural exchanges already existed. Doubtless the force of circumstances had led us, as it had led America, England, the Soviet Union, India, and other States, to negotiate with the Chinese representatives, when in 1954 the Geneva Conference decided the fate of Indochina or when in 1962, under the same form and in the same city, the situation in Laos was somewhat defined. But the weight of evidence and of reason increasing day by day, the French Republic estimated, for its part, that the time had come to place its relations with the People's Republic of China on a normal, in other words a diplomatic, basis. We have met with an identical intention in Peking, and therefore on this point, former Premier Edgar Faure, requested to make an unofficial sounding on the spot, returned to Paris with positive indications. It was then that the two States arrived at an official agreement to carry out the necessary measures.

I have referred to the weight of evidence and of reason. In fact, there is in Asia no political reality, notably with regard to Cambodia, Laos, Vietnam, or to India, Pakistan, Afghanistan, Burma, or to Korea or Soviet Russia or Japan, etc., which does not concern or affect China. There is, in particular, neither a war nor a peace imaginable on this continent without China's being implicated in it. Thus it would be absolutely impossible to envision, without China, a possible neutrality agreement relating to the Southeast Asian States, in which States for so many reasons, we French feel a very particular and cordial interest—a neutrality which, by definition, must be accepted by all, guaranteed on the international level, and which would exclude both armed agitations supported by any one among them in one or another of the States, and the various forms of external intervention; a neutrality that, indeed, seems, at the present time, to be the only situation compatible with the peaceful existence and progress of the peoples concerned. But further, China's own mass, her value, and her present needs, the scope of her future, cause her to reveal herself increasingly to the interests and concerns of the entire world. For all these reasons, it is clear that France must be able to listen to China directly, and also to make herself heard.

Why, moreover, not consider what will perhaps be fruitful in the relations of two peoples, relations which thus have an opportunity to be established as a result of the contact instituted between the two States? Of course, we must avoid nursing too many illusions in this regard. Thus, in the realm of economic exchanges, what is done today and which can, certainly, be improved, will remain limited for some time to come. The same is true of the investments earmarked by us for Chinese industrial development. However, the case is different with regard to technology, whose sources, in France, are of increasing value and for which China is an infinitely broad field of application. Lastly, who knows if the affinities which manifestly exist between the two nations with regard to all things of the mind, taking into account the fact that at the deepest level they bear one another reciprocal sympathy and consideration, will not lead them to a growing cultural cooperation? This is, in any case, sincerely hoped for here.

Paris and Peking have thus agreed to exchange ambassadors. Need we say that on our part there is nothing in such a decision that involves the least approval of the political system which at present prevails in China? By entering, in her turn, and after many free nations, into official relations with this State, as she has done with others under an analogous regime, France merely acknowledges the world as it is. She believes that sooner or later certain governments, which still have reservations, will decide to follow her example. Above all, it is possible in the world's enormous evolution, that by mutliplying relations among peoples, the cause of all men will be served—that is, the cause of wisdom, of progress, and of peace. It may be that such contacts contribute to the attenuation—now under way—of the dramatic contrasts and oppositions between the different camps that divide the world. It may be that in this way human souls, wherever they are on earth, will meet each other a little sooner at that rendezvous which France gave the universe 175 years ago, the rendezvous of liberty, equality, and fraternity.

FRANCE MUST PARTICIPATE IN THE SETTLEMENT OF SOUTHEAST ASIA

As for Vietnam, the United States is unwarranted in considering itself "as being invested throughout the world with the burden of defense against communism." France, China, the United States, and the Soviet Union (England has been omitted) have primary responsibility for settling the war there.

The Geneva Agreements concluded in 1954 put an end to the fighting in Indochina. At the time, everyone seemed to desire it sincerely. These agreements included provisions which varied according to the countries in question, but which had in common the absolute exclusion of all outside intervention. Cambodia pledged not to enter into any

SOURCE: Tenth Press Conference, November 23, 1964 (New York: French Embassy, Press and Information Service).

alliance and not to allow any base on its territory. Laos was to pro-
hibit the presence of any foreign troops, with the exception of a French
military mission and an airfield used by France in Seno. The two Viet-
nams could not ally themselves with anyone, or introduce on their soil
any force from the outside, or receive armaments which would increase
their potential. Moreover, general elections were scheduled to take
place in Vietnam in 1956, so as to lead to the institution of a democratic Government and to reunification.

The 1954 agreements were not applied for long. That is the least that
can be said about them. Cambodia alone—thanks to its national unity
and to the very skillful and determined way in which it is led by its
Head of State—has known how and been able to remain intact, neutral,
and relatively peaceful until now. But in Vietnam everything conspired
to bring that country back to the troubled situation from which it had
just emerged, while Laos in its turn was caught up in domestic conflicts, aided from the outside.

Concerning Vietnam, it must be said that the existence of a communist State installed in Tonkin, from which our troops withdrew in
accordance with the agreements, and the shock caused in the south
by the withdrawal of our administration and forces, exposed the
country to new perils. It was a matter of knowing whether it could
find, in itself, a national cohesion and a solid government. It was then
that the Americans arrived, bringing their aid, their policy, and their
authority.

The United States, in fact, considered itself as being invested
throughout the world with the burden of defense against communism.
Since South Vietnam was running the risk of it, as the regime established in the north was aimed at imposing itself there, Washington
wanted to put this State in a position to protect itself. It can be added,
without any intention of being derogatory, that their conviction of fulfilling a sort of vocation, the aversion which they had to any colonial
work which had not been theirs, and finally the natural desire in such
a powerful people to ensure themselves of new positions, determined
the Americans to take our place in Indochina.

We know that, back in 1954, they sponsored the Diem government,
that Diem immediately and unfortunately assumed an unpleasant attitude toward us, that once Emperor Bao-Dai had left the country he
replaced him, that he did not carry out the scheduled elections and
lastly that in all fields, particularly those of defense, economy and
administration, he placed himself in the orbit of Washington. But, as
this policy was more and more unpopular, the day came when Diem

tried to disentangle himself from it, while the Americans began to have doubts about him. Then a military putsch removed the President and gave him a successor. After that, a new putsch invested another one, the latter closely linked with the war action which the United States is supporting, staffing, financing, and arming.

War action, indeed, for although the subversive elements of the Vietcong had disappeared from South Vietnam after the 1954 agreements, they reappeared there under the pretext that the agreements were not being applied. Guerrilla fighting and some action carried out by constituted units are spreading more and more over the territory. At the same time, the populations, whatever their opinion of communism, are less and less inclined to support a cause and an authority which in their view are intermingled with those of a foreign State. Thus it seems that, locally, a military solution cannot be expected.

Some people imagine, it is true, that the Americans could seek it elsewhere by carrying the war to the north as far as it would be necessary. But, although they certainly dispose of all the desired means, it is difficult to assume that they wish to take the tremendous risk of a generalized conflict.

Lacking a decision by war, it is peace which thus must be made. Now, this implies returning to what was agreed upon ten years ago and, this time, complying with it, in other words, this implies that in North and South Vietnam, in Cambodia and in Laos, no foreign power any longer intervene in any way in the affairs of these unfortunate countries. A meeting of the same order and including, in principle, the same participants as the former Geneva conference would certainly be qualified to make a decision and to organize an impartial control. That is what France is proposing to all the States concerned, certain that, unless plunging Asia first and without doubt, at a later date, the entire world into very serious trials, this will have to be done, and the sooner, the better.

This meeting, to which each must come without conditions or recriminations, would successively deal with the international aspects of the Laotian, Cambodian and Vietnamese situation and of which the essential is, in advance, their neutrality. No other road can be visualized which can lead to peace in Southeast Asia, provided that once the theoretical agreement is concluded, if it is to be, two practical conditions be realized. The first is that the powers which directly or indirectly bear a responsibility in what was or is the fate of Indochina and which are France, China, the Soviet Union, and America, be effectively resolved to be involved there no longer. The second is that massive economic and technical aid be furnished to all of Indochina by the States which have the means for it, in order that development replace cruel division. France, for her part, is ready to observe these two conditions.

WE HAVE BECOME INDEPENDENT

On April 27, 1965, De Gaulle, reviewing some six years of effort, finally proclaims the independence of France.

In today's world, where all problems arise, where the dangers could reach the infinite, where the needs and ambitions of States clash fiercely, what is the action of France?

Let us recognize that having once been a Colossus of a people by virtue of population, wealth, and power, we are returning from afar to play our international role once more. For, one hundred years ago, our demographic and economic growth, and consequently our strength, began to decline. Then came, one after the other, the two world wars which ruined and decimated us, while two great countries, the United States and Russia, in their turn rose to the summit. In a situation of diminished strength at that time, the temptation to give up—which is to a weakened people what apathy is to a humiliated man—could have drawn us toward a decadence from which there would have been no return. All the more as, having once been accustomed to being always in the forefront, sometimes not without presumptuousness, our relative decline might have caused us then to doubt ourselves too much. We might have become discouraged after comparing our statistics to those on the total population of each of the two giant countries, or the global production of their factories and their mines, or the number of satellites they are launching around the earth, or the mass of megatons which their missiles are capable of carrying for destruction.

Indeed, after the burst of French confidence and pride which lifted us from a fatal abyss during the last war and despite active forces which reappeared in our country with renewed vigor, a tendency toward self-effacement momentarily emerged to the point of being established in doctrine and in policy. That is why some partisans would have liked to bind us, body and soul, to the totalitarian empire. That is also why others professed that we must not only, as is sensible, remain the allies

SOURCE: *Foreign Affairs No. 175* (New York: French Embassy, Press and Information Service), pp. 1–4.

of our allies so long as a threat of domination stood in the East, but that we must also become absorbed into an Atlantic system, within which our defense, our economy and our commitments would necessarily depend on the Americans' weapons, material hold and policy. The same people, with the same intention, wanted our country—instead of participating, as is normal, in organized cooperation among the free nations of the Old Continent—to be literally dissolved in a Europe described as integrated which, lacking the incentives of sovereignty of the peoples and responsibility of the States, would automatically be subordinate to the protector across the ocean. Thus, there would doubtless still be French workers, farmers, engineers, professors, officials, Deputies and Ministers. But there would no longer be France. Indeed. The vital fact of these last seven years is that we have resisted the sirens of surrender and have chosen independence.

It is true that independence implies conditions, and that they are not easy ones. But, as can be seen, we are succeeding in meeting them. In the political sphere, we must, without renouncing our American friendship, behave like the Europeans we are and, in that capacity, attempt to re-establish, from one end of our continent to the other, an equilibrium based on understanding and cooperation among all the peoples who live on it as we do. That is exactly what we are doing by reconciling ourselves with Germany; by proposing a real solidarity of the Six to our neighbors on both sides the Rhine and the Alps; by resuming with the Eastern countries, as they emerge from their crushing constraint, the relations of active understanding which formerly linked us to them.

With respect to the problems in the rest of the world, our independence leads us to act in accordance with our present concept, which is: that no hegemony excercised by anyone, no foreign intervention in the internal affairs of a State, no prohibition made to any country on maintaining peaceful relations with any other is justifiable. On the contrary, in our view, the supreme interest of mankind dictates that each nation be responsible for itself, free from encroachments, aided in its progress without conditions of allegiance. Hence our reprobation of the war which is spreading in Asia day by day and more and more, our favorable attitude toward the efforts of human liberation and national organization undertaken by various countries of Latin America, the assistance we are giving to the development of a good number of new African States, the relations we are forging with China, and so on. In short, France now has a policy, and it is being made in Paris.

From the viewpoint of security, our independence requires, in the

atomic age we live in, that we have the necessary means to deter a
possible aggressor ourselves, without detriment to our alliances, but
without our allies' holding our fate in their hands. Now, we are giving
ourselves these means. Doubtless, they force us to an effort of renewal
which is praiseworthy. But these means cost us no more than those
which we would have to furnish for Atlantic integration, without thereby
being sure of protection, if we were to continue to belong to it as
subordinate auxiliaries. Thus we are reaching the point at which no
State in the world could bring death to us without receiving it on its
own land, which is without doubt the best possible guarantee.

In the economic, scientific, and technical domain, to safeguard our
independence, being required to face the enormous wealth of some
—without, however, refusing to practice all types of exchanges with
them—we must see that our activities, for the essential part, remain
under French management and French control. We must also meet, at
whatever cost, the competition in advanced sectors which determine
the quality, the autonomy, the life of industry as a whole; which involve the maximum of studies, experiments and perfected tools; which
require great numbers of the most highly qualified scientists, technicians, and workers. Finally, when it is opportune, in order to combine
our inventions, our capabilities, and our resources in a given branch
with those of another country, we must often choose one of those
which is closest to us and whose weight we do not think will over-
whelm us.

That is why we are imposing a financial, economic, and monetary
stability upon ourselves which frees us from resorting to outside aid;
we are converting into gold the dollar surpluses imported into our
country as a result of the American balance of payments; we have
over the past six years multiplied by six the funds devoted to research; we are setting up a common industrial and agricultural market
with Germany, Italy, Belgium, Holland, and Luxembourg; we are tunnel-
ing through Mont Blanc in cooperation with the Italians; we are developing the Moselle River along with the people of Germany and
Luxembourg; we are joining with England to build the world's first
supersonic passenger aircraft; we are ready to extend this French-
British collaboration to other types of civil and military aircraft; we
have just concluded an agreement with Soviet Russia concerning the
perfection and use of our color television process. In sum, however
large may be the glass offered to us, we prefer to drink from our own,
while touching glasses round about.

Certainly, this independence which we are once more practicing in all areas has not failed to surprise, and even to scandalize various circles for which France's vassalage was the habit and the rule. They speak of Machiavellism, as if the clearest conduct did not consist precisely in following our own path. They are alarmed at our isolation at a time when there have never been more people flocking around us. In addition, the fact that we have reassumed our faculty of judgment and action in regard to all problems sometimes seems to displease a State which may believe that, by virtue of its power, it is invested with supreme and universal responsibility. But, who knows if, some day, the advantage which this friendly country may have in finding France on her feet will not by far outweigh the annoyance which it now feels about it?

Finally, the reappearance of a nation whose hands are free, which we have again become, obviously modifies the world interplay which, since Yalta, seemed to be limited to two partners. But since this division of the world between two great powers, and therefore into two camps, clearly does not benefit the liberty, equality, and fraternity of peoples, a different order, a different equilibrium are necessary for peace. Who can maintain this better than we—provided we remain ourselves?

Men and women of France, as you can see, for us, for everyone, as ever, France must be France!

Vive la République! Vive la France!

INDEX OF NAMES

❖

Adenauer, Konrad, 23, 105, 167, 179, 185, 186, 191, 192
Alexander, Harold, 131
Attlee, Clement R., 126

Bao-Dai, 237
Barrès, Auguste Maurice, 3
Bergson, Henri, 9
Beria, Lavrenti P., 6
Bidault, Georges, 37, 121, 225
Bierut, Boleslaw, 127
Bismarck, Otto von, 150
Boisson, Governor General, 205
Boncour, Paul, 225
Bonnet, Henri, 214
Byrnes, James F., 214

Caffery, Jefferson, 212, 214
Canning, George, 15
Castlereagh, Robert Stuart, 15
Chiang Kai-shek, 228, 233
Churchill, Sir Winston, 10, 16, 116, 117, 122, 123, 126, 127, 131, 196, 201, 203, 223, 224, 228
Clausewitz, Karl von, 9
Colbert, Jean-Baptiste, 4

de Retz, Cardinal, 6
Debré, Michel, 45, 60, 106
Dulles, John Foster, 193
Duverger, Maurice, 27

Eboué, Felix, 87
Eden, Anthony, 117
Eisenhower, Dwight D., 21, 105, 108, 109, 181
Erhard, Ludwig, 23, 167, 191

Fontaine, André, 24, 103
Franklin, Benjamin, 218

Gambetta, Léon, 3
Giraud, Henri H., 132, 207
Grosser, Alfred, 26, 27

Hegel, Georg W. F., 2, 3, 9
Himmler, Heinrich, 14
Hitler, Adolf, 100, 212
Hobbes, Thomas, 5, 15
Hopkins, Harry, 123, 204, 210–213, 216

Kennedy, John F., 22, 143, 145, 173, 174, 197
Khrushchev, Nikita S., 6, 104, 106, 107–108

Lafayette, Marquis de, 218
Lenin, Nikolai, 6
Lübke, Heinrich, 185
Luther, Martin, 128

Machiavelli, Niccolo, 242
Macmillan, Harold, 21, 105, 109, 143, 197, 202
Maglione, Cardinal, 121
Malenkov, Georgi M., 6
Mao Tse-tung, 6, 127, 234
Maurras, Charles, 3
Metternich, Prince Klemens W. N. L., 15
Mikolajczyk, Stanislaus, 127
Mussolini, Benito, 5, 203

Nagy, Imre, 6

Ngo Dinh Diem, 237
Nogues, Auguste, 205

Pétain, Henri Philippe, 9, 205, 207
Peyrefitte, Alain, 232
Pinay, Antoine, 73
Pleven, René, 86
Pompidou, Georges, 60

Renan, Joseph Ernest, 3
Reynaud, Paul, 212
Richelieu, Duc de, 4
Roosevelt, Franklin D., 10, 64, 119, 122, 123, 196, 203, 204, 205, 206–210, 211, 213, 223, 224, 226, 228

Segni, Antonio, 179
Spaak, Paul-Henri, 21
Stalin, Joseph V., 6, 118, 119, 120, 122, 123, 126, 127, 151, 203, 223, 224, 228

Tito, Josip Broz, 6, 124
Tolstoy, Leo, 9
Touré, Sékou, 10
Trotsky, Leon, 6
Truman, Harry S, 126, 127, 204, 213–216, 226

Weygand, Maxime, 4, 205
Wilhelm II, emperor of Germany, 100
Wilson, Maitland, 131

INDEX OF SUBJECTS

❖

Africa, French involvement in, 172; independence of colonies, 10–11; as nuclear testing site, 138–139; rejection of 1958 French Constitution, 10–11; World War II effort in, 131
African colonies, *see* Colonies, French
Agriculture, *see* Economy
Algeria, *colons*, 11; Communism and, 93–94; conflicting groups in, 11; French policy toward, 93–94; independence of, 11–12; insurrection in, 34, 84, 91; Melun talks, 91; Moslems, 91; Statute of, 91; U. S. view of, 231
        See also Army, French
America, *see* United States
"Anglo-Saxons," 14, 17, 196
Armée de Métier, 10
Army, French, effect of nuclear weapons on, 13; Fourth Republic and, 10; Free French Forces, 97; functions of, 5, 133–137; insurrection in Algeria, 9, 10, 34, 42–45: withdrawal, 175; Liberation, role in, 128–132; morale of, 22; NATO, role in, 174–175; necessity for, 5–6, 9; obedience to State, 9–10; preservation of, 12; reorganization of, 112; weaknesses of, 130–131, 150
        See also World War II

Atlantic Alliance, *see* NATO
Atomic weapons, *see* Nuclear weapons

Balance of power doctrine, as applied by De Gaulle, 16–17, 96, 116–127, 147–150
Bayeux speech, 33–36, 45
"belle et bonne alliance," 119, 121
Berlin, *see* Germany
Brazzaville, Conference of, 85–87

Cambodia, 236–237, 238
China, Algeria and, 11; De Gaulle's European concept and, 116; French recognition of, 23, 230, 235–236; and Limited Test Ban Treaty, 13; relations with Soviet Union, 6, 21, 234; rise of Communism in, 234; tribute to, 233–236; world role of, 17, 104, 164, 220, 235
        See also Communism; Soviet Union
Coexistence, *see* Soviet Union; Khrushchev, Nikita
Colonies, French, aid to, 84; Anglo-American interference with, 84, 86; European influence on, 88; policy toward, 10–12
        See also Africa, French; Algeria; Decolonization; individual names of countries

245

Colons, see Algeria

Common Market, European unity and, 23, 110, 155–156; French economy and, 65, 113, 159–160; rejection of Britain, 23, 27, 117, 196–202

Communism, in China, 234; criticism of, 81; economic theory of, 65–67; European ambitions of, 101; in France, 17–18, 34, 37, 40, 65, 70, 121; personality cult discussed, 6; in postwar Europe, 18, 215; in United Nations, 227; United States attitude, 236–237

Crimea, *see* Soviet Union

Cuban crisis, 144

Dakar, 86; address at, 89–91

Decolonization, De Gaulle's motives for, 11–12; process of, 84–94

Détente, 105, 107, 108, 109

Dictatorship, 23, 29

Disarmament, French policy on, 14–17, 22–23, 107, 129–130, 138–142

    See also Nuclear weapons

Dumbarton Oaks Conference, 23, 224

East Germany, *see* Germany

East-West Conflict, arms race, 138–139; Cold War thaw, 104, 107–108; French role in, 103–113; summit meeting, 103–109

Economy, agriculture, future of: 79, reform of: 69, role of Common Market in: 199; finance, 82–83, 241; industrial and trade agreements, 241; nationalization of, 68–71; recovery of, 75–83; reform of, 18–19, 65–75: reduction of deficit, 73–74; social security, 69, 73–74; technology, 76–77

Education, 77, 79

England, *see* Britain

Europe, dependence on United States, 21; as economic community, 198–202; Franco-German role in, 26; Franco-Soviet pact and, 119–121; German problem and, 191–195; internal balance destroyed, 126–127; unification of, 16–17, 24, 26–29, 101, 110, 112, 114, 151–167, 184–186

Europe des patries, 29

Fifth Republic, compared with Fourth Republic, 24–25; Constitution of, 33–39, 45–56, 59–63

Foreign policy, De Gaulle's concept of, 12–13, 14, 21; delineated, 143–150; independence of France, 239–242

Fourth Republic, army under, 10; compared to Fifth Republic, 24–25; constitution of, 41–43; economy of, 64–65; leadership provisions under, 7–8, 36; nuclear development under, 13

Franco-German alliance, *see* Germany; United States

Geneva Agreements (1954), terms of, 236–237

Geneva Disarmament Conference, 130, 139, 141–142, 148

Germany, American-German relations, 163–167, 177; Berlin dispute, 23, 178–184: conferences on (1962), 176: NATO and, 193: war over, 181–184; Franco-German relations, 9, 15, 16, 23, 99, 116, 176, 185–186: Franco-German treaty, 166–167, 177, 186–191 (text of); neutralization of, 176, 180–181; rearmament of, 27, 99–102; unification of, 16, 28, 108, 112; World War II, postwar treatment of, 19, 119–120, 123–127: Reich, 20, 100, 192–194

    See also Disarmament; NATO; Nuclear weapons; World War II

Grands ensembles, 26

Great Britain, Anglo-American unity, 196; Common Market rejection of, 196–200; economy separate from Europe, 199–200;

Great Britain *(Continued)*
Nuclear force, 146, 197; relations with France, 14–15, 98, 116–120; World War II: role in, 131–132, postwar role, 19–20, 99–101, 122–127
See also Balance of power; Common Market; Germany; NATO; United States
Guinea, 10–11, 85

Hydrogen bomb, *see* Nuclear weapons

Indochina, French war in, 75, 232, 236–237; insurrection in, 84–85; U. S. intervention in, 237
Isolationism, *see* United States

Laos, 237–238
League of Nations, 223, 227–228
Lebanon, 91
Lublin Committee, 120, 124, 127

Madagascar, 18, 91, 94
Mali, Federation of, 89–90
Mediterranean Fleet, *see* NATO
Memorandum of September 23, 1958, 21, 23, 103
See also NATO
Mexico, De Gaulle's visit to, 231–232
MLF (Multilateral Force), *see* NATO
Morocco, 85, 91
Munich Conference, 105

National defense, *see* Army: French, NATO: Nuclear weapons
Nationalism, American, 26–27; concept of, 25, 27, 29: in Europe, 161–163; French, effect on Algeria, 11; NATO *vs.*, 171–173
Nation-state, concept of, 1–9, 14, 15, 24, 27, 90; isolationism and, 29
NATO (North Atlantic Treaty

Organization), American influence in, 16, 21, 26; delineated, 168–169; effect of European change on, 168–175; European unity and, 163–167, 170–171; Franco-German treaty and, 177; French role in, 21–22, 23, 26, 28, 103, 109, 230–231: independence from, 171–173: Memorandum of September 23, 1958, 168–169; German unity and, 193; history of, 171–172; Mediterranean Fleet withdrawal and, 170–171; MLF, 28, 142–147; necessity for, 136–137; nuclear policy of, 22
Nuclear weapons, Arms race, 138–139; Berlin dispute and, 181–184: European fate in war over, 115; French nuclear force, 13, 109, 112, 145, 146, 149; hydrogen bomb, 14; necessity for, 12–14, 129, 134, 136–142, 149–150; peace and, 107–108; Sahara tests, 137, 138, 139; test ban treaty, 13, 137–142; in World War II, 126–127
See also Britain, Disarmament, NATO, Soviet Union, United States

Politique, la, 5, 9, 64, 128
Poland, *see* Soviet Union, satellites of
Potsdam Conference, 20, 105, 203
President of French Republic, election of, 51–54, 55–56; powers of, 8, 36–37, 42–43, 44: in Fifth Republic Constitution, 48–51; succession of, 53–54, 59

Ralliament du Peuple Français (RPF), 34
Reich, *see* Germany
Resistance, French, 1, 17, 33, 98–99
Rome, Treaty of, 113, 159, 166, 167, 186, 198, 199
Ruhr Valley, 100
Russia, *see* Soviet Union

Saar Valley, 100

St. Cyr (academy), 2
Senegal, 90
"Six, the," *see* Common Market
Socialism, economic theory of, 65–66
Soviet Union, Communism in, 164; Crimea, 122–127; French-Soviet relations, 16–17: "belle et bonne alliance," 199–121; Germany, neutralization of, 178–184; imperialism of, 93; nuclear role, 136–142: in Berlin, 176, 181–184: coexistence, 151; satellites of, 16, 104, 124, 183, 194, 216; Poland, 120–121, 124; Sino-Soviet dispute, 6, 21, 234; role in United Nations, 229; U. S.-Soviet relations, 104, 107–108, 220–221; World War II, postwar role, 101, 122–127
    See also Communism; Disarmament; Nuclear weapons; United States
State, *see* Nation-state
Summit meeting (Paris, 1963), *see* East-West conflict
Syria, 91

Technology, *see* Economy
Teheran Conference, 105
Test Ban Treaty, *see* Nuclear Weapons
Third Force, *see* Europe
Third Republic, criticized, 38; French Army and, 10; leadership provisions under, 7–8
Tunisia, 85, 91

U-2 incident, 108
United Nations, birth of, 223–225; Charter, 226, 228; 1965 crisis, 227–229; Franco-Soviet pact and, 121; General Assembly, 225, 226, 227, 228; inadequacy of, 225–227; Roosevelt's image of, 224; Secretary-General, 228, 229, Security Council, 225, 226–227; small countries' role in, 225; United States influence in, 164
United States, anti-Americanism, 15, 96, 153–154; economy, postwar, 214–215: European competition with, 221; European role, 21, 27–28, 164–165, 201: ambitions, 14: postwar, 19–20, 99, 101, 122–127: Roosevelt's policies, 206–210; French–U. S. relations, 21, 98, 112, 203–206, 211–212: Franco-German treaty dispute, 177: French independence, 216–222: French nuclear force, 145; isolationism of, 29, 95, 210; "liberalism" of, 6–7; nuclear power, 136–142; presidential system, 61–63; Santo Domingo affair, 23, 231; Soviet–U. S. relations, 104, 107–108, 220–221; in Vietnam, 237
    See also Disarmament, Germany, Great Britain, Nationalism, Nuclear weapons, NATO, United Nations
UNR (Gaullist party), 35

Vatican, the, De Gaulle's visit to, 121–122
Versailles, Treaty of, 228
Vichy government, 18, 67, 121–122, 130, 131, 205
Vietnam, Vietcong, 238; war in, 237–238; negotiations, 230, 232–233, 236–239
    See also United States

World War I, 211–212
World War II, European operations, 131–132; French Liberation and recovery, 17–20, 33, 211; French role, 210–213: postwar, 212–213: relations with Allies, 14–15: unpreparedness for, 12, 130–131; postwar period, 25–26, 97–102, 122–127; West Germany, *see* Germany

Yalta Conference, 19–20, 105, 116, 119, 122–126, 163, 203, 224, 242
Yaoundé, conference of, 94